THE SOCIOLOGY OF CARDI B

This powerfully written and co-authored book creatively engages with the topics of Black and Latinx femininity, motherhood, sexuality, racial and ethnic identity, and political engagement through the life and artistic work of Hip Hop artist Cardi B. The authors highlight examples from Cardi's lived experiences and artistry using a trap feminist framework as a starting point for sociological conversations about Black women and the trap.

The authors weave foundational histories of Black sociology, Black feminism, and institutional inequalities along the lines of race, class, and gender. Drawing from moments in Cardi B's public life—her rap lyrics, her behavior at New York Fashion Week, questions about her racial and ethnic identity, the unveiling of her pregnancy, her engagement with politicians, and her responses to social media comments and critics—this book argues for the merits of addressing Black feminist theory from the bottom up—that is, to take seriously the knowledge production of Black women by attending to and creating space for hood chicks, ghetto girls, and ratchet women.

By centering the lived experiences and social positions of the Black women Cardi represents, the authors expand Black feminist discourse and entrust Black women to define themselves for themselves. This book is an important contribution to scholarship for students, scholars, and readers interested in sociology, Hip Hop, pop culture, and women's studies.

Aaryn L. Green is a sociologist, instructor, student affairs professional, diversity consultant, writer, and speaker from East Cleveland, Ohio.

Maretta Darnell McDonald is an affiliate faculty member in the Sociology Department at Virginia Tech.

Veronica A. Newton is a tenure-track Assistant Professor of Race in the Department of Sociology at Georgia State University.

Candice C. Robinson is Assistant Professor of Sociology and DeLaney Faculty Scholar at Washington and Lee University.

Shantee Rosado is Assistant Professor of Afro-Latinx Studies in the Africana Studies Department and Latino and Caribbean Studies Department at Rutgers University-New Brunswick.

THE SOCIOLOGY OF CARDI B

A Trap Feminist Approach

*Aaryn L. Green, Maretta Darnell McDonald,
Veronica A. Newton, Candice C. Robinson and
Shantee Rosado*

Routledge
Taylor & Francis Group

NEW YORK AND LONDON

Designed cover image: Joycelyn Adeoye | DaredtoPaint
www.daredtopaint.com

First published 2025
by Routledge
605 Third Avenue, New York, NY 10158

and by Routledge
4 Park Square, Milton Park, Abingdon, Oxon, OX14 4RN

Routledge is an imprint of the Taylor & Francis Group, an informa business

© 2025 Aaryn L. Green, Maretta Darnell McDonald, Veronica A. Newton, Candice C. Robinson and Shantee Rosado

The right of Aaryn L. Green, Maretta Darnell McDonald, Veronica A. Newton, Candice C. Robinson and Shantee Rosado to be identified as authors of this work has been asserted in accordance with sections 77 and 78 of the Copyright, Designs and Patents Act 1988.

ISBN: 978-1-032-02744-9 (hbk)
ISBN: 978-1-032-02742-5 (pbk)
ISBN: 978-1-003-18498-0 (ebk)

DOI: 10.4324/9781003184980

Typeset in Sabon
by Apex CoVantage, LLC

Dedicated to the ancestors throughout the diaspora. To our sociological foremothers. To women Hip Hop pioneers. To the girls growing up hard or who are second guessing themselves and their sense of belonging. To the hood chicks, ghetto girls, and ratchet women in and adjacent to the trap, and in and adjacent to the academy, all around the world. We see you. We the shit!

CONTENTS

ABOUT THE AUTHORS

Aaryn L. Green

Aaryn L. Green is a sociologist, instructor, student affairs professional, diversity consultant, writer, and speaker from East Cleveland, Ohio. She received her PhD in Sociology from the University of Cincinnati in 2018. Her research focuses on race, popular culture, and media, emphasizing the contributions of Black women. She has published on these topics in peer-reviewed journals such as *Sociological Inquiry*. Dr. Green has contributed commentary on diversity, equity, inclusion, and social justice to digital outlets such as Al Jazeera's AJ+. For the past ten years she has worked with and advocated for historically underserved students at various universities and nonprofits throughout the Midwest. Dr. Green resides in the Washington, DC area and is currently Interim Director of Research, Professional Development, and Academic Affairs at the American Sociological Association. She enjoys live music, traveling with friends, cooking, and HBCU marching bands.

Maretta Darnell McDonald

Maretta Darnell McDonald is an affiliate faculty member in the Sociology Department at Virginia Tech. Dr. McDonald was a 2022–2024 University of Wisconsin-Madison, Institute of Research on Poverty National Poverty Fellow, a 2021–2022 American Sociological Association (ASA) Minority Fellow, and a member of the inaugural 2021–2022 cohort of ASA/NSF Doctoral Dissertation Research Improvement Grant awardees. Dr. McDonald earned her PhD in Sociology at Louisiana State University in 2022. Her current research interests are racial inequality, criminology/criminal justice, family, gender, spatial inequality, and public policy. Her primary research examines the association of child support policies and practices with macrolevel spatial and racial inequality, which brings all these areas into conversation with each other. She has published multiple book chapters and public scholarship pieces. As a professed Hip Hop and sneakerhead, Dr. McDonald loves to listen to music (especially live), buy new colorways of Nike Air Max 95s, spend time dancing with her biological and chosen family, and go to Black cultural events and spaces.

Veronica A. Newton

Veronica A. Newton is a tenure-track Assistant Professor of Race in the Department of Sociology at Georgia State University. Her areas of specialty are intersectionality, critical race theory, Black feminisms, and qualitative methods. Her work is embedded in critical race feminism, examines systemic racism and patriarchy within higher education, and how these systems impact Black college women. Dr. Newton's solo authored book project, titled *There's Racism in the Building and Patriarchy in the Yard: Black Women Navigating Discrimination at a HPWI*, is currently under contract with SUNY Press's Critical Race Studies in Education Series. Dr. Newton is originally from St. Louis and now lives in Atlanta with her cat Mister Whiskers. In her free time, she does trap karaoke and trap yoga and attends concerts and music events in the city.

Candice C. Robinson

Candice C. Robinson is Assistant Professor of Sociology and DeLaney Faculty Scholar at Washington and Lee University. Her research agenda is motivated by a commitment to understanding the often-overlooked and discredited contributions of Black Americans to American society in the areas of civic engagement, social movements, theory, and sociology broadly. In addition to this book, Dr. Robinson's solo authored book project is on Black Middle Class contributions to the National Urban League and its auxiliary the National Urban League Young Professionals. A native of St. Louis, MO, she earned her sociology degrees from Hampton University (BA), University of Iowa (MA), and University of Pittsburgh (PhD). Outside of her research and teaching, Dr. Robinson enjoys music and traveling, and is active in a wide variety of civic, cultural, and service endeavors.

Shantee Rosado

Shantee Rosado is Assistant Professor of Afro-Latinx Studies with a joint appointment in the Departments of Africana Studies and Latino and

Caribbean Studies at Rutgers University-New Brunswick. She holds a PhD in Sociology with a certificate in Latinx and Latin American Studies from the University of Pennsylvania. Dr. Rosado's research examines racial identities and inequalities among Latinxs in the United States and in Latin America, as well as Black women (including Afro-Latinas) in Hip Hop. Dr. Rosado's first solo book project, tentatively titled "Latinxs and the Emotional Politics of Race and (Anti)Blackness in the U.S.," examines how emotions shape the racial ideologies of 1.5- and second-generation Puerto Ricans and Dominicans in Central Florida.

PREFACE

We were surprised that our panel titled "The Sociology of Cardi B," had a standing room-only audience at the 2018 Association of Black Sociologists (ABS) Annual Meeting in Philadelphia. ABS is one of the most welcoming academic environments we have experienced, thus we knew that it would be the perfect opportunity to discuss Cardi B's release of her first album, *Invasion of Privacy*, and the media surrounding it. As one of the first panels of the day, we thought the crowd would be smaller and would comprise mostly younger women scholars. None of us thought that we would encounter a multi-generational and multi-gendered group of new and long-esteemed scholars who were eager to hear our thoughts on bridging our shared discipline of sociology with Cardi B. Our presentations, organized and moderated by Candice C. Robinson, were titled:

- "White Media and the Appropriation of Authentic Black Womanhood," presented by Aaryn L. Green
- "Cardi Gotta Baby by Offset: A Nonmaritial Childbearing Case Study," presented by Maretta Darnell McDonald
- "Cardi B: Pregnant While Twerking or Twerking While Pregnant," presented by Veronica A. Newton
- "Policing Cardi B's Blackness: Critical Analysis of 'Commonsense' Notions of Race," presented by Shantee Rosado

We ended that morning with excitement about how well the conversation went and had no further plans to publish the work together until we saw our names featured in *The Philadelphia Inquirer* and *XXL Magazine* highlighting the panel. At that point, we realized the conversation was not over.

A year later, at the 2019 ABS Annual Meeting in New York City, we reconvened after many people requested another opportunity to hear our thoughts on the Sociology of Cardi B, especially in Cardi's hometown. In a larger room and amid many traveling delays, we held presentations in the following order:

- "Lessons from Developing the Sociology of Cardi B," presented by Candice C. Robinson
- "Act Like You Got Some Sense: Cardi B, Respectability, and the White Gaze," presented by Aaryn L. Green
- "Living Her Best Feminist Life: Cardi B's Struggle Against Marianismo," presented by Maretta Darnell McDonald
- "From Stripper to Rapper to Cultural Icon: Cardi B and Trap feminism," presented by Veronica A. Newton
- "Cardi B and the U.S. Political Imaginary," presented by Shantee Rosado

Once again, a lively question and answer followed that further pushed our thinking of why Cardi B is so interesting to so many people, how our own positions as Black women scholars in the academy relate to her experiences, and why the overall conversation is important. A day after the presentations, following a series of scholars and fans tagging her on Twitter about the presentations, Cardi B replied in a tweet with "Wow!"

In the time since those two years of presentations and conversations traversing the topics of Black feminism, identity, motherhood, media, politics, race and ethnicity, trap feminism, and the white gaze, we have begun to affectionately call ourselves some combination of the "Cardi Crew," "Cardi Scholars," and/or "Academic Bardi Gang." With this explicit admiration of Cardi B, it is reasonable to think that we are conducting a biography or an analysis of every move Cardi B makes. After all, we are fans that follow her, but we are also sociologists. Therefore, this book builds on those presentations and emphasizes our hard-earned, well-practiced sociological imaginations that allow us to recognize Cardi B's experiences as kindred to all Afro-Latinas and Black women. To the surprise of many who assume how a PhD should act, we see ourselves in a woman like Cardi B. We have aspirational goals of self-expression and fight for the authentic professional success that she represents. Like her, we too have difficulty fitting into the paradigms of what the world suggests Black women should be. As Black feminists and sociological scholars, we furthermore have difficulty fitting into what our chosen career paths suggest we should do given its exclusionary history.

To be clear, we do not want to suggest that all Black women's experiences are inherently the same. For example, in approaching this equally co-authored book, we attempted to find common threads in our biographies as Black women outside of our shared identities as Black feminists and sociological scholars, and as you may have guessed, we couldn't. We were varied in who we are. We hail from different socioeconomic backgrounds, cities, regions, ethnicities, ages, educational training, research interests, and even favorite Cardi moments and songs. Although it should not have shocked us, there were no two of us that were alike beyond our unifying experiences as Black women in the United States and our love for Cardi B.

Our varied personal and professional backgrounds in part inspired us to write this book as a space to question what we'd been taught about fitting into sociology, feminism, and Black womanhood. In the words of queer Black feminist scholar Audre Lorde (1984), "it is axiomatic that if we do not define ourselves for ourselves, we will be defined by others—for their use and to our detriment" (45). Lorde's iconic sentiment is a stark reminder: we must use our particular embodied knowledge and cultural experiences to acknowledge all the ways we exist as Black women to maintain and elevate the relevance of sociological theories. Until we are seen by ourselves and others as experts on our own lives, we cannot develop theories that apply to our lives. We can be Black women and different kinds of Black women at the same time. Our varied experiences as Black women strengthen this work as we take our training, lived experiences, and readings of previous scholars altogether to push the bounds of what it means to be a sociologist, a Black woman, a Black feminist, and more specifically, a trap feminist.

With this background as the foundation, our own experiences, and our training, we knew that this book needed to be a Black feminist project that may look a lot different than other books. In taking this balance between the similar and the separate, we felt it was important to unify ourselves by making this book an intentionally equally co-authored project, not an edited volume. This choice alone caused us to reconceptualize what co-authorship and collaborative work looks like.

In short, *The Sociology of Cardi B* is based on the fact that as Black women, *we* are the experts on our own lives no matter how those lives are lived. Not by conducting a biography of Cardi B or a study of the trap, but by letting Cardi B and women in, from, and adjacent to the trap speak for themselves. If we want to develop theories that forward equality and justice for all, then we need to get out of the gated hallways of academia. And while we hope a wide variety of people read this book, we unequivocally are writing this book to encourage and louden the voices of women like us—self-expressed Black women, who have our own way of knowing and doing. After all, writing this book has survived in the face of a global pandemic, COVID-19 sickness, an attempted coup, and the Dobbs Decision—the overturning of Roe *v.* Wade. It has also survived the authors' completion of five separate and distinct dissertations (none on Cardi B), new jobs within and outside the academy, cross-country moves, annual reviews for tenure, family member's sickness and death, break-ups, and marriages. Of course, we can't forget to mention, it has also stood true in the face of Cardi's ever-evolving career. In this book-writing process, we stayed true to trying something new, and we did not give up. In the words of Cardi B, "Good girls do what they told, Bad bitches do what they want."

ACKNOWLEDGMENTS

Cardi Collective

We would like to give a very special thank you to the Association of Black Sociologists. Without this conference and without a space for Black sociology, we would have not been able to develop this project and have the ability to continue this sociological discourse. The feedback, guidance, mentorship, and femtorship support have been unwavering for this project and for us as scholars.

We would like to thank our developmental editor Mary Gustafson and our press editor Tyler Bay. Thank you both for believing in this project and staying the course with us to get it off the ground and in press. We truly appreciate all of your time and effort for supporting each of us as writers and as sociologists.

We would also like to thank the artist, Joycelyn Adeoye of Daredtopaint, who created our cover art. You took our ideas and concepts and then returned to us a visual masterpiece that encapsulates everything Sociology of Cardi B is and more. Thank you for lending your talent to our project.

We would also like to acknowledge our reviewers whose excitement about the book confirmed the importance of this project. Thank you for your questions, critiques, and suggestions that helped us develop this book.

We would also like to thank our emotional support pets who have been writing and riding with us since day one. Our BardiGang cats Mister Whiskers, our sixth author, and Jorge, our final editor. They made our zoom meetings manageable. Lol:)

Aaryn L. Green

To my Mommy (the writer, artist, and street philosopher), Linda D. L. Green: You got a little Black girl from one of the poorest cities in the nation to believe that she and others like her were powerful, and you taught me all people deserve equal humanity. That idea of community shaped who I am and motivates all I do. To my grandma Thomsena Green, I know your prayers have covered me all the way from Orangeburg, South Carolina. To my late grandmother Shirley A. Lee, you saw Cardi B on TV and called me one day from your hospital bed. You thought she might mention this book (lol). I am sad you could not see the finished product, but I thank you for being an early believer that this book matters. To my Lee and Green families: Thank you for sacrificing time and space to allow me to dream big. To my late God sister, Cherae Jemison, you were my introduction to the trap. You took me with you everywhere, put me up on game, made mistakes so that I wouldn't have to, and you loved and protected me fiercely. I have felt your presence throughout this journey, and it's girls and women like you who matter most to me.

To my Cincinnati Framily and mentors: Thank you for edits on early drafts, for constant encouragement, and space to vent. To my Ronis and closest friends from home: Thank you for the laughs, the kick its, for gassing me up and keeping me grounded.

To East Cleveland, Ohio, especially the women and girls: Thank you for being a community despite the less-than-ideal circumstances. It was with you where I first learned that the very real effects of racism, sexism, and poverty are still not strong enough to eradicate Black joy and community. No matter how far I go, you will forever be my home base.

Lastly to my co-authors: Thank you for your brilliance, vulnerability, accountability, and steadfastness. You are the baddest bitches in sociology and academia and I mean that! Period!

Maretta Darnell McDonald

First, I would like to thank Dr. Barbara Scott—my academic mom—who took a chance on a stranger and pulled me into the wonderful world of the Association of Black Sociologists. My connections to my amazing co-authors were fostered by this one moment of kindness. Dr. Scott, I will forever be grateful. To my kids and gbabies, Audri, Greg, TJ, Markil, Makai, Treyshon, G3, Chip, Levi, Demi, Mozy, Tru, and A'Mina: Thank you for understanding while I was writing yet not understanding when I should be present. To my brother/cuz, Lyndon for being so hyped about this book and continually trying to connect us to the "source." I would like to thank all my sisters, especially Sharonda, who made sure I stayed a human who danced to Cardi B more than I sat at this desk and wrote about her. To Dr. Kate Jensen: Thank you for creating a place in your Feminist and Gender Theory course to discover the concepts that started my Cardi B journey and allowing me to do a presentation that was academic and ratchet at the same time. To Dr. Catherine Jacquet whose Black feminism course was not only a place to learn but also a place to unlearn. Thank you for giving of yourself as my professor in that course and as my friend forever more. A big thank you to RWC for creating a space to get the words on the page and whose continued presence, encouragement, and listening ear helped keep me focused and committed when times were hard. Lastly, thank you to my mentors and mentees, especially Drs. Lori Martin, Sarah Becker, Ifeyinwa Davis, and Doctor-to-Be Mahalia Crawford, who supported and continue to support all my ideas no matter if they don't fit nicely packaged in a linear research agenda Rubik's Cube. #BardiGang #CardiB-Collective—we did it. And we did it hella good too. Lastly for real . . . in the words of Erica Campbell "I luh God. You don't luhGod. What's wrong wit you?"

Veronica A. Newton

I would like to give a special shout-out to my co-author Candice for being our unofficial book manager who helped coordinate meetings, emails, documents, and anything else you can name to keep us all on the same page! To my sister scholar Dr. Jelisa Clark for being a listening ear for me as I have worked on this book. You have heard it all, and I could not have gotten through this without your endless support and feedback on my work. Thank you sis! To my mom, Dr. Julia Burke, your unwavering love, support, and excitement to share my work will always be heartfelt. Thank you for shaping me into being a strong writer. I've learned from the best. I would also like to give a shout-out to my mentors who have guided me since I was a master's student. Thank you Dr. Derrick Brooms and Dr. Regina Dixon-Reeves for always believing in my work and my potential as a Black sociologist. I made it! I'd also like to mention Dr. Dawn Hicks Tafari, who first invited me into the scholarship and pedagogy of Hip Hop feminism, thank you big sis! Thank you to all of my academic friends and to my ratchet friends. I appreciate y'all's continued excitement for this book project. Your encouragement was truly motivating. Shout-out to my study buddy, Mister Whiskers, who always sits next to me as I write. Lastly, a huge acknowledgment to Cardi B for being a dynamic, outspoken woman whose music continues to motivate me personally and professionally. #BardiGang

Candice C. Robinson

I want to first acknowledge my co-authors for taking this wild ride with me. Moving from engaging in a conversation about Cardi B at a conference for fun to writing a book is a far jump, but I'm glad we did it!

Professionally, I want to acknowledge Dr. Earl Wright II for being the first to suggest we move this from a presentation to some other written form; my dissertation committee members and the supportive faculty at the University of Pittsburgh who never discouraged me from following this passion project in addition to my dissertation; my ABS RAMP mentor Dr. Amanda Lewis for assistance in locating our developmental editor; my former colleagues at UNCW, with a special thank you to my TA Sarah Krueger for her compiling support and Dr. Erin Michaels who was regularly a listening ear as I worked through the many moving parts of the book; to RWC who have been part of the process from the early days; and to Dr. Aria Halliday for our conversations on Black feminism and Hip Hop (and playing a little Cardi at my Dissertation defense).

I would also like to acknowledge and thank all the friends (including but not limited to Hamptonians, sorors, YP, Facebook, and "internet friends") who have hyped me up in writing this book, regularly asking "where is the link?!?!!" and promising to buy multiple copies—there is not enough space to name all of you but know your support was felt all along the way.

Finally, as always, I want to thank and acknowledge the people who are closest to me, my husband Tristan McCoy, my mom Brenda Howard, sisters Crystal and Amelia Robinson, my Great Aunt Aretha (Williams) Stroy, and all my extended family who went from "Cardi B?" to "Cardi B!"

Shantee Rosado

I'd like to start by thanking the trap feminists in my family: My great grandmother Virginia, who used to sew clothes for the sex workers on Calle Luna in San Juan, Puerto Rico. My grandmother Eva, who taught me from an early age that as Black Puerto Rican women, we had to josear (hustle) to get ahead in life. My mother Serena, who embodied that hustling spirit everyday as a single mother of three who was "pobre, pero nunca sencilla" (poor, but never simple). And my sister Cindy, my aunt Xiomara, and all of my primas, who taught me that growing up in the PJs should never stop you from dreaming of more.

To my co-authors, the academic BardiGang, thank you for being so incredibly supportive and encouraging, even as I nitpicked our chapters to death. Your patience, guidance, and warmth were a blessing throughout this process. So much love to you all.

I would like to thank my brother, Eddie, for being my lifelong teacher and coach. ¡De Carolina pal mundo, bro! Much love to the entire Rosado family for being my support system, always.

Last, but certainly not least, I would like to thank my husband, Jim. For all the conversations, meals, support, and editing along the way. And for fully and unequivocally embracing me as the ratchet, trap feminist I am. ¡Te amo!

GLOSSARY

African Diaspora: the dispersal of peoples from the African continent, which was significantly shaped by the Transatlantic Slave Trade spanning the 16th–19th centuries.

Afro-Latinx/a/o: an individual with African ancestry who is from Latin America. The term was created by activists to specifically highlight the importance of African culture and heritage in Latin America, where it has been, and still is, erased from understandings of the region.

Agency: the capacity and ability of individuals to act independently and make their own free choices.

Black feminism: (a) the active practice of valuing, centering, understanding, and empowering all Black women regardless of their social standing in society; (b) focusing on Black women's lived experiences and how their lives are impacted by their race, class, gender, sexuality, and nationality.

Black feminist thought: (a) a social theory developed by sociologist Patricia Hill Collins to conceptualize the knowledge developed by the lived experiences of Black women; (b) the understanding that Black women's lives are informed by racism, sexism, classism, and sexuality; (c) a framework to assess how Black women navigate society, define themselves, and work collectively to empower one another.

Black sexual politics: a concept developed by Black feminist scholar Patricia Hill Collins to describe the relations, interactions, and communities of Black men and Black women's racial, gender, sexual, and class dynamics impacted by Black culture and the larger white society.

Civic engagement: a spectrum of activities in which people get involved in political and community affairs.

Class: a group of people within a society that possess a same/similar socioeconomic status as defined by wealth and/or income. Class is used to rank a person or group of people in comparison to others within a society.

Colorism: the preferential treatment or attitude that people of lighter complexions are prettier, better, or more attractive than people of darker skin tones.

Culture: a way of life including widespread values (about good or bad), beliefs (about what is true), and behavior (what people do every day). According to the American Sociological Association, culture refers to the languages, customs, beliefs, rules, arts, knowledge, and collective identities and memories developed by members of all social groups that make their social environments meaningful.

Deviance: actions, language, or behaviors in society that are perceived as violations of rules or norms.

Deviance as resistance: (a) a concept developed by Cathy J. Cohen that describes participating in behaviors that disrupt social norms deemed appropriate in public; (b) embracing attitudes and behaviors that challenge respectability politics.

Diaspora: the dispersal of peoples from their homeland to two or more outside locations.

Ethnicity: (a) used to refer to a group or subgroup of people who share and identify around distinctive cultural background(s) such as ancestry/place of origin, heritage, language, customs, or food; (b) not the same as race although it is often used or thought of as interchangeable in the United States.

Gender: socially constructed categories that normalize and differentiate certain behaviors, actions, and activities based on masculinity and femininity. It includes both gender identity and expression. Often used in binary ways, however, gender is a fluid entity that relates to how someone views themselves.

Gendered racism: a term coined by Philomena Essed to describe the oppression that Black women and women of color experience at the intersection of race and gender.

Heteronormativity: the assumption that heterosexuality is the normal and "appropriate" sexuality for all people. It also refers to how society is structured in a way that privileges heterosexuality.

Hip Hop: a genre of music that is male dominated that originated in the United States that speaks to the experiences, expressions, and cultures of Black people. The six foundational elements of Hip Hop are DJing, MCing, beatboxing, breakdancing, graffiti, and fashion.

Hip Hop feminism: a term coined by Joan Morgan in the late 1990s; Hip Hop feminism refers to the movement of putting Black feminist foundations into the context of Hip Hop music and culture.

Hood feminism: a term made mainstream by Mikki Kendall to address the marginalization of poor Black women in feminist movements. Hood feminism challenges mainstream feminism by pointing out its exclusion of marginalized women (including trans women) and its lack of attention to poor women's basic needs, such as access to adequate housing and food.

Misogynoir: a term coined by Black feminist Moya Bailey that specifically speaks to misogyny directed at Black women.

Misogyny: the attitude that women are less than men and should be treated as such; hatred toward women.

Patriarchy: male domination over women; when men have systemic power over women.

Race: socially constructed categories based on real or perceived physical differences between groups of people. It may include phenotypic characteristics such as skin color, facial features, hair, and size, among others.

Racism: (a) the structural and systematic power to oppress, discriminate, deny, and alter life chances of individuals based on their race; (b) racial prejudice plus social and institutional power.

Rap: (a) commonly seen as shorthand for "rhythm and poetry"; (b) etymology connected to "rapport" or "repartee," which means witty or clever talking; (c) rhythmically speaking over music, beats, and sounds to share prose or messages that represent one's life, upbringing, culture, wants, desires, and ideas; (d) an extension of MCing, which is one of the six fundamental elements of Hip Hop.

Ratchet feminism: a form of feminism that disrupts notions of respectability politics and centers "ghetto" women. Differs from trap feminism in that it does not have its roots in male-dominated music.

Ratchetness: as defined by Brittney Cooper, this concept can be described as Black women's agency and framework to challenge respectability politics.

Respectability politics: beliefs/ideals stating that conformity to white, patriarchal, and mainstream standards of appearance and behavior will protect a person who is part of a marginalized group, specifically Black people and Black women. A transfigured version of the politics of respectability, a concept introduced by Evelyn Brooks Higginbotham.

Sexism: structural and systematic power to oppress women.

Sexuality: sexual identity, attraction, behaviors, and practices that express one's desires and orientations.

Social norms: socially enforced rules or expectations within a society or group.

Sociology of Cardi B: a concept developed by the authors of this book that combines sociology, Black feminism, and trap feminism to describe the feminism that rapper Cardi B practices within her music, personal life, and career; and an approach that shows the multifacetedness of Black women and Afro-Latinas.

Trap: the term "trap" was first introduced to Hip Hop lexicon by the Atlanta rapper T.I. Trapping refers to drug dealing and stashing large amounts of drugs in an abandoned house (referred to as the trap house or "bando").

Trap feminism: (a) a term coined by Sesali Bowen to describe the lived experiences of women who society has deemed as inappropriate and unproductive; (b) a feminist theory that centers Black women who live and embody the trap (see trap), who use their voices and their music to speak up and out, express themselves sexually, and state their truths; (c) a framework that disrupts every notion of respectability and embraces Cathy J. Cohen's concept of "deviance as resistance."

Trap feminist politics: civic and political engagement that emerges from the lived experiences of hood chicks, ghetto girls, and ratchet women and centers the needs of these women in policy and institutional decisions.

Uses of the erotic: (a) a concept developed by queer Black feminist scholar Audre Lorde to describe women's pleasure sexually and nonsexually; (b) teaches us to embrace our eroticism and to self-define our joys; (c) different from the patriarchal definition of the erotic, meaning women's pleasure is centered.

White gaze: the assumption that the default reader or observer is coming from a perspective of someone racialized as white; a concept introduced by W.E.B. Du Bois and coined by author Toni Morrison.

White patriarchy: white male domination over systems, structures, and institutions which relegate women of color to the bottom of the social hierarchy.

White supremacy: (a) a structure that systematically keeps whites at the top of the social hierarchy while simultaneously keeping Black people at the bottom; (b) the belief that white people are a superior race and should therefore dominate society, typically to the exclusion or detriment of other racial and ethnic groups, specifically Black people.

Womanism: a term coined by Alice Walker describing women who seek joy and pleasure from other women (sexually or nonsexually); a woman who lives a women-centered life where their activities, interests, and focus are on women.

INTRODUCTION

You may have picked up this book due to the "Sociology" or "Feminism" in the title, others of you were drawn to "Cardi B" or the "trap." Some of you may be academics or students while still others may simply be fans of Cardi B. Many of you might have been drawn to this book because you wanted to know: how do all these things fit together? No matter what brought you here, this book provides an opportunity to take seriously the intellect of Cardi B and people like her—women in and adjacent to the trap: the hood chicks, ghetto girls, and ratchet women. In this book, we recognize the value of a trap feminist sociological perspective, and we use the lens of trap feminism to elucidate the intellectual prowess, knowledge production, and feminism demonstrated throughout the public life of Cardi B.

In 2016, Cardi B expressed her bold stance about feminism in one powerful sentence on Instagram (IG),[1] "The problem is that being a feminist is something so great and y'all don't want me to be great, but too bad" (Thompson 2016).

A key thread throughout this book is a conversation about a question: Why don't "we" want Cardi B—and women like her, to be great? To answer this question, we take the opportunity to situate the experiences and knowledge of Black[2] women—who make choices that are often deemed unacceptable or reprehensible but are actually often misunderstood—within the history and constraints of structural conditions (racism, sexism, and classism), social institutions (government, education, and media), and individuals under the influence of white-centric patriarchal viewpoints. While the allure of Cardi B is often the spotlight when talking about this book, this project more specifically and intentionally elevates the voices of

DOI: 10.4324/9781003184980-1

marginalized Black women for Black women and Black girls. By the end of the book, you will be able to note how the experiences of marginalized Black women relate to the concepts of feminism, the white gaze, race and ethnicity, motherhood, and politics. All concepts that cannot be untied from our[3] racialized, gendered, and classed identities.

While we unapologetically wrote this book for Black women in and adjacent to the trap, we want this to be a book that has a dialogue with everyone from the trap to the classroom to the boardroom and more. We want to make space for our students, colleagues, and everyone else we interact with to not only engage with the experiences and knowledge of Black women but also celebrate Black womanhood even if they are not Black women. Once again, we turn to the words of Cardi B, but this time from the foreword of Tamika Mallory's book, *State of Emergency: How We Win in the Country We Built* (2021):

> This conversation is for everybody; every voice belongs at the table.

We use the rest of this introduction to answer some commonly asked questions—like why we chose to write about sociology, feminism, Cardi B, and trap—and to provide you with the foundational information you will need to read the rest of this book.

Sociology and Feminism

Simply put, sociology is the scientific study of society. As an academic discipline, the field of sociology is dedicated to understanding how and why groups of people function individually, together, and as part of social structures. The expectation of sociology is that scholars engage in rigorous theoretical and empirical research that is then published in journals that have been properly vetted and reviewed by fellow scholars and colleagues.

The history of sociology in the United States traces its origins to Yale University—the first to include sociology within a course, the University of Indiana—as the first to hold a course titled "Sociology," the University of Kansas and the University of Chicago—the first official sociology departments,[4] and the Atlanta Sociological Laboratory at Atlanta University—the first successful program of collective sociological research in the United States (Wright II 2020). Century-old journals, the *American Journal of Sociology* and *American Sociological Review*,[5] are often credited as the standard of sociology scholarship due to their longevity, perceived impact on the discipline and public, and ability to be seen as "generalist"—meaning scholarship that is relevant and applicable to most sociologists. Except for the Atlanta Sociological Laboratory, the history of those institutions and journals emphasize(d) and center(ed) "rigorous" scholarship that was devoid of practical application to everyday people, the public that we study. Historically, the term "rigorous scholarship" has been applied only to sociological research and texts (1) produced by white, highly educated, heterosexual men and (2) of interest to people in positions of power— white, highly educated, heterosexual men. People who did not and do not fill these categories, those who are nonwhite, not men, less educated, and/ or not heterosexual, were often considered problems to be studied and "fixed." Like other marginalized groups, Black women were not seen as intellectual people with agency who were capable of making choices and creating theories that improved our lives. Rather the presumption was made that we and people like us are making all the wrong decisions to be recognized in contemporary society. Historically (and even today), "mainstream sociology" would not deem the five of us as legitimate sociologists. Furthermore, Cardi B would not have even be considered worthy of an intellectually serious conversation. In summary, many of the early participants of the discipline of sociology through the American Sociological Association (ASA) worked hard to intentionally exclude people based on racism, sexism, classism, and elitism (Romero 2020).

For much of the 20th century, the study of race or Blackness, gender, feminism, and/or solving community problems were seen as subfields of "mainstream sociology" (which would have been better named "white male academic sociology"). Despite these exclusionary efforts, there have always been scholars who do not fall in line with the expectations of white and male sociology, white feminism, and white scholarship devoid of public facing engagement. Predating the 120-year history of ASA, the list of these distinguished scholars includes W.E.B. Du Bois and colleagues at the Atlanta Sociological Laboratory, Anna Julia Cooper, and Ida B. Wells-Barnett. By the 1970s, sociology expanded to include the Association of Black Sociologists (where we held the first panel for this book), Sociologists for Women in Society, and Society for the Study of Social Problems (Bernard 1973; Brunsma, Embrick, and Nanney 2015; Reed and Taylor 2018; Romero 2020). These named groups are often the organizational homes of scholars conducting research on Black sociology, feminism,[6] and public sociology. Noting this history, we follow the traditions of Anna Julia Cooper (Black feminism), W.E.B. Du Bois and the Atlanta Sociological Laboratory (Black sociology), and Ida B. Wells-Barnett (public sociology). This book is Black sociology, Black feminism, and public sociology— scholarship that has been deemed "less" by the standards of white sociology but does not base itself solely on those standards. In the next section, we will provide a brief history about Black sociology and Black feminism, but first we note what Toni Morrison said of racism in 1975:

> The function, the very serious function of racism is distraction. It keeps you from doing your work. It keeps you explaining, over and over again, your reason for being. Somebody says you have no language, and you spend twenty years proving that you do. Somebody says your head isn't shaped properly so you have scientists working on the fact that it is. Somebody says you have no art, so you dredge that up. Somebody says you have no kingdoms, so you dredge that up. None of this is necessary. There will always be one more thing.
>
> *(Morrison 1975)*

Therefore, this is not an exhaustive list of all the ways our foundational literature for this book is different from "mainstream sociology," or to prove the rigor of this work, but rather to provide you with the information you need to engage in this urgent conversation about feminism and sociology. In the following, we briefly outline the histories of the scholarship we draw from in Black sociology and Black feminism, focusing on how the intersection of these allows us to follow the traditions that understand and address social problems.

Black Sociology

Black sociology (Wright 2020) proposes that race, racism, and colonization are not secondary but central to understanding of the structural problems. Therefore, race is undoubtedly a key thread throughout this book. Watson (1976) defines Black sociology as:

> The systematic study of social interaction and social change among Black people, and in intergroup relations from the viewpoint of Black sociologists. The focus is on the construction of theories of social organization and social change that will contribute to an understanding of Black people's behavior and help point the way to release Black people from social oppression.
>
> *(118)*

Put another way, Black sociology is framed by five primary conditions: "1) the research be led, primarily, by Black Americans; 2) the research center on Black Americans; 3) the research be interdisciplinary; 4) the findings, whenever possible, be generalizable; and 5) the findings, whenever possible, have social/public policy implications" (Wright and Calhoun 2006).

The history of Black sociology is traced to W.E.B. Du Bois in the 19th century, credited as the first Black person to receive a PhD from Harvard and considered the first person to conduct rigorous theoretical and methodological research in sociology. His theoretical work engaged in conversations about who Black people are, their roles in power structures, and variations within the Black community as one of many ways to understand the United States. The research methods he and other Black sociologists engaged with through the Atlanta Sociological Laboratory from 1896 to 1917 includes the use of census data, surveys, and interviews that produced conclusions and theories published in articles, books, and data visualizations. This work was the standard of scholarship on all people, but more specifically on Black people. In the words of W.E.B. Du Bois himself in his oral history (Du Bois 1961),

> nevertheless, it's fair to say that for the next 25 years there wasn't a book published on the Negro problem that didn't have to depend upon on what we were doing at Atlanta University. It was the first study of sort. Ours was the first institution in the United States, white or Black, that had any course on the history of the American Negro or Negro history in general. So, it was a good beginning.

While the work of W.E.B. Du Bois has rightfully been discussed in recent years across books, articles, and special issues about his impact on the discipline of sociology and academia (Morris 2015; Itzigsohn and Brown 2020; Burawoy 2021; Wright and Morris 2021), Black sociology does go beyond his work. Recently, the work of Ida B. Wells Barnett has also been intentionally highlighted as part of Black sociology, given its emphasis on social and public policy implications. Wells-Barnett was a thought-provoking Black woman scholar who engaged in rigorous research methods. She chronicled the lynchings that occurred throughout the US South at the turn of the 20th century when mainstream sociology and society did not bother tracking them. In 2022, we finally saw the policy implication of her work, conducted over 100 years ago, through the passing of the Emmett Till Anti-Lynching Act.

In 1973, Joyce Ladner edited the anthology, *The Death of White Sociology* (Ladner 1998 (1973)), to trace this lineage and to center the work of Black scholars. In their chapter, Bracey, Meier, and Rudwick (1998 (1973)) note that the first half century of Black sociologists included work from "George Edmund Haynes, Betram W. Doyle, Ira De A Reid, Oliver

Cromwell Cox and Allison Davis; and the class volumes by Charles S. Johnson, E. Franklin Frazier, St. Clair Drake, and Horace Cayton." Their works transverse the topics of family, education, disenfranchisement, social class, and Black experiences in Philadelphia, Chicago, and New York. Black sociology carves out a space to center people who have been historically othered in the discipline and the United States.

The Sociology of Cardi B is in line with the five components of Black sociology outlined earlier: (1) this book is led by Black women; (2) the research here centers Black people with an expansion into the African Diaspora through Cardi B; (3) the research is inherently interdisciplinary, meaning it transcends beyond just sociology, given our emphasis on areas such as ethnic and gender studies; (4) the findings are generalizable, given the experiences of Black women tell us about the world around us; and (5) incorporating the experiences of Black women makes it possible to make better social and policy decisions about the world around us. In conducting Black sociology, we are carving out a space not just for Black women, but for Black women who are part of the trap. In addition to conducting sociology and Black sociology, we engage with a trap feminist standpoint throughout this book through the lineage of Black feminism.

Black Feminism

Parallel to Black sociology is the concept of Black feminism. Like Cardi B, feminism is often misunderstood. Scholarship in the sociology of gender and feminisms historically centers on the experiences and knowledge of white women. However, for many Black women, feminism has never been about the experiences of white women. Even if we add Black, Hip Hop, hood, or trap, feminism at its core is about incorporating the experiences and voices of all women who are marginalized, including those in the hood or trap. Meaning, women who are placed in subordinate positions in a patriarchal society that often emphasizes the experiences, thoughts, voices, and beliefs of men—which include those in the hood or trap. Same as if your sociology does not recognize the vast ways people engage in the world; if your feminism is not including the women on the margins, you are not doing good feminism. Furthermore, the structural impacts of race, gender, and class are embedded within our theories, analyses, and discussions throughout the book. By incorporating those who are the most powerless, we gain a critical understanding of the racialized, gendered, and classed oppressions they encounter, but also the power, skills, hustle, creativity, and joy they employ to successfully navigate society.

Our work here builds on the long history of Black feminism from within and beyond the academy. Using one's voice to speak up and speak out, even (or, especially) when it goes against the grain, is one of the most powerful tools used by Black feminists. This ability to speak our own truths and control our own narrative is the result of a feminist practice that reaches back to Anna Julia Cooper. Born as an enslaved person in 1858, Cooper published her first book, *A Voice from the South by a Black Woman in the South* in 1892, a text that was published the same year as the first sociology department was developed and before W.E.B. Du Bois completed his PhD in 1894. In that book, she presented a disciplined argument for centering the education of Black women in the fight for equal rights. In 1925, at the age of 67, Cooper became the fourth African American woman to obtain a doctor of philosophy.

Scholar Patricia Hill Collins[7] used her landmark book *Black Feminist Thought* (1991) to conceptualize and define a Black feminism that keeps the pressure on society to see Black women as full human beings. Collins states that the basic components of Black feminist thought, its thematic content and epistemology, or knowledge, are shaped by Black women's position in the economic, political, and ideological terrain. In line with this, each generation of Black feminists pushes for new understandings of the constraints and opportunities defining their lives. For example, Hip Hop feminism was formally introduced in academic conversations by Joan Morgan in her groundbreaking text *When Chickenheads Come Home to Roost: A Hip-Hop Feminist Breaks It Down* (Morgan 1999). There, she defines Hip Hop feminism as an extension of Black feminism that acknowledges and complicates the intersections of race, gender, Hip Hop[8], and misogyny within Hip Hop music and culture. Rather than critique, deconstruct, or draw boundaries, Hip Hop feminists embrace living in contradictions, which allows us to complicate and better understand the Hip Hop generation, politics around Hip Hop's cultural influence, and Black women's role in Hip Hop (Durham, Cooper, and Morris 2013). Hip Hop feminism's goal is to reach audiences outside of the constraints of academia and traditional white feminism.

Moving into the 21st century, Black women scholars who came of age with the development of Hip Hop feminism extended the concept through their own work. The Crunk Feminist Collective (Cooper, Morris, and Boylorn 2017) is one example of a group of Hip Hop feminist scholars who extended Morgan's work. Crunk Feminism allows us to see and understand how "getting crunk" serves as a form of Black resistance. It pushes us to speak up and speak out by utilizing what Lorde (1984) calls "the uses of anger" as a response to oppression. By showing the power of anger and rage, Crunk Feminism gives Black women "permission" to embody a femininity and feminism that disrupts the bounds of hegemonic femininity. The Crunk Feminist Collective carved out a space for Black women to embrace ratchet culture while naming and calling out patriarchy, misogynoir, and sexism within Hip Hop culture and music.

Hip Hop feminists call out the double standards between male and female rappers, as well as the over-critique of female rappers. Over the last decade, they have adopted an unapologetic pro-sex stance (Durham et al. 2013) while disrupting respectability politics of honor and self-respect. Female rappers are critiqued for explicitly discussing their body parts sexually, while male rappers are not. In fact, male rappers including lyrics on the size of their penis is a norm in Hip Hop lyrics. Additionally, female rappers' lyrical skills tend to be criticized more harshly than male rappers, as men debate whether women can "really rap." Hip Hop feminism notes that men have established themselves as the gatekeepers of Hip Hop, which often results in female artists being overlooked simply because they are women. Overall, Hip Hop feminism's professed goal is to give us more flexible tools to discuss Black sexual politics in music, by using it as a "lens to view the continuing reliance on normative notions of respectability as the primary way to understand gender and sexual politics in the public sphere" (Durham et al. 2013:726).

With the rise of Black women rappers like Cardi B, City Girls, and Megan Thee Stallion, there has been a shift in popular culture to embody the aesthetics of ghetto girls without actually understanding their lived experiences as Black women (Bowen 2021). These artists have come on the Hip Hop scene and used their platforms to speak truth to their lived experiences as Black women who grew up in the hood or the trap. To earn the title of trap feminist, women from the trap use their smarts to hustle, survive, thrive, and/or use their authentic voice to speak up and out to the powers that be. With these women in mind, *hood feminism* (Kendall 2020) and *trap feminism* (Bowen 2021) have put words to this approach to engaging with feminism, feminisms that we identify with throughout our book. Hood feminism defined by Mikki Kendall focuses on the Black women that mainstream white feminism has left behind. She focuses on the Black women who fall outside of respectable womanhood, who experience criminalization and gender violence, all while calling out the constraints and limits of white feminisms' view of equality for all women. The authors of this text agree with Kendall's sentiment in that our feminisms cannot leave anyone behind. This is where we wanted to build from her critical yet important intersectional work on feminism. Trap feminism is discussed in greater detail in Chapter 1.

Whether we are talking about Black, Hip Hop, hood, or trap, feminism at its core is about paying close attention to the unique struggles, hopes, and joys of people who endure intersecting oppressions. These groups include poor Black women, inclusive of queer Black women and femmes, disabled Black women, and working-class Black women, among others

(Luna and Pirtle 2021). *The Sociology of Cardi B* pushes the field of sociology to acknowledge and center the contributions of trap feminists as necessary to the expansion of Black feminist scholarship. We present the sociology of Cardi B to push forward a new, even more inclusive model of feminism. Until every Black woman is included in our conceptualization of feminism, we will be thwarted in our attempts to achieve not only well-informed theories that can guide our sociopolitical decisions toward justice and equality but any semblance of justice and equality for all. And if your Black feminism is not including or acknowledging the Black women of the trap, it is incomplete. We can only imagine what Anna Julia Cooper would think of Cardi B or us; possibly, she would not approve of our bold self-expressions. But the burgeoning movements of Black feminist scholars, in and outside of academia, have widened our paths.

In sum, while we recognize that the differences between these terms are worth considering, when *we* say sociology, we mean Black sociology, and when *we* say feminism, we mean Black feminism.

Cardi B and "Trap"

In addition to engaging a discussion on the terms sociology and feminism, this book engages in a discussion on Cardi B and trap. We use Cardi B's public life as a *framework* to magnify the many structural and interpersonal elements of the parallel and immeasurable experiences of Black women's lives. For many, at first glance, Cardi B may seem like she is just another Black woman rapper and former stripper talking about her pussy and sex with "funny" phrases like "Hoes Don't Get Cold" or "A woman's going to have beef with me foreva." For us, yes, she is all those things, and she is more. She is:

- A Black hood chick former stripper from the Bronx.
- A Sexually Expressive, Scorned, and Idolized, Afro-Latina Hip Hop Rapper and Reality TV Star.
- A wealthy woman who threw one of her red Elie Saab platform heels at her nemesis while wearing a Dolce and Gabbana gown at New York's highest fashion event.
- A bilingual woman who brags publicly and often in English, Spanish, and Spanglish.
- A sexually expressive mother who raps about both the money-moving power of her wet ass pussy *and* the joy of raising adorable kids with her beloved husband, the rapper Offset.
- A self-proclaimed feminist who's discussed policies in one-on-one meetings with President Joe Biden and Senator Bernie Sanders.

It is no surprise that 152.5 million people (including all five of us) follow Cardi B on IG; her authenticity is captivating. When we expand our sociological imaginations, the seeming contradictions of Cardi B's public life collapse into a cohesive yet complicated model of womanhood and trap feminism—a concept previously defined by Corey Miles (2020) in his article "Black Rural Feminist Trap: stylized and gendered performativity in trap music" and Sesali Bowen in her acclaimed memoir, Bad Fat Black Girl: Notes from a Trap Feminist (2021). In *The Sociology of Cardi B*, we elaborate on the specific ways Cardi B represents trap feminism—a feminism that centers Black women and girls who live and express themselves "in ways that have been deemed inappropriate, reductive, and unproductive" (Bowen 2021).

Some people have asked, why not focus on the sociology of Lil Kim, Trina, Nicki Minaj, Remy Ma, another Black woman rapper, or all Black women rappers? While other celebrities captivate us and identify as feminists (e.g., Beyonce and Oprah), we engage with Cardi B due to her unique willingness to share her unfiltered thoughts and experiences with the public. Controlling one's own narrative is one of the most powerful tools women can use to counter stereotypes about themselves. Unlike previous women rap and Hip Hop artists, Cardi grew her massive following on Vine, Twitter, and IG by posting truth-telling videos about her impoverished Bronx childhood, her wild dating history, her butt injections and breast implants, and her life as a stripper. Because she can control and has controlled her own narrative on social media, Cardi's authentic voice is not easily silenced by anyone, including the men who have historically dominated the Hip Hop scene.[9]

Although all five of us are proud fans of Cardi B, we chose to push forward *The Sociology of Cardi B* because we knew she was about so much more than her irresistible rapping voice. By sharing her experiences as a self-proclaimed gangsta bitch and a poor Black girl and Afro-Latina in the Bronx, Cardi B has not only garnered the attention and pocketbooks (31 million records sold so far) of her fans, but she has also given voice to the complexities and ever-expanding boundaries of feminism. As sociologists in academia, we have personalized the importance of this expansion; in many academic settings, women who speak and/or act like Cardi B are still rejected or ignored. Many of our current sociological theories are flawed at best and at worst, our theories inform policies that exaggerate the oppression of the marginalized groups we are trying to "help." Cardi's unabashed sexuality and refusal to succumb to white notions of respectability cause most people to discredit her and women like her as nothing more than someone who needs to be helped. However, for the same reasons that people discredit Cardi B and women like her, we center the voices of Black women in and adjacent to the trap. Each of us know colleagues who feel forced to adjust how they dress, speak, and act to be taken seriously according to white notions of respectability. And sometimes, it is us that feel this way. Something we note as an experience of Cardi B as well. In her forward to Tamika Mallory's book (Mallory 2021), Cardi asks Black feminist scholar Angela Davis:

> Sometimes because of the haters, I feel like I should just shut up, but I know I can't. It's too serious. Dr. Davis, please tell me and people like me, how do we activate? Are we welcome? How does someone like me, someone who has no political background, who's a little loud, a little unbuttoned, how does that girl or boy from the bottom do their part?
>
> *(Mallory 2021:xvi)*

Angela Davis, a Black feminist scholar, responds, "Dearest Cardi," with all the care of taking Cardi seriously, and goes on to say:

> Yes, of course you are welcome, and you know that you are especially needed at this moment. Just as this movement requires the sturdy shoulders, forceful words, and steady leadership of our sister Tamika, we also need your vision, your creative power, and your unabashed political interventions. You inspire Tamika—and you inspire all of us. Young activists today recognize that structures have to be transformed, systems must be changed, and that we need a revolutionary approach to racism, misogyny, climate change, homophobia, and transphobia.
>
> *(Mallory 2021:xvii)*

To move sociology and feminism forward for Black women, Angela Davis and our foremother scholars have told us that we need to pay the closest attention to the women on the margins, including the women of the trap, women who are seen as too radical or ratchet or undeserving for academia, white-centric sociology, and society. Carrying this torch, we must advocate for a sociology and a feminism that not only *recognizes* but also *relies* on the knowledge and theories produced by and for the most marginalized women among us. Using sociology and feminism, we can finally interrogate why "we" don't want Cardi (or women like her) to "be great."

The Sociology of Cardi B: A Trap Feminist Perspective

To bring out the "*Sociology*" in writing *The Sociology of Cardi B*, we took on the roles of well-educated, humble learners, not superior preachers. We support the exchange of ideas between the ivory tower and the trap, and the advancement of theories not based on the knowledge produced in well-appointed university offices, but reliant on the knowledge produced by Black women in and from the trap.

We use our sociological imaginations to position the content of Cardi B's public-facing life as an anchor for a critical sociological discussion about the complexities and urgency of a more diverse Black feminism; a feminist theory and praxis that includes the trap and a varied sociology that centers Black sociology. We realized that to expand our sociological imaginations, we had to sit in the discomfort of imagining the reactions of people who were not like us. Many people do not want to face, much less learn from, the unapologetic sexuality and trap feminism exemplified by Cardi B. With this, our hope is that you can sit in the discomfort long enough to expose the fallacies of "all-inclusive" feminism—that is often defaulted as white, and discover the power of sociological theories based on the knowledge produced by women who live or lived in the trap—women like Cardi B. Remember that being uncomfortable is the first sign that your sociological imagination is being pushed into new territory.

In *The Sociology of Cardi B*, we adopt the standpoint of trap feminism to acknowledge and center the intellectual contributions of Black women in and from the trap. As Black feminists and sociologists, we respect the intellectual contributions and expertise of hood chicks, ghetto girls, and ratchet women. This book theorizes and operationalizes trap feminism as a tool to understand the everyday life of the women who reside in the trap. *The Sociology of Cardi B* challenges the current and past constraints of white mainstream sociology as well as Black sociology and Black feminism. We use the theories of Black sociology, Black feminism, and Hip Hop feminism to deepen our understanding of ratchet Black women's engagement with society. We center Black women's experiences through a discussion of Cardi B's public life and feminism to highlight, discuss, and focus on the knowledge, culture, music, and politics that hood chicks and ratchet women embody daily. We argue for looking at the world through the eyes of women who have been forgotten or deliberately excluded by mainstream feminism; Trap feminism not only helps us understand Black women but also provides us with a broader and critical understanding of society.

We wrote *The Sociology of Cardi B* to provide theoretical frameworks and practical applications for those seeking to engage in research and sociological Black feminist scholarship that includes "non-respectable" women. We are also here to expand and support the sociological relevance and seriousness of Black feminist scholars, Black cultural icons, and Black sociology.

Du Bois once stated of sociology that people often are doing "car window sociology," where they observe groups rather than engage with them

(Morris 2017). Because we subscribe to the idea that Black women are experts on their own lives, we know we need to do more than roll down the car windows (Du Bois 1903). In *The Sociology of Cardi B*, we stop the car in the center of the trap and use our sociological imaginations to illuminate the inherent feminism practiced by women in, from, and adjacent to it. Our goal is to push forward a truly inclusive concept of feminism that includes the full self-expressions and life experiences of marginalized Black women. Some may use these descriptions of marginalized Black women to pigeon-hole, judge, or simplify the public expressions of a woman like Cardi B. However, in this book we recognize that we would lose the nuanced, critical perspective of marginalized Black women from the hood if we do not incorporate their lived experiences—which means we lose our chances to evoke a truly all-inclusive feminism.

Organization of Chapters

We use the foundational histories of Black sociology and Black feminism, our own experiences, and our sociological training to create this Black feminist project. We unified our diverse personal experiences and interests in Cardi B as well as our professional experiences across university types and locations to intentionally create an equally co-authored and collaborative project rather than an edited volume (names are alphabetical). With this as the foundation, the following chapters use a trap feminist standpoint along with sociological theories and methods, to address the life, artistry, politics, culture, and feminist stance that Cardi B employs in her life. The chapters in this book help us answer important sociological questions but are by no means exhaustive of all the things that Cardi is, says, and does. We engage in a trap feminist approach, praxis, and application to unpack and discuss areas of our collective expertise, including the topics of motherhood, identity, politics, trap music, the Hip Hop industry, and sex positivity.

In Chapter 1, "What Is a Trap Feminist Standpoint?," we define trap feminism, discuss its importance for the Black women who reside in and represent trap spaces in urban neighborhoods, and highlight the ways that Cardi B's life story and her professional experience embody trap feminism. Using theoretical analysis, we demonstrate that Black feminists reproduce respectability politics unless their feminism includes the knowledge produced by Cardi B and all Black women deemed as ghetto or ratchet. Lastly, this chapter calls for the centering of trap feminists within Black feminism as well as respecting, loving, and embracing trap feminists and their production of knowledge from the trap.

In Chapter 2, "Cardi B's Bad Behavior: Resisting White Gaze and Respectability," we contend with comments about the "inappropriateness" of Cardi B's behavior in public. Specifically, we use the physical altercation with rap icon Nicki Minaj at a 2018 New York Fashion Week (NYFW) event as a case study to understand the white gaze, respectability, and resistance. We use conceptualizations of the white gaze to suggest that the criticisms of Cardi B and women like her are often laced with respectability. We frame Cardi's refusal to alter her behavior in white spaces as a form of resistance, and we conclude that much of the public's criticism of Cardi's actions is due to an internalization of the white gaze. Lastly, we detail how a retreat from centering the white gaze and respectability politics creates space for respecting and valuing the contributions and knowledge of those who are typically pushed to the margins.

Chapter 3, "Cardi B Living Her Best Feminist Life," seeks to answer the question: What is Cardi B's feminist praxis? Her art is used as data to answer this question. We conducted a content analysis using the song lyrics of Cardi B's first studio album, *Invasion of Privacy*, as data to shed light on her relationship with feminism. The results of this study show that Cardi B's art reflects a complicated relationship with marianismo, a unique set of gender expectations brought to the United States with Latinx immigrants.

In Chapter 4, "Policing Cardi B's Blackness" we analyze public debates in the media about Cardi B's Blackness. These debates focus on Cardi's appearance as a "racially ambiguous" woman and her ethnic background as the daughter of Caribbean immigrant parents. We argue that concerns over Cardi B's Blackness (or lack thereof) elucidate broader conflicting racial ideologies across the African Diaspora, as well as concerns about race in the United States. These questions include the following: Who counts as Black? Is Blackness about appearance, ancestry, lived experiences, culture, politics, or all of these? And who gets to decide? We advocate for an African Diasporic understanding of Blackness paired with trap feminism to better understand Cardi B's racial self-identification and lived experiences as an Afro-Latina.

In Chapter 5, "Cardi Put the WAP on Offset: Trap Feminist Motherhood," we center Cardi B's expressed viewpoints and lived experiences of motherhood and sexuality. Her controversial performances often cause debates about how Black women should act and behave as mothers. She expresses a positive enthusiastic view of sex as a natural part of human life. Controlling images (Collins 2002) present Black women's sexuality as deviant, however, Cardi B challenges normative notions of women's sexuality by subversively disrupting these images of Black womanhood and motherhood.

In Chapter 6, "Cardi B's Trap Feminist Politics," we turn our attention to Cardi B's political engagement and activism. Since her time on the reality TV show *Love & Hip Hop: New York*, there has been no shortage of examples of Cardi B showing her commitment to politics. We examine Cardi B's civic and political engagement by focusing on her work in electoral politics as well as her activism surrounding issues of race, class, gender equality, and immigration rights. Using Black and trap feminist theories, we argue that Cardi's political engagement highlights (and defies) societally enacted boundaries that determine who is allowed to be part of the political process. Specifically, we show how Cardi B's experiences uncover the need for a more inclusive democracy. Throughout the chapter we analyze how the public, political pundits, and politicians received Cardi and conclude with the ways we see her political engagement continuing in the future.

Throughout this book, we raise questions concerning current and future understandings of feminism, motherhood and sexuality, gender, race and ethnicity, and political engagement using a combination of trap feminist sociological theorizing and the words and lived experiences of Cardi B. While Cardi B encompasses several often-excluded identities in sociological conversations, the conclusion chapter discusses areas that still need additional research. We then encourage readers to deconstruct their relationship with previous assumptions about how individuals ought to exist without the white gaze, respectability politics, and gendered standards on womanhood. Finally, we push for readers to reconsider their policing of Black women. In doing so, we encourage readers to recognize the complexities of lived experiences even when they are incongruent than our expectations. Reading this book from the viewpoint that Black women are the experts on their own lives and that they navigate the trap, the hood, and society in ways that best fit their lives will help you better grasp the importance of a trap feminist standpoint.

We hope you ride with us as we go on a journey to discover new truths about sociology and feminism. We are inspired by the words of Zora Neal Hurston, who stated, "Sometimes, I feel discriminated against, but it does not make me angry. It merely astonishes me. How can any deny themselves the pleasure of my company? It's beyond me." You may not "like" the conversation within this book; however, it is a good conversation. This book will make you think. So, in the words of Cardi B: You may not want us to be great. Too bad.

Notes

1 Cardi B chose to delete her Instagram and social media in 2018 immediately after rapper Azealia Banks made comments about her. She subsequently has returned to Instagram but is known to delete her social media posts when it suits her (Nunez 2018).
2 Although in 2023 it should go without being said, we intentionally capitalize the B in Black.

3 Similar to Patricia Hill Collins in Black Feminist Thought (1991), we use "we" and "our" to acknowledge how we too are Black women who have lived in and/or adjacent to the trap.

4 The official first department depends on what you consider to be a department. The University of Kansas was the first to hold a department in 1889 with the Department of History and Sociology. The University of Chicago is the first to hold a solely Sociology Department (Wright 2020).

5 *The American Journal of Sociology* was founded in 1895 at the University of Chicago. *The American Sociological Review* was founded in 1936 as the official journal of the American Sociological Association.

6 Throughout this text we say feminism or feminist rather than clarifying a difference between feminist sociology. We contend that feminism is inherently sociological.

7 In recognizing the history of sociology, we note that Patricia Hill Collins was the first Black woman elected as the President of the American Sociological Association. In total, sociology has elected three Black women as President (years served in parenthesis): Patricia Hill Collins (2008–2009), Prudence Carter (2022–2023), and Adia Harvey Wingfield (2024–2025) (American Sociological Association 2024).

8 In line with Iglesias and Harris (2022), we capitalize Hip Hop throughout this text.

9 Rapper and producers Snoop Dogg, Jermaine Dupri, and CeeLo Green have notably criticized Cardi B for her provocative lyrics that involve sex. All people who Cardi herself has responded to unabashedly and candidly (www.revolt.tv/article/2020-12-12/63965/snoop-dogg-criticizes-cardi-b-and-megan-thee-stallions-hit-song-wap/; www.rollingstone.com/music/music-news/cardi-b-jermaine-dupris-female-rappers-response-858199/).

1

WHAT IS A TRAP FEMINIST STANDPOINT?

The standpoint theory of trap feminism is a sociological theory that centers and celebrates the life experiences of hood chicks, ratchet women, and ghetto girls—women living in or adjacent to the trap—women like Cardi B. In *The Sociology of Cardi B*, we adopt the standpoint of trap feminism to answer a call to action issued by Black feminist scholar Patricia Hill Collins, the 100th and first Black woman leader of the American Sociological Association. In her groundbreaking book, *Black Feminist Thought: Knowledge, Consciousness, and the Politics of Empowerment*, Collins urges Black feminists within academia to expand their concept of Black feminism by bridging the gap between the knowledge, culture, and theories of the streets and the insular theories created within the ivory towers of academia. To do this, we must recognize Black women outside of academia as curators of knowledge who develop reliable theories that apply to their lives. In other words, our research needs to reflect the agency of hood or hood adjacent Black women and see them as the ultimate experts on their lives.

Only through the wide lens of trap feminism can we discern the feminist stance and advanced intellect of hood Black women. Once we recognize their expertise, we can finally place their knowledge at the center of our sociological studies and theorizing. Collins challenges us to stop ignoring the knowledge produced by Black women and start questioning the legitimacy of the so-called knowledge produced mostly by white men. In essence, the standpoint theory of trap feminism de-marginalizes poor Black women in our sociological studies and our feminism by naming the ways of knowing and pointing out the strategies of resistance that hood chicks,

DOI: 10.4324/9781003184980-2

ghetto girls, and ratchet women engage in to demonstrate power in all aspects of their lives. In short, trap feminism is a standpoint theory that celebrates and focuses on self-defined womanhood and motherhood from the perspective of hood Black women. Trap feminism centers or focuses on the Black women who society has labeled as ratchet (Love 2017)— Black women who refuse to display their gender and womanhood according to white-centric standards. Trap feminism also provides a platform for women to discuss their sexual desires by disrupting the restrictive ideals for what women can or should talk about when it comes to their bodies and sexual pleasure (Bowen 2021).

To explain why a trap feminist approach to sociology is important for all Black women, but especially for Black women who live in the trap or who grew up in the trap, we first go deep into the definition of trap feminism, a feminism that denounces and avoids reifying white patriarchal standards of womanhood within Black feminist spaces and literature. Then, we discuss how we use and apply trap feminism to Black women's sexuality, gender roles, and femininity. Finally, we highlight the feminism found in the lyrics of Black female rappers like Cardi B, City Girls, Megan Thee Stallion, and Gangsta Boo. In creating and performing their songs, these women embody trap feminism by boldly using their voices and lyrics to state their demands and desires in ways that represent who they are as women.

Our analysis of Black womanhood and Black femininity enables us to move beyond mere inclusion to the explicit centering of ratchet girls, hood chicks, and ghetto girls by combining sociology, Black feminism, Hip Hop feminism, and trap feminism to describe the feminism practiced by Cardi B. Cardi B understands the power of her voice, and she uses her voice to speak up for herself and to speak out on issues and concerns regarding her career, family, or politics. Black women's ability to speak back, speak up, and speak out (Evans-Winters 2015) is rooted in a Black feminist practice. In spaces where we have typically been erased or dismissed, voices like Cardi's disrupt oppressive white ideologies and bring awareness to sociological topics from a trap feminist standpoint. Understanding the power of your voice is a hallmark of trap feminism—regardless if you talk in slang, an accent, or African American vernacular,[1] trap feminists speak their minds in the way that fits them.

So, what exactly is trap feminism as a theory? The term trap feminism was coined by Bowen (2021) in her book *Bad Fat Black Girl: Notes from a Trap Feminist*, which discusses her journey with feminism, her love of southern Hip Hop, and her understanding of the trap as a self-defined trap feminist. Building off Bowen's framework, we define trap feminism as a feminist theory that aims to refute classist, white, male, and/or patriarchal expectations of how Black women should behave, speak, and act in public. More specifically, trap feminism challenges the expectations of respectability politics (Higginbotham 1993) for women. You'll learn more about respectability politics in Chapter 2, but here we define respectability politics as the strict rules and social norms that dictate appropriate human behavior in public spaces. Since these societal norms are based on standards created by white folks, these norms work to silence the voices of Black women. If the voice, style, and life experience(s) of a Black woman does not fit into the preferred white-centric narrative of womanhood, she is seen as a subordinate who deserves to be chastised and ignored. On the other hand, Cardi B speaks to the importance of celebrating self-defined womanhood. She does not want to be compared to anyone else and understands that each woman should have the ability to define who they are for themselves.

In 2016, Cardi B took to twitter to state:

> I'm going to encourage any type of woman. You don't have to be a woman like me for me to encourage and support you and tell you, "Yes, b—h, keep on going."[2]

Black feminist writer Audre Lorde (Lorde 1984) stated in her book *Sister Outsider*, "that it is axiomatic that we define ourselves for ourselves, or else we will be defined by others for their use and to our detriment (45)." Trap feminists understand the power of self-definition based on cultural standards that make sense from the perspective of their lives in the trap. To sum this up, using one's voice to speak up and speak out is one of the most important tools of feminism. Trap feminists know how to use their voices to speak their minds, even if their standpoint is unpopular or discredited based on the language or slang they use. They speak out in ways that are viewed as unacceptable to the dominant white society by embracing the trap, hood politics, and oppositional behavior (Cohen 2004).

Our understanding of trap feminism begs several questions: Why do we continue to subscribe to white-centric definitions of womanhood to define ourselves as Black women when we were excluded from the category of woman in the first place? Why are we still using a white-centric standard to define Black womanhood? And lastly, why do we, as Black women, judge other Black women who do not subscribe to white-centric, classed, social norms?

Trap Feminist Standpoint

To fully understand and apply trap feminism, it is important that we have a theoretical framework to use when discussing trap music, trap culture, and

Hip Hop music from the perspective of trap feminists. We define trap feminism as a standpoint theory (Collins 1991) that centers the hood chicks, ghetto girls, and the Black women who live and embody the trap. Our book is rooted in Black feminist thought (Collins 2000; Hull et al. 1982), which is a theory that names Black feminism in practice and states that Black women are producers of knowledge based on their lived experiences, which make them experts on their own lives. We then build off of Hip Hop feminist standpoints (Cooper et al. 2017; Morgan 1999), which take a feminist perspective to Hip Hop music providing us with a framework to discuss patriarchy, misogyny, and women's roles in Hip Hop. Building from Black feminist thought and Hip Hop feminism, we use Miles's (2020) article "Black Rural Feminist Trap: stylized and gendered performativity in trap music" and his understanding of the trap beyond the male perspective; and lastly, we use Bowen's (2021) concept and definition of trap feminism to guide our trap feminist standpoint theory.

Both Miles and Bowen state that trap feminism (1) "is an intellectual framework, consciousness, and day to day way of being that speaks to a type of hustling that creates space, both physical and ideological, in response to a gendered racial capitalism that intends to keep us confined" (Miles 2020:10) and (2) "acknowledges the ways in which Black girls might benefit from and enjoy performing racialized gender in ways that have been deemed inappropriate, reductive, and unproductive" (Bowen 2021:15). Trap feminism provides the opportunity for ghetto girls and hood chicks to embrace trap culture and music in ways that allow for women to self-define their lives based on their environment in the trap.

A core element of trap feminism is the active disruption of behavioral norms, standards of beauty, dress, and expressions of sexuality. Trap feminists disrupt the social norms of how women should behave, speak, talk, and dress in public—norms associated with respectability politics. According to the respectability politics that set middle-class standards for gender norms (Higginbotham 1993), Black women who reside in urban, low-income areas are unladylike, uncouth, and unworthy of respect because they engage in oppositional behaviors that are stigmatized (Cohen 2004). These behaviors include talking loud and dancing in public, using profanity, and showing off body parts in public that are seen as sexual (boobs and booty). Social norms dictate appropriate behavior for women, calling out the act of wearing body-revealing outfits in public as low-class, uncouth, and even ratchet (we'll explore more of this in Chapter 3). In a patriarchal culture like ours, women who use curse words are labeled crude and disrespectful (Kendall 2020). But from a trap feminist perspective, these behaviors are seen as admirable resistance to oppressive social norms.

Trap feminists manifest their own definitions of Black womanhood while also creating their own standards of beauty for their hair, makeup, nails, and style (Kendall 2020). Cardi B is known for her long colorful nails and colorful wigs, which are viewed as ghetto by mainstream beauty standards. Her former gang affiliation and occupation as a stripper, as well as the many visible tattoos on her arms and thighs, disrupt the white-centric beauty standards for how women should show up in the world. According to Eurocentric standards of beauty, women are expected to present themselves in a soft, feminine, subservient manner, with flawless skin and hair (Hunter 2016). Scars from fighting and tattoos are seen as masculine and hard, which are features women should not wear proudly, as Cardi does (Jones 2010). For the cover of her single, "Bodak Yellow," Cardi B embodies the complexities of trap feminism by adorning herself in a long red wig and a short dress that gives fans a clear view of the large peacock tattoo on her thigh.

No matter where she appears in public, Cardi B does not give up her authenticity for the sake of oppressive white-centric standards or social norms. Cohen (2004) refers to this non-assimilation as "oppositional behavior" or deviance as resistance to the dominant white society. In other words, when Black people deliberately engage in behavior that is considered unproductive or dysfunctional by white society, they are taking a stand against white oppression. By creating and maintaining her own standards and sticking to them wherever she goes, Cardi B is showing us her capacity to define herself for herself without regard for societally approved norms. She does not change her vocabulary and vernacular to accommodate the preferences of white people. Instead of developing the habit of code-switching in white spaces, Cardi B continues to embody the trap and her Latina roots as the self-proclaimed "Trap Selena." Selena[3] is a musical icon and Mexican American Tejano singer and is known as the Queen of Tejano music. She was an idol for many Latinos and is still beloved to this day throughout many music genres. Trap Selena speaks directly to who Cardi B is as an Afro-Latina and where she grew up in the Bronx. In response to people's outrage about Cardi's use of Selena's name to describe herself, Cardi tweeted, "I said Trap Selena because who didn't want to be Selena? She is a alter ego that everyone wanted to be and I want the world to know how much I love her" (Twitter; @iamcardib; 12/06/2017).[4]

Moreover, trap feminists like Cardi B set their own standards and self-define their womanhood (Bowen 2021). They wear what they please in public, regardless of classed expectations on how women should dress; this can include but is not limited to sexy clothing that shows off the body. Trap feminists use their voices to share their narratives and to speak truth to their power as Black women. Additionally, trap feminists are emboldened by their sexuality and use it as a source of power in their lives (Cooper et al. 2017; Morgan 1999). In general, as a standpoint theory, trap feminism focuses on trap culture, voices, and lived experiences all from the perspective of ratchet and ghetto Black women.

Radical and Ratchet: Why We Need a Trap Feminist Theory

We call on Black feminism to create connections grounded in history that carve out space for the lived experiences and voices of trap feminists across Black feminist and Hip Hop feminist spaces. In addition, we draw attention to the patriarchy within the trap; the voices and experiences of hood Black men often eclipse the voices and experiences of hood Black women. This male-centric view obfuscates the fact that Black women and girls must create their own tools of survival to protect themselves from the violence within their neighborhoods. In the trap, Black girls learn early on that no one is coming to save them, so they must learn how to save themselves (The Combahee River Collective 1982).

Black boys *and girls* deal with violence in low-income neighborhoods (Anderson 2000), and Black girls are often victims of male violence (Morris 2016). In their 2010 book, *Fighting for Girls: New Perspectives on Gender Violence*, scholars Chesney-Lind and Jones tell us how Black girls learn that they must stand up for themselves (Chesney-Lind and Jones 2010). This means that Black girls often defend and protect themselves by fighting Black girls and boys. In her acclaimed book, *Between Good and Ghetto*, author Nikki Jones (2010) unpacks the reasons why Black girls use fighting as a survival strategy in their neighborhoods and schools. While women and girls who fight are deemed unladylike, ghetto, or ratchet by Western norms and respectability politics, Jones's ethnography demonstrates that even the Black girls who are considered "good girls" must fight and stand up for themselves within their schools and neighborhoods. In Jones's study, both good and ghetto girls got into physical altercations to build a reputation, so people knew not to mess with them. Therefore, Jones (2010) discusses the paradox inner city Black girls face, as they attempt to find a balance between femininity and fighting for their survival.

Cardi B's reputation as a girl fighter completely disrupts the notion that women should be soft. She has openly shared stories about carrying a razor in her mouth when she was younger to defend herself in case she got into a fight. On *Love & Hip-Hop: New York*, Cardi's altercations with the other women on the reality show often went viral. In Chapter 2, you'll learn more about the trap feminism and oppositional gaze that Cardi B expressed in the infamous fight with Nicki Minaj at the 2018 New York Fashion Week. By examining and exploring the daily lives of women who live in the trap through a feminist lens, we can better understand their worldview and perspective. Using one's voice to share lived experiences is a powerful feminist tool that Black women have been using to speak out about their lives. Cardi B did this when she took to her social media platforms to share stories about growing up in the Bronx, stripper stories, dating tips, and advice on men.

Additionally, trap feminism calls for Black feminism to shift our focus back toward the women who are oppressed through race, gender, and class or, in this case, the hood chicks, ghetto girls, and ratchets. As Hip Hop feminists and Black feminists, we should not only be using our standpoints to eradicate systems of oppression; we should also be using our feminism as a lens to see and hear each other and to validate each other as Black women. bell hooks calls this the oppositional gaze (hooks 2010). As a tool of Black feminism, the oppositional gaze allows us to see one another through our self-defined views of womanhood. This is especially important in a society that views Black and Brown women as disposable. If our Black feminist practice does not include the voices of ghetto girls, hood chicks, and Black women who experience classism, racism, and sexism, then we must revisit our practices to ensure all Black women are seen, heard, and validated.

Radical and Ratchet: The Importance of Trap Feminism in Practice

If our Black feminist praxis does not center girl fighters, hood chicks, and ghetto girls, then our feminism is not radical enough. Black feminism can be used as a tool to dismantle the patriarchy and racism, but if that feminism is not accessible to the women who live at the margins of society, then our feminist praxis is not ratchet enough. Black feminism provides us with tools that allow us to define ourselves and create and set the standards that best serve our lives. By liberating us from respectability politics and white-centric standards of beauty and social norms while employing and embracing ratchet politics (Love 2017) and hood politics (Kendall 2020), trap feminism expands the power of marginalized Black women. Ratchet and hood politics recognize and celebrate ratchetness and other forms of Black politics that are in opposition to white-centric norms (Payne 2020). Using Cooper's (2012) definition of ratchetness, which can be described as Black women's agency to challenge respectability politics, trap feminism serves as a radical practice that actively disrupts the classed and gendered expectations placed on Black women by celebrating and acknowledging the value of their oppositional or ratchet behavior (Cohen 2004). In other words, trap feminism gives Black women permission to talk, dress, speak, and behave according to trap aesthetics in public and private spaces. As you'll see in Chapter 5, this includes twerking in public as an act of joy, liberation, and freedom that also disrupts white social norms. Because we do not subscribe to white patriarchal definitions of womanhood, trap feminists do not view twerking in public as ghetto or ratchet. Therefore, we do not begrudge women for twerking in public. Instead, we acknowledge the creativity and power of twerking. A trap feminist might join in and twerk as an act of solidarity and celebration. Embracing a trap feminist standpoint provides more space for all Black women by calling out the damage done by applying European standards of beauty and white patriarchal definitions of womanhood to Black women. Trap feminists know that white-centric standards will not ever serve the needs of Black women and should not ever be used to judge the behavior or the style of Black women.

During enslavement, Black women were excluded from the legal category of "woman" since African Americans were not considered people under the law (Haley 2016; hooks 2015). Only white women were included in the legal category of women, which explains why existing gender expectations and standards of beauty are based on white womanhood. Moreover, during enslavement, Black women were not viewed as humans, they were seen and categorized as property. Therefore, enslaved Black women were often victims and survivors of rape from white men; however, these men were not held accountable for sexual assault because legally Black women were not women (Roberts 2017). In other words, Black women were viewed as unrapable. It was not until the passing of the 14th Amendment in 1868 that Black people were granted Black citizenship and were categorized as people; and it was not until much later, in 1965, when Black women gained the right to vote with the Voting Rights Act of 1965.

Even after Black women were legally categorized as women, their Blackness placed them outside of white-centric standards of beauty for women (Haley 2016). These standards of beauty are centered on middle-class white femininity which again excludes Black women because of our race and class. Even middle-class Black women do not fully meet these beauty standards because their Blackness does not afford them the same privileges that are given to middle-class white women (Collins 2000, 2004). Wealthy and successful Black women who subscribe to all aspects of white culture can still be viewed as ghetto or ratchet. Overall, Black women, regardless of their social class, are often critiqued, condemned, and stigmatized by white society because of racist and sexist stereotypes.

We have been sold the idea that if we subscribe to white social norms of femininity, sexuality, and womanhood we will be respected as women (Hunter 2016; Lorde 1984). However, we as Black women know this is not a truth but rather an ideology we are forced to align with to make whites feel more comfortable when we are in public spaces. Therefore, the condemnation of Black femininity as deviant (Haley 2016) does not afford Black women the opportunity to be seen as women according to white norms because womanhood was historically and culturally meant to be for white women only. For that reason, it is important to embrace and practice trap feminism in our daily lives so that we liberate ourselves from social norms that were never meant for us.

The Erotic as Power: Trap Feminism and Sexuality

Instead of being oppressed or ashamed, trap feminists are empowered by their sexuality, and they feel free to assert that power through their body language, speech, and/or their style of clothing. As you'll see in Chapter 3, the theme of sexuality is woven throughout Cardi's song lyrics. Cardi's ability to state her desires in a frank and often comedic manner demonstrates ownership of her sexual power. This bold assertion of sexual prowess may be jarring to people who subscribe to respectability politics. According to the standards of these people, women should not even discuss, much less demonstrate, their sexuality in public.

One of the most important values of trap feminism is sex positivity, which can be defined as having positive attitudes toward sex and sexual activity, feeling comfortable about one's sexual identity, and embracing and expressing one's sexuality in public and private. Trap feminists' stance on sexuality disrupts dominant white standards of sexuality and gender by using the erotic as a source of power. Lorde (1984) explains that our understanding of the erotic has been discussed only from a patriarchal lens which centers men's pleasure and solely views the erotic as sexually explicit. Lorde defines the erotic as

> a measure between the beginnings of our sense of self and the chaos of our strongest feelings . . . and the assertion of the lifeforce of women; of that creative energy empowered, the knowledge and the use of which we are now reclaiming in our own language, our history, our dancing, our loving, our work, our lives.
>
> *(54–55)*

In other words, the erotic as power is not about having power over others but having power over oneself. The erotic as power is about Black women's liberation from patriarchal sexual repression. Viewing the erotic as a source of pleasure allows for women to fully embrace their sexuality. This is exactly what trap feminists are doing when they use their voices to speak on their sexual desires or twerk in public. Trap feminists give power to their erotic because they understand the power of women's sexuality. Instead of being repressed by their sexuality, trap feminists are free to express and define their sexual desires based on their own pleasure and sexual needs. They find power in defining and using their sexuality for their own enjoyment and pleasure. Cardi B has been open about her sexual orientation and often raps about finding sexual pleasure in women and enjoying free expression of her sexual desires for women and men. Moreover, Cardi's music videos are often highly sexual and sensual but rarely include men and almost never center on male pleasure.

Trap feminists like Cardi B, Megan Thee Stallion, and the City Girls disrupt the patriarchal Hip Hop perspective of men wanting "a lady in the streets, but a freak in the bed," as the rapper Ludacris[5] would say. This sentiment not only restricts Black women's sexuality but focuses on male sexual pleasure as well as the respectability politics that dictate how women should behave in public and in private. According to the patriarchy, women should not be "freaks" or share their sexual side in public. In fact, virginity is seen as the ultimate form of femininity, something we will discuss in depth in Chapters 3 and 5. Trap feminists disrupt this notion by viewing their sexuality as a positive attribute. They are not ashamed of their sexuality, and they do not adhere to patriarchal values concerning sex. People who do subscribe to these values view sexually empowered women as ratchet, sluts, thots, and unladylike. Even within the Black Community, open discussions of sexual activity and sexuality are deemed taboo for women and are viewed as a private matter that should be talked about only in private spaces.

In addition, Black Patriarchy within the Black Church stigmatizes sexual activity which contributes to the lack of a dialogue about Black sexual politics (Collins 2004) within Black spaces. Trap feminists make space for us to not only talk about sex but also envision sex from a Black woman's perspective. By centering Black women's sexuality in their music, trap feminists force us to reckon with a new image of Black women's sexuality, one that is free from the white patriarchy's criminalization of Black women's bodies. The erotic as power is not inherently sexual but can be used as a form of gratification—sexual and nonsexual (Brown 2019). Because our book describes the trap feminism of a Hip Hop star, we'll now look at a few songs that embody trap feminism's themes of the erotic as power, sex positivity, and women speaking up and out against men [mg4] [mg5] and the patriarchy. The four songs discussed in the following demonstrate the ways that trap feminists speak back to men, speak up for their desires, and speak out when discussing their dating standards.[6]

"Up" by Cardi B

Cardi B released her single titled "Up" in 2021. With a catchy beat and lyrics, she once again captured listeners and fans with her sex-positive attitude and voice. In the song she is schooling women on setting standards for themselves when it comes to interactions and relationships with men. Cardi speaks out by proclaiming that "make a nigga act right, broke boys don't deserve no pussy," followed by women in the back shouting "I know that's right!" This is collective recognition and agreement from other women, that broke boys or men who lack financial independence have not earned the right to have sex with you. Cardi is trying to make us understand, or is spitting game, to women so that we can interact with men in ways that make them "act right" based on our wants and needs. In verse 2, she speaks out by stating: "niggas out here playing, gotta make 'em understand. Ain't no ring on my finger, you ain't going on the gram." In other words, you shouldn't be Instagram official with a guy without an engagement ring demonstrating your partner's commitment to you. Setting standards that make men or your partner take you seriously, while also knowing your sexual worth, is the overall trap feminist message of this song.

"WAP" by Cardi B and Megan Thee Stallion

In 2020, Cardi B and Megan Thee Stallion released the song and music video for "WAP," which celebrates female pleasure and orgasms. "WAP," which is an acronym for "wet ass pussy," is the ultimate female anthem with bold, sex-positive lyrics that demonstrate women being in control during sex. "WAP" became pop culture slang and took the media by storm. From conservative politicians to the movie character Madea,[7] to ballet dancers, to veterinarians bathing cats at the clinic, and environmental scientists[8] using the song to bring awareness to climate change, "WAP" has become a social–political cultural phenomenon. Regardless of one's perspective of the song "WAP," Cardi B and Megan the Stallion have brought the erotic as power into mainstream society—demonstrating the power of trap feminists' voices.

"Pussy Talk" by City Girls ft. Doja Cat

City Girls, a rap duo (JT and Yung Miami) from the inner-city of Miami, also use Lorde's concept of the erotic as power to discuss the power of their pussies. In the song, "Pussy Talk," Yung Miami proclaims that her pussy is "from the hood, ghetto and from the projects." In the chorus of "Pussy Talk," JT and Yung Miami state that their pussies speak multiple languages (English, Spanish, and French) and count money from different countries. In other words, they have so much pussy power that men from a variety of racial and ethnic backgrounds are attracted to them and want to spoil them with money, trips, and gifts—this is how much power their eroticism holds. Yung Miami celebrates the joys of riding in private planes and vacationing on private islands while she raps about the worldwide love of men from Japan to Cuba. In these lyrics, City Girls are letting the audience know that they have global sexual appeal to all men. This is an important trap feminist observation because according to gendered racism, ghetto girls are supposed to be relegated to the projects for their whole lives as undesirable ratchet women. City Girls not only changed that narrative but also celebrated and embraced their global appeal by speaking truth to the sexual power of hood chicks.

In "Pussy Talk," City Girls also point out the importance of money and wealth when choosing sexual partners. They state that men with money are attractive—if you do not have any money, then neither they nor their pussies will talk to you. In other words, no money means no date and no sex. In Chapter 3, we also discuss the importance of sex and money. From a patriarchal perspective, this exchange of money for sex would be seen as an example of prostitution. To the contrary, a trap feminist standpoint highlights the importance of money to women who live in the trap. Because these women are financially strained and they understand the gendered power dynamics of dating men within the patriarchy, it makes perfect sense to reject the advances of men without money and to pursue men with money. This demand also speaks to an understanding of the erotic as power, which encourages Black women to seek pleasure in their lives. Overall, City Girls show us their sexual appeal as hood chicks while also boldly stating their wants, needs, demands, and appeal to men, globally.

"Where Dem Dollars At?" By Gangsta Boo

In 1998, female rap artist Gangsta Boo, a member of Three 6 Mafia, released a song titled "Where Dem Dollars At." This song was essentially a clap back to Memphis rappers' 8Ball and MJG's song "Sho Nuff," which is a misogynoiristic rap song about strippers getting money from men, featured on the soundtrack for the film *Players Ball*. The female anthem, "Where Dem Dollars At" is a counternarrative to "Sho Nuff," showing that gangsta chicks use an active voice, not a passive voice as Bowen (2021) discusses, to demand money from men. This is an important trap feminist observation because it demonstrates how Gangsta Boo reclaims her power within the male/female dynamics of the trap. Moreover, Gangsta Boo's song, which was remixed by DJ Paul, focuses on getting money instead of getting and maintaining a man. She explains, "I be screaming about that cheddar every goddamn day." She also proclaims that any men that are in her presence better have money, asking "where dem dollars at?" to make it worth her time. Gangsta Boo demands money and respect from a man— which is a different narrative than the "ride or die" chick, who is down for her man even when he puts her in a bad situation.

In her second verse, Gangsta Boo questions why some women have children by men who have no money. She is demonstrating her understanding of the cost of having children; the emotional and household labor that is expected by women and mothers' places them in an extremely difficult emotional and financial position. As she asks, "Where dem dollas at, nigga?" she is challenging existing gender roles for women by stating that women should not submit to men, especially if they do not have money. Her stance is that her time is money, so if a man wants to hang with her, he needs to be making money, which would give Gangsta Boo agency to move about society, which is required in a capitalist system historically dominated by white men.

Boo's standpoint in this song is an early example of what the authors of this book term a trap feminist standpoint. Gangsta Boo grew up in the Memphis projects in the 1990s. Although the term trap had not yet been popularized, Gangsta Boo is a product of her environment, and her lyrics are influenced by her experiences in the hood. Her solo underground album, *Hypnotized Minds*, which was produced and promoted by Three 6 Mafia, also reflected her lived experiences as a woman living in the projects. During this time, southern Hip Hop was not popular, so it was extremely difficult for female Hip Hop artists from the South to become mainstream. Gendered racism kept Gangsta Boo and other women like her at the bottom rank of underground Hip Hop at that time. Perhaps if we had social media back then, her music would have gotten to more audiences. Sadly, Gangsta Boo passed away in January of 2023. RIP Gangsta Boo.

In general, trap feminist rappers redefine gender roles, call out the patriarchy, and speak out about their demands, desires, and wants in their songs. The songs discussed here unpack some of the lyrics from a trap feminist standpoint. City Girls, Megan, and Cardi are disrupting normative notions of femininity and are redefining Black women's sexuality by celebrating it. Gangsta Boo questions the patriarchal standards that leave women broke and dependent on a man. These women are essentially breaking the stereotypes and the male-dominated narratives that have plagued Black women for centuries. Trap feminists are subversive and go against the grain when it comes to strict ideal types for women, gender roles, and using their eroticism as power.

Trap Feminism and Sexuality

So why is it important to use a trap feminist standpoint to view Black women's presentation of sexuality to the public? First, trap feminists' sex-positive standpoint speaks to the Black womanist tradition of embracing Black women emotionally, physically, and sexually. Walker (1983) gives us multiple definitions of womanism, which speaks to Black women loving other women sexually or nonsexually as well as women who prefer women's culture and emotional flexibility. Second, trap feminists teach us to value and embrace our sexual power as well as give us different ways to envision ourselves as sexual beings. Hip Hop feminists have been doing this work since the 1980s and 1990s (i.e., Lil Kim, Foxy Brown, Trina the Baddest Bitch). In fact, Black female rappers have always been vocal about embracing their sexuality. Trap feminists, like their Hip Hop feminist sisters, embrace Black women as sexual beings while disrupting middle-class notions of sexuality for women. Trap feminists are often very explicit in their lyrics while rapping over a trap beat and adding adlibs of excitement and sexual expression. Additionally, trap feminists, unlike female rappers of the 1990s and early 2000s, have used social media as a platform to express and display their sexuality to the public through images and videos. This gives trap feminists the ability to control their bodies, narratives, and sexual expression.

Third, trap feminists' use of sexually explicit lyrics paints a raw, unfiltered image of Black women's sexuality that is not approved by white-centric patriarchal standards or respectability politics. Trap feminists' songs and music videos give us permission to rap and dialogue about sex and sexuality on a daily basis from a sex-positive standpoint. In other words, the unedited lyrics of Black female rappers allow for us to engage in Black sexual politics to discuss sexuality from a trap feminist standpoint. This is extremely important since Black women live in a patriarchal society that represses our sexuality, our bodies, and ultimately our power. Lastly, like most industries, the music genres of rap and Hip Hop are male dominated and male centered, leaving little room for Black female rappers and their experiences to be heard and accepted on a mainstream level. Therefore, trap feminists use their voices and head-turning lyrics to disrupt misogyny by making us listen to them and by inspiring us to think about our sexual power in different ways. This is an extremely powerful tool that can assist in the liberation of Black women.

Furthermore, Lorde's (1984) *Uses of the Erotic: The Erotic as Power* calls for Black women to tap into our erotic power and to use it as a resource for making changes in our lives. Trap feminists respond to this call by using the erotic as power to share narratives of sex positivity and sexual freedom in their song lyrics. Audre Lorde reminds us that Black women as oppressed people have been conditioned to distrust, stigmatize, vilify, and abuse these types of erotic power. This is exactly what happens when we have been socialized to adhere to white standards of femininity. Black women are often uncomfortable with exploring our inner erotic power for fear of stigmatization and, in turn, shame other women who have been able to tap into their eroticism and use it as source of power; we deem these women as ratchet. By condemning them, we are participating in our own oppression by perpetuating the stigmatization of Black women's sexuality. Lorde (1984) warns us that men have misnamed the erotic and have used it against women. The erotic as power is not only sexual, but it can be used as a tool to sexually liberate Black women and to create a mainstream sex-positive Black feminism. Moreover, "the erotic offers a well of replenishing and provocative force to the woman who does not fear its revelation, nor succumb to the belief that sensation is enough" (54). Here lies the power of trap feminists.

By detailing even this short lyrical history, we can see that Cardi B inherited a certain type of female rap which has helped her to blaze a new trail. Historically, the competitive nature of rap has been male centered and dominated, and female rappers were forced to attach themselves to male rappers or compete over very limited spots. Women were either excluded or tokenized, only allowing for one female rapper's voice—and this tokenization continues today in mainstream Hip Hop. Record labels and the music industry, which are also sites of patriarchy, tend to pit women against each other for the top spot. However, Cardi has taken a different approach to being the "one" top female artist. Her music collaborations demonstrate her understanding of the power of Black women working together or what Black feminists (and early generations of female rappers)[9] would call sisterhood (which we also discuss in Chapter 6). Her music has opened the doors for more Black women rappers to gain mainstream popularity, control their own narratives, and create their own image. Cardi has collaborated with lots of female artists, including Lizzo, Normani, Megan Thee Stallion, and others outside of the Hip Hop genre. Cardi's support for other female rappers, both mainstream and underground, demonstrates her understanding of sisterhood and feminism. She does not view these women as competition or a threat; instead, she stays empowering women and shows her support. This is an important feminist observation because in Hip Hop and rap, being the greatest is part of the rap game. Female rappers continue to drop "female anthems" that encourage women to be bold, blunt, and badass bitches. Cardi B has blown the top off the pot of the macaroni and cheese,[10] she has inspired and empowered women globally to use their voices and their power to demand respect from everyone, especially men.

Conclusion

So, why is Cardi B an example of a trap feminist? Because she (1) disrupts gendered expectations for women (2) uses her voice to speak her mind and give voice to silenced women of the trap, and (3) brings all facets of who she is in terms of race, ethnicity, class, gender, and sexuality into all public spaces, whether that be online or in person. As we show throughout the book, all of these factors define trap feminism in practice. Our role as feminists should not be to discourage Black women and girls from being ratchet or to ostracize them and hold them to middle-class social norms and values. Our role as feminists is to see and accept Black women and girls for who they are and where they are without judgment (Miles 2020). If a Black woman is proud of her ratchetness and street "cred," we must embrace her version of Black womanhood and femininity (Love 2017).

Moreover, it is important for us to listen, acknowledge, and better understand the lived experiences of trap feminists. We are better able to see the perspectives and worldviews of women in and adjacent to the trap by focusing on their narratives. Listening to music from trap feminists like Cardi is the first step to hearing their narratives. However, we must do more to respect and stand up for our trap feminist sisters so that we see them as full human beings. You do not have to embody, appropriate, or emulate trap feminists to understand the importance of trap feminism. Trap feminism allows for an understanding of difference across womanhood without being inauthentic to the hood and the streets. A trap feminist standpoint allows us to acknowledge and recognize the knowledge produced by hood chicks; their lived experiences make them experts on their own lives. Trap feminism aims for us as Black women to see ghetto girls and hood chicks as women worthy of respect, love, and support. We must get ratchet or apply a ratchet lens to have a radical Black feminist praxis that liberates Black women from respectability politics and white gendered expectations of femininity and womanhood.

Overall, it is important that Black women have power over our own lives, especially our sexuality, since it has been controlled by the white patriarchal system since enslavement. It is crucial that Black women understand and embrace our sexuality since men often use our bodies as sexual objects for their own pleasure. Reclaiming and self-shaping our perspective of sexuality as sex positive will allow Black women to break free from patriarchal standards of womanhood and sex. Trap feminists' sexual expression emboldens women to express and demand our sexual desires be met for our own pleasure. Trap feminism pushes us to celebrate, focus on, understand, and acknowledge Black and Brown women who mainstream society has deemed as ghetto, ratchet, uncouth, or hood. Trap feminism disrupts every notion of respectability politics or the social norms of how women should behave, speak, talk, and dress in public. Trap feminists create their own standards to live by, use their voices to speak on their lived experiences, and understand the importance of the erotic as power.

Trap feminists embrace ratchet politics to carve out spaces for women of the trap while simultaneously dissolving the class boundaries that have been upheld by middle- and upper-class Black women. Lastly, trap feminists do not adhere to patriarchal gendered expectations for how women should act and speak in public. Instead, trap feminists self-define their woman-hood, have their own standards of beauty, and embrace their sexuality on their own terms. Cardi B is a great example of a trap feminist because she embodies all the aspects of trap feminism on multiple platforms, such as politics, motherhood, and culture, as you will see in the following chapters. A trap feminist praxis can help lead the way to celebrating (and focusing on ghetto girls and trap queens. Cardi B is a trailblazer) who carves out more space for women like her to be seen and heard without judgment. Her collaborations and features on songs with new female rappers demonstrate her trap feminism in practice in how she moves in her daily life.

In an article by Footwear News,[11] Mr. Christian Louboutin[12] spoke very highly of Cardi stating that "her freedom, her liberty of speech and basically her commitment to everything [makes her stand out]. She stands and fights for what she believes in, she's the opposite of politically correct." This quote succinctly encapsulates how Cardi embodies trap feminism by being authentic to who she is at all times and in all spaces, even venues and events originally created for white elites. She does not participate in respectability politics as she navigates these spaces, she stays true to being a "regular, degular, smegular girl from the Bronx." The following chapters continue the discussion on the Sociology of Cardi B while expanding a trap feminist standpoint to topics of culture, motherhood, politics, feminism, and Blackness.

Notes

1 African American vernacular or Ebonics is our own language that deviates from standard English.
2 https://blavity.com/watch-cardi-b-dispel-myths-takes-feminist.
3 Selena is the Queen of Tejano Music and is on the Billboard list of top Latino Artists of All Time.
4 In 2018, Cardi B did an interview on the J Cruz show with LA radio station Power responding to backlash from her lyric. She discussed her love for Selena and how she looked up to her and respected her. Cardi stated that she was not comparing herself to Selena but that she wanted to give Selena a shout-out in her verse on Motorsport.
5 Ludacris is an Atlanta-based rapper who is known for his catchy lyrics.
6 Cardi B's album *Invasion of Privacy* will be discussed in Chapter 3.
7 Tyler Perry plays the character Madea in numerous films.
8 Wet Ass Planet by Hila the Earth.
9 MC Lyte, Latifah and others did work together; so Cardi is reintroducing the collaborative spirit to the genre after it was gone for many years.
10 Referencing the lyrics in "WAP" regarding macaroni in the pot.
11 https://footwearnews.com/fashion/designers/cardi-b-christian-louboutin-paris-fashion-week-1203189292/.
12 The Italian shoe designer who created "red bottoms heels."

2

CARDI B'S BAD BEHAVIOR

Resisting White Gaze and Respectability

Cardi B's rise from sex worker to rap superstar occurred in front of millions. As new levels of success thrust Cardi B into mainstream pop culture, critics and fans alike began to discuss if and how her behavior should change given her new-found fame. Nothing brings this more to light than the infamous 2018 altercation at the Plaza Hotel between Cardi B, Nicki Minaj, and their camps during New York's fashion week (NYFW).

Wearing a red Dolce & Gabbana gown, Cardi and her entourage crossed paths with Nicki and her entourage on the first-floor balcony of Harper's Bazaar's ICON party during a performance by Christina Aguilera. After an exchange of words and tempers flared, Cardi attempted to approach Nicki. When security guards intervened to stop Cardi's approach, she removed one of her pricy red spiked heels[1] and hurled it at her nemesis.

Reporters, social media commenters, and bloggers gleefully shared the image of Cardi leaving the event with a visible knot on her forehead[2] but a satisfied smirk on her face; soon the photo went viral, circulating on social media platforms for weeks after the incident. In addition, the shoe-throwing incident was caught on camera and eventually released for all to see. Since celebrities are especially prone to being scrutinized in the public eye, it is no surprise that this altercation in front of some of the world's top designers garnered (and continues to garner) indignant and supportive responses from the public. Even now, the altercation at NYFW is revisited annually on social media, as Cardi has continued to participate and host her own events at national and international fashion weeks.

DOI: 10.4324/9781003184980-3

In the immediate aftermath, media professionals and everyday fans regarded Cardi as an embarrassment.

> Twitter user @TwigHoff wrote, "Cardi B sis you made it out the hood. You winning, stop this shit. Putting on a show for them white people at NYFW. NO SIS NO you embarrassing us."

"Puttin on a show for them white people at NYFW" reflects the idea that Black Americans, Afro-Latinos, and other people of color should alter their behavior or face the consequences of offending white people. These consequences and the pressure to avoid white scrutiny are connected to the concept of white gaze[3]—the understanding that white people are always looking, that whiteness and white perspectives are the standard, and that anything that deviates from whiteness is subject to scrutiny and control.

In this chapter, we engage the context of trap feminism to suggest that criticisms of Cardi B and women like her are often framed by the white gaze and laced with respectability politics that grant overwhelming power to white perspectives and opinions. We use the public reactions to Cardi B's altercation with Nicki Minaj as a case study to highlight the historical relationship between the white gaze and the policing of behavior for Black people, namely Black women.

First, we overview the impact of the white gaze on Black peoples' behavior by revisiting the theories of W.E.B. Du Bois, Michael Foucault, Patricia Hill Collins, Evelyn Brooks Higginbotham, bell hooks, and Toni Morrison. Then we detail how the white gaze has been used specifically to police and manage the behavior of Black people, namely Black women, throughout the generations and particularly within popular culture.

By framing Cardi's seeming refusal to alter her behavior in white spaces as a form of resistance, we argue that much of the public's criticism of Cardi's actions is due to an internalization of the white gaze. We conclude by detailing how a retreat from centering the white gaze and respectability politics creates space for valuing people who are typically left out and pushed to the margins and how trap feminism aids us in making this shift.

Theorizing the White Gaze and Power

The idea of gaze, looking at or surveilling another, has historically been studied by sociologists and philosophers to understand how groups internalize authority and alter their behavior (Du Bois 1903; Foucault 1977; hooks 2003; Browne 2015; Yancy 2017). The influence of the gaze is so strong that people do not need to see who or what is surveilling them to modify their behavior. Students in a classroom, domestic workers in wealthy homes, convicts in prison yards, and workers on the factory floor modify their behavior under the gaze of teachers, homeowners, prison guards, and shift supervisors whether the authority figures are present or not; the mere belief in the gaze serves to modify behavior. The public supervision and surveillance that are embedded in these systems effectively encourage obedience and conformity to the rules set by those in power because people fear the consequences of punishment or embarrassment (Foucault 1977). While everyone in society is subject to power and surveillance in some form or fashion, Black theorists have spent generations illustrating the power whiteness tries to exercise over Black lives and bodies and also theorizing about how white supremacy is fundamentally tied to the concept of the gaze.

One of the founders of the discipline of sociology that we discuss in the introduction, W.E.B. Du Bois,[4] thought deeply about Black Americans' internal struggle to balance their own self-perception and worth with constant surveillance by white Americans. In 1903, Du Bois coined the concept of "double consciousness" to describe the fact that most Black people are highly aware of being watched and analyzed by white people who perceive them negatively. Du Bois argued that because Black people are "always looking at one's self through the eyes of others," (p. 10), they must learn to differentiate between white perceptions and their own views. This double consciousness, this awareness that Black people are being watched, does not entirely dictate our lives—Black people have always found ways to exist and resist (which we detail in Chapter 6) (Blain 2018; Allen and Miles 2020)—but still, the white gaze continually intrudes upon our work, our dreams, our families, and our entertainment.

Later in the 20th century, Michel Foucault,[5] commonly referenced as part of the traditionally white sociological canon, expanded Du Bois's concept to broader society. His work on the power of surveillance to influence behaviors echoes Du Bois's argument that systems and people with power have the ability to surveil everyone (or create the appearance of surveillance) and therefore control them (Foucault 1977). We extend Foucault's theory on the power of surveillance to the systemic nature of racism and suggest that the white gaze contributes to establishing and maintaining the racial hierarchy of a white supremacist society. Foucault's theory did not consider race, but thinking about his work in conjunction with the theories offered by Du Bois begs the following questions: Which races have the power to look at and surveil others? Which races have the ability to enforce punishment or consequences on those who do not conform and obey? What are the consequences for not acknowledging the gaze of the more "superior" race and/

or not conforming to its will? As history has shown, the consequences of refuting the white gaze can prove deadly to Black people.

In her development of *Black Feminist Thought* ([1989] 2000), one of the literary staples of the Black feminist tradition mentioned in Chapter 1, Patricia Hill Collins expanded on Du Bois's concept of double consciousness and introduced the concept of the "outsider-within." This concept was born out of the experiences of Black women who worked as domestics in wealthy white homes. The "outsider-within" ([1989] 2000) captures the unique position of Black women who worked in white homes for generations as well as the perspectives they gained on the inner workings of white supremacy by virtue of being in such intimate proximity to its perpetrators. Rendered close but invisible, as subordinates who were expected to be silent and rarely seen, Black housekeepers were in a good position to understand (and challenge) whiteness. As self-identified outsiders-within, most Black women are especially aware of the white gaze, its impact on behavior, and how to navigate and resist it (Collins [1989] 2000).

Contemporary Black feminist thinker bell hooks expanded upon the ideas of Du Bois's double-consciousness and Foucault's theory of surveillance to include Black representation within the media. hooks (2003) argued that films and television shows depict Black lives and experiences in ways that please a white audience. Even when Black life is represented by Black people in these mediums, it is often framed by whites' feelings, understandings, and interpretations. In the book *The Black Image in the White Mind: Media and Race in America*, authors Robert Entamn and Andrew Rojecki (2000) conclude that a significant amount of white people hold stereotypical beliefs about Black life and that the dominant pattern within TV and film is to promote media images that support those beliefs in overt and covert ways. hooks (2003) argued that the media assumes and caters to white audiences even when including people of color on the screen, because white people are the gatekeepers, the ones in control. Since pleasing white gatekeepers and audience members is the goal, media portrayals forgo authenticity and complexity in favor of stereotypical and one-dimensional forms of Black representation.

Beloved author Toni Morrison is credited with popularizing the term "white gaze" and often spoke about the importance of decentering whiteness in her work. When reflecting on a reviewer who once suggested she include white people in her work, Morrison said,

> [it's] as though our lives have no meaning and no depth without the white gaze, and I have spent my entire writing life trying to make sure that the white gaze was not the dominant one in any of my books.
>
> *(Morrison 1998)*

Because Morrison created authentic Black characters who were not bound by what white people saw and thought, she spent a significant amount of time explaining and defending her decisions; whiteness has become such a norm that it was hard for white audiences to accept their absence in her work. The pressure of deciding whether or not to alter behavior under the watch of white people has plagued Black people in every facet of their life for generations, especially in the US context.

Surveillance and "Good Behavior" through Slavery, Jim Crow, and Beyond

Historically, being visible to white people has placed Black people in greater danger of being policed, harassed, or worse (Collins [1989] 2000). To appease whites in public spaces, Black Americans and many people of color have needed to adopt certain racial etiquette.[6] Understanding the history of this racial etiquette helps us to see that this centuries-old fear of white judgment persists—even in 2018, when Cardi B confronted Nicki Minaj. We see the impact of these deeply rooted beliefs about "proper" behavior in the presence of whites across traditional journalism, mass media, and social media.

The systemic oppression that has underwritten the lives of African descendants in the Americas has always included an element of surveillance, requiring Black people to be keenly aware that they are being watched and judged, and as a result, controlled. In her book, *Dark Matters: On the Surveillance of Blackness*, Simone Browne (2015) discusses how Black people have historically been treated as a spectacle to be looked upon by whites, from their "examination at slave trafficking forts and ports, through the Door of No Return,[7] and on slave ships during the Middle Passage voyage from Africa to the auction blocks and plantations of the New World" (42). On southern plantations, slave quarters were positioned in accordance with the idea of constant white surveillance; enslaved people assumed that they were being watched even when not working in the fields (Browne 2015).

This impression of constant surveillance was enforced until the end of the Jim Crow era in the 1960s. Being on your best behavior[8] was a survival tactic for hundreds of years. Examples of legally enforceable racial etiquette included knowing where and when not to make eye contact with whites—especially white authority figures, being sure to use formal greetings like "ma'am" and "sir" when speaking to any white person regardless of age, and yielding sidewalks and seats when in the same space with whites (Ritterhouse 2006; Schultz 2005). This racial etiquette was especially important in the segregated Jim Crow South. This practice was designed to reinforce the racial hierarchy of white supremacy in everyday interpersonal exchanges (Schultz 2005). Given that Black people were routinely imprisoned and lynched by white domestic terrorists for minor affronts, practicing this racial etiquette when interacting with whites was seemingly (and often in reality) the only way to ensure Black people's safety.

Unwritten racial guidelines also played out along gender lines. The presence of white women increased the enforcement of these social rituals for Black men. In his work detailing the complicated daily interactions of Blacks and whites living in the rural south, Mark Schultz (2005) found that the presence of white women aggravated the enforcement of racial etiquette by white men. Therefore, Black men had to be especially careful of their behavior in the presence of white women. White men came to understand that their manhood was determined by how well they protected white women from Black men, and this meant more surveillance of, and exercised power over, Black men in public spaces—usually by the strict enforcement of racial etiquette (Higginbotham 1993). This system reinforced white male superiority and reduced the humanity of Black men by making them feel small. In public and sometimes private spaces, Black men learned to be hyper-aware of the watchful eyes of white men because failure to follow the rules was likely to be met with violence.

From the late 1800s through the 1950s Jim Crow era, Black women faced the same threats as Black men along with the additional burdens of the white *and* Black male gaze. The degree of oppression Black Americans experienced during this period led them to believe that assimilation to white standards was the key to survival and opportunity. By displaying "respectable behaviors" that mimicked white middle-class American values, Black people thought they could lessen the effects of racial discrimination (Higginbotham 1993). During a time when racial violence was high and racist rhetoric and stereotypes[9] permeated popular culture, many Black people believed that the keys to their advancement were a good education, a professional job, and a stable nuclear family unit. Born out of the white gaze, respectability soon became a politic that many Black people internalized and passed down through the generations (Higginbotham 1993; Wolcott 2001). The "politics of respectability" (coined by Black feminist Evelyn Brooks Higginbotham) suggest that certain behaviors—speaking too loudly, using African American Vernacular English or Spanglish, wearing certain hairstyles and clothes—are not appropriate for white spaces because they perpetuate stereotypes that translate into having a lower socioeconomic status or being "ghetto."

A Black woman had to be a "respectable" Negro and a pillar of femininity to navigate the dual burdens of white supremacy and the need to be attractive and nonthreatening to Black men (Collins [1989] 2000; Higginbotham 1993). This means Black women became champions of assimilation to white dominant frames—they straightened their hair, worked as domestic workers in white homes while maintaining their own homes, and took a backseat to Black male religious leaders while trying to be involved in movements for racial equity (Higginbotham 1993; Robnett 2000). For Black women, surveillance came in the form of white men and women and Black men watching and policing their race and gender—an intersectional form of surveillance and oppression that still exists (and is still resisted) today Collins ([1989] 2000).

In her analysis of Black Baptist women who championed the politics of respectability from 1880 to 1920, Higginbotham (1993) writes,

> Their assimilationist leanings led to their insistence upon blacks' conformity to the dominant society's norms of manners and morals. Thus the discourse of respectability disclosed class and status differentiation . . . women's emphasis on respectable behavior found expression in the writings of most black leaders of the time, male and female alike, and was perceived as essential to racial self-help and dignity.
>
> *(187–188)*

As Higginbotham explains, the "politics of respectability" created a chasm between Black women who were middle- or upper-class and those with poor or working-class backgrounds. With this extensive history of racialized and gendered surveillance, it's no wonder that women like Cardi B, who resist racial etiquette in white spaces, are seen as especially problematic. Cardi embodies many of the traits that are deemed undesirable based on the politics of respectability. As her star rises, she becomes more visible in white spaces and is faced with the burden of navigating respectability and representing her race and ethnicity on a massive scale. As Cardi's wealth, social influence, and stardom increase, she is more susceptible to the burden of having to navigate white gaze, male gaze, and respectability politics. If a woman with Cardi's resources and influence is still subject to these social constraints, it goes without question that women still in or near the trap are also navigating and challenging these issues. In doing so, these women must constantly balance their right to authenticity and self-determination with real-life threats to their livelihood, motherhood, womanhood, and more. Cardi's celebrity provides us a space to investigate what non-celebrity women from the trap might be able to do when given access to resources, power, and support.

Black Celebrity, Respectability, and Crossing Over into White Audiences

Cardi B's resumé provides evidence that she has achieved major crossover in the music industry.[10] An artist who broadens their appeal to more audiences is likely to receive better recording contracts, more endorsements, larger musical venues, access to new business ventures, and other unique opportunities. While it is not the goal of every artist to cross over, the financial benefits are undeniable. For Black and Latino artists who start out in distinct musical genres like Hip Hop or reggaetón, achieving crossover is usually synonymous with becoming more appealing and accessible to white audiences (Roy and Dowd 2010). Because of the pressure to place more consideration on their appeal to white audiences, crossover artists might alter or altogether abandon some parts of their public-facing identity to gain acceptance by white audiences. Interestingly, white tastes include the paradox wherein white audiences enjoy being spectators of what they see as "real" Blackness, albeit from a safe distance (Entman and Rojecki 2000; Park et al. 2006).

The 1950s and 1960s were a period in which the politics of respectability was quintessential; the training protocols instituted by Motown Records provide a glaring example of the pressure inflicted upon Black entertainers who wanted to achieve financial success (Demby 2013). Motown, a Black-owned record company, dominated the US music scene with iconic acts such as Smokey Robinson and the Miracles, The Temptations, and The Supremes. Motown founder and CEO Berry Gordy instituted rigorous artist development as a way to reach beyond Black audiences. Motown artists, many of whom had low-income backgrounds, were required to attend a "finishing school" that focused on etiquette, charm, and media training. Twice a week, Black artists were taught how to speak, walk, sit, eat, and more. Maxine Powell, a founding member of the artist development department for Motown, taught artists that refining their behavior and image was key to gaining access to places from which Black artists were often excluded. "They did come from humble beginnings," Powell said, "some of them from the projects, some of them were using street language, some were rude and crude." Powell told artists that she was training them for two places, "The White House and Buckingham Palace" (Demby 2013).

As a result, Motown became synonymous with success and sophistication. Many argue that Motown performers directly influenced the desegregation of the airwaves and white venues like the Copacabana, The Ed Sullivan Show, and various venues across Europe (Demby 2013). The contributions of Maxine Powell and Motown artists created space for future Black artists. The need to "polish" these artists was motivated by the reality of white supremacy. White audiences still held open biases against Black people in public spaces while enjoying Black music in the privacy of their cars and homes. White audiences also had the privilege to enforce racial etiquette and pose very real threats to Black artists' economic and physical safety. As a result, Black artists had an incentive to appear non-threatening and to adhere to respectability in order to have successful careers.

Still during the time of Motown, Black artists resisted white supremacy by touring throughout the deep south in areas where they were unwanted and unwelcome by white audiences. As an act of resistance, Dionne Warwick would turn her back to the white side of a segregated audience while catering to the Black side. As Motown evolved, artists like Sam Cooke and Marvin Gaye intentionally included lyrics that challenged the social structure. Since the days of Motown, there have been Black artists who have rejected the notion of intentionally crossing over (think of conscious rappers of the 1980s like Public Enemy and the gangster rappers of the early 1990s like N.W.A.).[11] Nonwhite artists who achieve market success and increased visibility continue to deal with the delicate balance between assimilating to white norms and the pressure of (mis)representing their entire race in the public eye (Jackson 2014).

It is important that we start to recognize the act of resistance inherent in both the refusal to alter behavior around white people and the internal rejection of anti-Blackness. So much power has been associated with white surveillance and authority that resistance to the white gaze is a revolutionary act. Trap feminism can help us make the transition from judging women of certain backgrounds to understanding the power of their authenticity in the presence of the white gaze. Poor Black women in, or adjacent to, the trap are judged harshly for not being obedient or respectable, but a trap feminist lens encourages us to accord respect to these women as knowledge producers. Intentionally and unintentionally, these women teach us how to thrive by showing us how to resist and circumvent white male power structures that have surveilled and policed us for far too long. Therefore, Cardi B, an Afro-Latina artist known for her authenticity, becomes a point of entry to discuss both the history of the gaze and how the internalization of respectability affects our view of Black women from poor and working-class backgrounds.

Trap Feminism and Resisting the White Gaze and Respectability

A trap feminist frame helps us identify the influence of the white gaze and respectability that fueled the responses to Cardi and Nicki Minaj's altercation at New York Fashion Week. The root of the disagreement between Cardi B and Nicki Minaj is still unclear to many, but it seems to be at least partially influenced by the sudden comparisons and competition caused by Cardi's quick rise to fame in the music industry. Unfortunately, women in Hip Hop are often pitted against one another. Hip Hop feminist scholars have attributed this competitiveness to the misogyny in Hip Hop culture that limits the presence of female artists or excludes them altogether

(Morgan 1999; Bowen 2021). Until the very recent influx of women megastars in rap (including women like Cardi B, Megan Thee Stallion, and City Girls), there has been an unstated rule that only one female MC can be at the top of the rap game at a time, despite the acceptance of multiple successful male MCs who are allowed to coexist.

Nicki Minaj held the top position in the rap game for many years, even before the release of her record-breaking debut album *Pink Friday* in 2010.[12] Her talent, image, and ability to connect with and mobilize her fanbase on social media came at a time when mainstream women Hip Hop artists were almost entirely nonexistent. The themes in Minaj's music were focused on the hood, quick money, dominating men from the trap, and using violence when necessary. According to the definitions outlined in Chapter 1,[13] Nicki could also be considered a trap feminist rapper at certain points in her career. Her massive presence and extreme success ushered in a new era of Hip Hop for women looking to be Hip Hop stars. She is often credited by Hip Hop aficionados and newer artists as having a major influence on the most recent generation of rappers, which includes Cardi B. Even with her celebrity, Minaj was often compared to and eventually began to feud with her predecessor, rap icon Lil Kim. Nicki and Kim's feud was related to whether or not Nicki Minaj was copying and/or stealing Lil Kim's style and persona without paying proper homage to the icon. Like the feud with Lil Kim, Nicki Minaj and Cardi B's public conflict has included subliminal song lyrics, snide statements in interviews, and full-out online wars between their fanbases. No matter the underlying reasons that sparked their feud, the Harper Bazaar's party described at the beginning of this chapter brought the beef between Cardi and Nicki to a peak.

The aftermath of the altercation at the NYFW party stirred up a lot of interesting responses. Nicki Minaj initially remained silent for days while Cardi took to her social media platforms to immediately explain what angered her to the point of wanting to throw blows, saying, "When you mention my child, you choose to like comments about me as a mother, make comments about my abilities to take care of my daughter is when all bets are fuckin off!!" (@iamcardib 2018). Cardi went on to say that she does not lead the life of an average citizen—she knew that she was not likely to run into Minaj at the grocery store—so in Cardi's mind, NYFW was an opportune time to confront Minaj. Eventually, Nicki Minaj responded to the incident and denied that she ever made or supported disparaging remarks about Cardi's child or her mothering. Minaj addressed the incident fully on her Apple Music radio show, Queen Radio, saying,

> The other night I was a part of something so mortifying and so humiliating to go through in front of bunch of upper echelon—and it's not about

white or black—it's about upper echelon people who are you know, people who have their lives together, the way they passed by looking at this disgusting commotion I will never forget. I was mortified. I was in [an] Alexandre Vauthier gown, okay, off the motherfucking runway, okay, and I could not believe how humiliating it all felt because we—and I use "we" loosely and I'm going to clarify "we"—how we made ourselves look . . . [Cardi B] left looking the way you left looking so that people could point their fingers at our culture and our community and laugh at us some more?

(Episode 8, Minaj 2018)

An analysis of these different responses from Cardi and Nicki brings forth an interesting topic of discussion: what happens when trap behavior is displayed on the national stage. In *Bad Fat Black Girl: Notes from a Trap Feminist*, Sesali Bowen (2021) eloquently explains how a trap feminist framework helps us make sense of Cardi's actions. She writes,

Cardi was abiding by a code that demands direct confrontation over passive-aggressive politeness and cordiality. The code states that your opps can get it "on sight" and does not stipulate an appropriate time, place, or circumstance. Through this lens, their fight was unfortunate but appropriate, given their history.

(43)

Discussions about the melee and both artists' responses show us how some people of color cooperate with the demands of white gaze and respectability politics. Critiques of the fight were about more than just shock. Nicki Minaj and many others felt that the presence of white and rich people made Cardi's actions that much more reprehensible (Queen Radio 2018). Fans and commentators also reflected this sentiment on social media. When conducting a search of "Cardi B + Fashion Week + Fight" on Twitter, it's easy to find tweets that refer to Cardi B as ghetto, cheap, or embarrassing:

Iselalalala @Iseladuh September 8, 2018: No matter how much money a stripper has you can't teach her or buy her class and cardi b prove that at New York fashion week event
. . . #CardiVSNicki

Esteban Rangel @erange23 September 8, 2018: Cardi B has no class is disgusting. Like who fights at fashion week like she's such a ghetto ass bitch

Myleeze (@MyleezeKardash) September 10, 2018: Nicki right. Y'all think that photo of Cardi leaving NYFW is so raw, but that shit is EMBARRASS-ING. Y'all know how long it took for hip hop culture to be respected in fashion? . . . Puffy. Kanye West. Jay Z. Russell Simmons. Dapper Dan and more

FOUGHT so all these rap artists can be front row of these fashion weeks, sitting comfortable. What she did was mad disrespectful to the culture.

K (@vuittonroses) September 7, 2018: cardi b bugs me so much like how are you gonna come to a NYFW event in a designer gown and then try to fight someone like youre in middle school.. how completely embarrassing and classless.

Twig Hoff (@TwigHoff): Cardi sis you made it out the hood. Putting on a show for them white people at #NYFW NO SIS NO you embarrassing us (forehead slap emoji) #NickiMinaj #RahAli

Africa Unscripted September 11, 2018: Nicki Minaj is speaking volumes! Y'all really expected them to break out into a fight at New York Fashion Week? NEW YORK FUCKING FASHION WEEK?? Two black women?! Of course she was hiding behind security she handled that well, that is a classy event Cardi B needs to check herself.

The tweets quoted here are representative of commentary made not only on various social media platforms but also on blogs, television panels, and radio talk shows. Use of language such as "classless," "ghetto," and "embarrassing" suggests that some people believed that Cardi should have censored her behavior because she was at a wealthy white event. Hip Hop is generally still seen as a relatively young genre that is "lucky" to be invited into mainstream (read: white) spaces. Many people disregard the benefits that result from white peoples' paradoxical yearning to consume the "coolness" that Black people bring to an event and/or a space while also upholding their racial bias.

Nicki appeared to be astonished that Cardi would behave in such a way and in such a place as New York Fashion Week. Yet Nicki Minaj has a poor, Caribbean, New York (Queens) background. She promotes violence as a response to disrespect in her lyrics, and she has incited confrontations on public platforms. For example, Nicki called out pop star Miley Cyrus on stage at the 2015 MTV Video Music Awards after Cyrus called her "not too kind" and implied that Nicki was jealous because Cyrus's music video was nominated over Nicki's video (Halliday 2018). Although the MTV Awards might not be viewed as having the same prestige as New York Fashion Week, it is a predominantly white space filled with wealthy white people. This public moment of confrontation suggests that Nicki does not always conform to respectability in white spaces. While Nicki's background and previous behavior very much overlap with Cardi's experiences, Nicki's comments about the Fashion Week event suggest that respectability should have taken priority over any other response at that moment and in that space.

Cardi, on the other hand, did not base her behavior on white, middle-class standards of respectability or appropriateness for a high fashion event. She did not intend to ignore or talk out her differences with Nicki Minaj.

Cardi's frame of reference for an appropriate response was generated from her trap background as an Afro-Latina who was recently navigating the Bronx as a former gang member and sex worker. From the perspective of a hood chick, Cardi's actions and reactions make sense. Logically, Cardi might assume that Nicki Minaj would also demonstrate the experiences, feelings, and reactions of a hood chick. While Nicki and others might not agree with Cardi's choice of behavior, using a trap feminist perspective rather than one of respectability helps us better understand *why* Cardi decided a physical altercation was a viable and necessary response to the disrespect she perceived from Nicki Minaj.

Despite her initial claim that her outrage was not influenced by the race of the people present, Nicki went on to repeatedly imply that Cardi is not really Black. She accused Cardi of entering "her" (Minaj's) culture (Hip Hop) to suggest that Cardi is an outsider, even though Cardi not only is from the Bronx but also has been deeply influenced by Hip Hop throughout her life. On her radio show, Minaj recounted another conflict from Cardi's past. Cardi had called a Black woman "a roach" during an argument. Seemingly, Nicki Minaj brought up this old dispute to suggest that Cardi was anti-Black and anti-Black women. The complexities of race, ethnicity, and identity for Afro-Latinas will be further discussed in Chapter 4, but it is important to mention here that both Nicki Minaj and Cardi B have Black Caribbean roots and at least one Trinidadian parent. However, Nicki and Cardi have developed different ways of dealing with Black womanhood and Hip Hop stardom. In public, Nicki Minaj presents herself as different and more respectable than Cardi B. Minaj seems to have been embarrassed not just because she was thrust into an unexpected altercation but because the altercation occurred in the midst of wealthy white people who would probably blame the embarrassing melee on Minaj's (and Cardi B's) membership in the Black musical genre of Hip Hop. Despite saying otherwise in her initial response, race clearly did matter to Minaj as evidenced by her later reference to Cardi as an outsider. Based on Nicki's commentary during and after the event, it seems fair to assume that the presence of white people and the white gaze exacerbated her embarrassment during and after the confrontation at NYFW.

Since the NYFW party centered the white elite and fashion, some commentators seemed to believe that Cardi had the duty of not responding as her authentic self—the self that is based on her ratchet sensibilities and does not self-censor in the presence of wealth and whiteness. More than that, commentators suggested that Cardi deserved to be chastised for being her authentic self. The comments and stories about the horror of white partygoers witnessing Cardi's outburst harken back to the period between the 1800s and the 1950s, when Black women especially were expected to be on their "best behavior" in white public spaces: look nice, be grateful and gracious, and don't make white people uncomfortable.

According to the mandates of respectability politics, Cardi's career should have been decimated after her outburst. One might think she'd be banned from fashion week events and shunned by the fashion industry. Instead, Cardi made history as the first female rapper to grace the cover of the US version of *Vogue Magazine* one year later in 2019. Ironically, the cover and the spread inside the magazine highlighted Cardi B and her daughter—the same daughter who was at the center of Cardi's dispute with Minaj. Since that 2019 *Vogue* shoot, Cardi has been heralded as a couture fashionista, having been selected to wear vintage and custom pieces from some of the most well-respected fashion designers. In addition, Cardi has attended and hosted events for extremely wealthy, high-profile fashion events including the Met Gala and Paris Fashion Week. Many times, Cardi has been invited or escorted to these events by the famous designers themselves. While we cannot assume that Cardi lost no opportunities after the 2018 altercation, we can verify that her unabashed authenticity in that one moment did not lead to her downfall as many had predicted. In fact, forcing respectability can diminish rather than uplift the power of women from the trap. By refusing to be defined by respectability politics, Cardi has resisted being reduced to a single moment and has moved past the racialized, gender-based, and classist critiques hurled at her.

These historical remnants of respectability are evident when we look at responses to Cardi B's behavior and even more so when considering the policing that ratchet women or women from the trap navigate daily (even from their own communities). The idea that one is lucky or blessed to be in a white space is tied to a belief that these Black artists (and all Black people, really) don't deserve to be in white spaces; to prove their worthiness, Black people must show their gratitude by meeting white respectability standards. Sesali Bowen (2021) provides an alternative perspective saying,

> Trap feminism says that Black girls who have ever rocked bamboo earrings, dookie braids, Baby Phat, lace fronts, or those who have worked as hoes, scammers, call-center reps, at daycares, in retail, and those who sell waist trainers and mink lashes on Instagram are all worth the same dignity and respect we give Michelle Obama and Beyoncé.
>
> *(14)*

If we shift from judging to understanding women in the trap, we also create more space for understanding various forms of Black representation and ways of being. In Chapter 4 we will discuss how narrow-minded thinking and the evaluating and policing of Blackness do a disservice to

Blackness across the diaspora. Black people who are immigrants are cast aside along with Black people who do not dress, speak, and/or live according to American, hetero, middle- and upper-class standards. However, Black people who are deemed "non-respectable" are not less deserving of opportunities or protection from white supremacy.

Conclusion

The classic works of Black feminists like Patricia Hill Collins, Evelyn Brooks Higginbotham, bell hooks, and Toni Morrison along with the incorporation of a trap feminist standpoint help us to understand and unpack how the white gaze influences public responses to the altercation between Cardi B and Nicki Minaj at NYFW. More than that, their/our work lays a foundation for how Cardi's refusal to alter her behavior is an example of decentering whiteness. In the face of very real threats to their safety and livelihood, women who do not change their desired behavior in the presence of white people are performing an act of resistance. As outlined throughout this book, trap feminism is a framework that centers and makes space for marginalized women from and adjacent to the trap.

Cardi B's mega fame certainly made her more visible to white audiences, and as an Afro-Latina, this visibility made her easier to criticize. Still, Cardi and women that share her background have found ways to resist conforming to white standards (to an extent). This resistance looks like refusing to switch your aesthetic or your way of speaking to appear more intelligent, not changing your hairstyle simply because white standards deem it unprofessional and/or directly calling out someone who has wronged you, even (especially) if it makes other people uncomfortable.

Resistance means ignoring or defying the white gaze and not cowering in the face of perceived disrespect. Trap feminists resist the idea that there is only one acceptable way to be Black by refusing to internalize anti-Blackness in any form. Women who resist patriarchal notions of respectability are chastised even from within their own communities, but they lay hold to the right to be complex and nuanced and messy and still in process—actively working through and changing who and what they desire to be. In the next chapter, we explore how Cardi's lyrics lend themselves to highlighting this complexity.

The unique social position that Black women occupy empowers us to understand white supremacy and patriarchy intimately; this means that we can turn the oppressive gaze we experience back on our oppressors. bell hooks (2003) says that the gaze can be oppositional and a tool of resistance. She reminds us that if we can be looked at, we can also look back.

We can interrogate whiteness and all its ridiculous components and weaknesses. hooks reminds us that we do have agency, and with that agency we can poke holes and chip away at the systems that press against us. As Hip Hop feminism pushed Black feminism to be more inclusive, trap feminism pushes us all to consider that "the least" among us have something important and radical to say.

Notes

1 Cardi notably talks about being a lover of Christian Louboutin, a high-end designer shoe which ranges between $500 and upwards of $6000. Her breakout single "Bodak Yellow" makes a nod to the shoes identified by their infamous red bottoms, and since that time Cardi has collaborated with and become friends with the designer himself.

2 "There was a giant fist full of hair on the floor. One of Cardi's assistants came and grabbed it and took it with her." According to TMZ, a member of the security team tried to intervene and elbowed Cardi in the process, leaving the huge mound on her forehead seen as she left the party (https://heatworld.com/celebrity/news/cardi-b-nicki-minaj-fight-nyfw-party/).

3 The term was popularized by Black author Toni Morrison. White gaze is rooted in a lingering history where Black people are under constant surveillance and where their "best behavior" around white people (who have the power to oppress and harm them) determines their access to opportunities, at minimum, and life or death, at most (https://onlinelibrary.wiley.com/doi/10.1111/gwao.12564).

4 Du Bois's contributions are usually attributed to race theory alone, and often his work in advancing sociology as a science is overlooked by white scholars.

5 Foucault's work is commonly referenced as part of the traditionally white sociological canon.

6 Racial etiquette refers to a series of behaviors that were expected of Black people when in the presence of white people. This includes words, gestures, and mannerisms that intended to highlight and maintain the supposed inferiority of Black people to white people.

7 The Door of No Return refers to the West African ports, where Europeans forced millions of Africans who they illegally captured to board ships to the New World in the Americas, never to return to their home continent again.

8 A specific concept of racial etiquette that Black people adopted for survival.

9 Dating back to the late 1800s vaudevilles and minstrel shows, the first forms of American pop culture, exaggerated portrayals of Black culture and were often seen as accurate by white audiences. Analyses of interviews and focus groups indicate that audiences, white audiences especially, conflate these cinematic images with real-world race relations (Park, Gaddabon, and Chernin 2006; Rogin 1996).

10 Crossover refers to "a broadening of the popular appeal of an artist (such as a musician) that is often the result of a change of the artist's medium or style," (Merriam-Webster 2024).

11 N.W.A. (Niggaz wit Attitudes) was a Hip Hop group active between 1987 and 1991. Formed by teenagers in Compton, California, the group is credited with popularizing the subgenre of gangster rap/West Coast rap. The group was led

by Eazy-E and consisted of Dr. Dre, Ice Cube, DJ Yella, MC Ren, and Arabian Prince. Their descriptions of street life, poverty, police brutality, racism, sex, and more were viewed as obscene and controversial and became highly popular among audiences of all races. Their notoriety thrust Hip Hop into the political arena, resulting in the genre's artists and lyrics being used to advance racist political agendas and criminal justice policy.

12 *Pink Friday* was released in November 2010 and went on to sell more than three million copies. The album garnered many accolades including having the second-highest debut week in the history of female Hip Hop recording artists.

13 "Trap feminism disrupts the social norms of how women should behave, speak, talk, and dress in public—norms associated with respectability politics."

3

CARDI B LIVING HER BEST FEMINIST LIFE

In Chapter 2, we learned that Cardi B's oppositional gaze and complicated authenticity are hallmarks of trap feminism in the face of the white and the male gaze. In this chapter, we analyze Cardi's song lyrics to find further evidence of a trap feminist standpoint in her artistry. In a 2018 interview published by i-D magazine, Cardi B states:

> Being a feminist is real simple. It's that a woman can do things the same as a man. I'm equal to a n****. Anything a man can do, I can do. I can finesse, I can hustle. We have the same freedom. I was top of the charts. I'm a woman and I did that. I do feel equal to a man.
>
> *(Collins 2018)*

As an artist who declares herself to be a feminist, we wanted to see whether Cardi's song lyrics mirror her public authenticity and support her feminist stance. To find out, we used the scholarly tradition of examining the artistry produced by marginalized creatives for evidence of their societal viewpoints (Davis 1998). This tradition was established because, for centuries, Black artists have used their creative outlets not only to elevate Black aesthetics but also to push against European standards of music, fashion, and other artistic pursuits and create space for public expression about social issues (Collins 2002; Davis 1998; Ford 2015a, 2015b; Harrison 2002). In particular, Black women have used creative outlets to defend their dignity and fight for their rights as women and Black persons throughout history (Washington 1988). The history of Black women's creative civil and political engagement is discussed further in Chapter 6.

DOI: 10.4324/9781003184980-4

In some cases, Black women artists' lyrics clearly illustrate the political statements they are attempting to make about society.[1] On the contrary, the feminist stance embedded in Cardi B's lyrics is obvious only when we view her lyrics through the lens of trap feminism and Black feminism. For example, when Cardi raps the words, "boss bitch," hood chicks know she's complimenting herself or another woman who "handles her business," but any phrase that includes the word bitch is antithetical to white feminists who oppose the use of "derogatory" terms about women (Kleinman, Ezzell, and Frost 2009). By using trap feminism as a lens, we can see the interconnections between Cardi's lyrics and her personal experiences. In other words, we can see the deeper meanings of Cardi's lyrics by taking into account the social, communal, cultural, and familial structures that have influenced Cardi's life.

For our dataset, we chose to interrogate the lyrics of all 13 songs on Card B's first and only major studio album to date, *Invasion of Privacy*.[2] Because Cardi B performs these lyrics in front of millions and because she has writing credits on each song, we can infer that these lyrics reflect her political views and cultural experiences.[3]

Cardi's songs matter to us as sociologists because millions of people listen to her music. In 2018, *Invasion of Privacy* soared to number one on the Billboard Hot 100 Music chart along with two songs from that album, "Bodak Yellow" and "I Like It." In addition, Cardi's album has unique staying power; as the longest-charting debut album by a female rapper, the 2018 album could still be found on the top 200 Billboard albums as of October 2022.[4] These accomplishments highlight the sociological relevance of Cardi's music. By using her lyrics as a source of data, we can see if Cardi is "putting her money where her mouth is." In other words, Cardi B most definitely "talks the talk" of feminism outside of her lyrics, but does she "walk the walk" on her biggest platform?

By reading through the Spanish and English lyrics of all 13 tracks of Cardi's album *Invasion of Privacy* as one continuous text, we uncovered patterns and themes that potentially speak to how Cardi sees herself as a feminist. Her lyrics also provide us with an understanding of the ways in which her feminism is complicated by gender expectations and sexism. Furthermore, we must take into consideration Cardi's cultural background with full knowledge of her current public history.

We begin our foray into Cardi B's feminist standpoint by discussing the socio-historical gender expectations associated with Cardi's ethnicity as Trinidadian and Dominican and her nationality as American. Then we elucidate the major themes that emerge from a sociological reading of the lyrics written by Cardi and her co-lyricists for *Invasion of Privacy*. Lastly, we unpack four primary themes that emerged from the deep reading that reveal the complexities of Cardi B's feminism.[5] These lyrics do not only provide evidence of Cardi's feminist practice, but they also demonstrate Cardi's rejection of the patriarchal ideals of womanhood alongside her simultaneous embrace of certain traditional gender roles. Using a trap feminist lens, we can see how existing both inside the confines of societal ideals (e.g., desiring long-term relationships and children) and outside of acceptable social structures (e.g., stripping to make money in the trap) creates a form of feminism that leaves space for Black women to be all the things we need to be in order to survive.

Cultural Understandings of Womanhood

We ground our analysis of Cardi B's trap feminist standpoint by addressing the history of differing gender roles in the Caribbean and the United States in the historical context of global expressions of gender expectations. To understand this difference, we explore the gender ideology of the cultures in which Cardi was socialized. We see how race, ethnicity, class, and gender shape Cardi into the rapper we love (or for some, love to hate). This helps us discern both the presence and the lack of clear delineations between Cardi B's professed feminism and her societal conformity and nonconformity as a woman. Cardi B's feminism may come into question due to some of her lyrics. In some of her songs, the lyrics infer that Cardi buys into the traditional gender role of being a caretaker who puts her family first. While in other lyrics, the narrative appears to push against traditional restrictions on womanhood through self-actualization. We theorize that Cardi's life experiences—both as a poor Black woman in America and as a woman with Dominican and Trinidadian roots—heavily influence the behaviors and beliefs expressed in her songs. You'll read more about this in the next chapter, but let's just say that Cardi's Afro-Latinx background is complicated. Because Spanish colonists brought enslaved Africans to the shores of Hispaniola (present-day Dominican Republic and Haiti) and Trinidad in the 16th century, Cardi's heritage contains African and Spanish influences.

Histories of Resistance

The bold feminist stance in Cardi's lyrics is no surprise considering her ancestry. Both sides of Cardi's family come from countries with histories of enslavement and female resistance against it. In the Dominican Republic (the birthplace of Cardi's father), women have always been instrumental to the survival of African descendants. In the early 16th century, an enslaved Black woman who practiced natural medicine opened her home as a hospital to aid poor sick people in Santo Domingo. Because her existence was purposely erased from the history books, this Hispaniola heroine remains unnamed. However, historical documents along with oral histories revealed that a hospital was constructed to support her healing efforts.[6] Another example of the fighting spirit of Black Dominican women is the story of Ana Maria who led the last known sugarcane rebellion in 1796. Known as the "Queen of the Freed Slaves" for governing more than 200 escaped slaves in a maroon society[7] that boasted an organized military, Ana Maria and her followers fended off Spanish colonial troops for over a month. She and her soldiers stole ammunition and burned sugarcane fields in several strategic attacks against Spanish enslavers.

Enslaved women were also at the forefront of resisting slavery in Trinidad and Tobago (the birthplace of Cardi's mom). They filed complaints before the magistrates to challenge the enslavement of themselves and their children at two times the rate of enslaved men. Furthermore, women acted as leaders in rebellions and political movements in Trinidad and Tobago (Reddock 1994). These legacies of powerful resistance and leadership encouraged the independence of Trinidadian and Tobagonian women, which aligns with the philosophy espoused by Trinidadian professor, author, and social activist, Rhoda Reddock (1994), who wrote:

> The treachery and inhumanity of the sugarcane plantation experience brought to the fore the potentials for production, self-sufficiency, rebellion, and the relentless quest for personal autonomy still present in Caribbean women today.
>
> *(11)*

The cultures of resistance related to Cardi's ethnicity are passed down across generations through verbal histories into our present-day bank of knowledge about navigating the world (Collins 2002). This historical ideology contextualizes any themes that become visible when reading Cardi's lyrics. Additionally, the gender expectations tied to Cardi's Latine background shape her worldview. We also see how her US nationality forwards both an ideology of individuality and to a lesser degree, the feminism that shapes the words Cardi raps to those infectious beats.

Womanhood: As the Dominant Culture Sees It

A gender ideology relevant to Cardi B's identity as a Latina second-generation immigrant is that of marianismo (Gil and Vazquez 1996). Modeled after the traits of Mary the Virgin Mother of Jesus, marianismo is defined as the ideal form of womanhood within Latinx communities. Gil and Vazquex (1996) define marianismo as a position of "sacred duty, self-sacrifice, and chastity . . . [which is] about living in the shadows, literally and figuratively, of your men—father, boyfriend, husband, son—your kids, and your family." Women who ascribe to the tenets of marianismo have historically been seen as enjoying the benefits of male protection, power within the home, and financial stability.

Similar gendered expectations of women exist in the United States. While this is not reflective of societal reality, the idealized role for woman in our country is still that of the caretaker of the family while the ideal man is the breadwinner (Hansen 1999; Vernier and Hale 1920). To achieve the coveted status of white, middle-class, heterosexual ideals in family formation, girls in the United States are taught that the goal is to become demure and empathic caretakers while boys are taught to be bold, ambitious risk-takers (Moon and Hoffman 2008). Feminism provided a departure from these historical expectations for women in the United States, specifically for white, middle-class women. Meanwhile, other feminist frameworks emerged from different communities as a response to the racism of white feminism and exclusion of non-white women from decision-making in feminist circles. These extensions of feminism created by women of color reveal the different ways women use their agency to empower themselves.[8] Growing up as a Bronx native, Cardi B's concepts of race and gender would have been molded by messages from her peers, schools, media, and other socializing agents. Therefore, the lyrics she performs (thereby endorses) are influenced by how she was socialized and give us a glimpse into the feminism to which Cardi ascribes. Next, we focus back on her lyrics and how they are reflective and rooted in who she is as an Afro-Latina and trap feminist.

Analysis: "I Like Stunting, I Like Shining"

After completing an analysis of Cardi's lyrics, four themes emerged that speak to different aspects of gender expectations that Cardi pushed back against and grapples with:

(1) financial success
(2) open discussions about sexual behavior
(3) negative experiences in romantic relationships
(4) the word "bitch" as empowering and degrading

We examine these four themes and then discuss how they speak to Cardi B's feminist practice.

Financial Success: "I Went from Rag to Riches, Went from WIC to Lit"

Financial success is the most common theme in Cardi's lyrics. In almost every song on *Invasion of Privacy*, she raps about her increased income and wealth. When considering traditional and Latina gender ideology, a woman should not revel in her ability to take care of herself. Instead, she should rely on her male partner as the breadwinner and play her role as the caretaker. Although bragging about material wealth is central to Hip Hop culture (Price 2006), Cardi B's lyrics infer that stripping and rapping to make money is more about survival than Hip Hop bravado. In addition, Cardi B's discussion of her work ethic in the nontraditional jobs that brought her financial success reflect trap feminist principles. Trap feminism is a framework that makes room for the use of divergent mechanisms to make money (hustles) in order to survive the harsh economic conditions of disadvantaged neighborhoods. Profitable trap hustles for women include drug dealing, stripping, being a kitchen beautician, or buying food with food stamps and then selling "dinners." Remember, the trap is a place marked by underfunded schools, rampant municipal disinvestment, and a scarcity of high-paying jobs. Therefore, women in the trap must actively hustle to make a living. When we incorporate these facts into our socio- logical imagination, we can see the trap feminist knowledge produced in Cardi's lyrics about stripping and hustling.

Further aligning with trap feminism, Cardi B's lyrics also reflect her refusal to rely on a man to be her economic savior; trap feminists do not wait for someone to rescue them and whisk them off to a life of luxury. Cardi B used all the tools at her disposal—her attractiveness, talent, authen- ticity, and personality—not only to survive the trap but also to create a new reality that includes the ability to live in a big house and buy whatever she wants, including a brand-new luxury car "off the lot." In other words, her lyrics suggest that Cardi's upward socioeconomic mobility is the result of her ability to hustle—a fundamental tenet of trap feminism.

To sum it up, living in areas of concentrated disadvantage limits one's ability to use traditional means to move up to a better neighborhood (Alva- rado and Cooperstock 2021). Therefore, Black women in the trap often co- create or adopt unconventional paths to financial security, much like their male counterparts. For everyday Black women, these paths might include braiding hair, working multiple part-time jobs, and selling waist trainers. Cardi B's unconventional means included stripping, finessing men, social media, Hip Hop, and reality television.

Cardi's lyrics also highlight the hard work she performed to become a top rap artist who creates successful records that earn her millions. She brags about owning and wearing expensive jewelry, designer clothes and shoes, and buying and enjoying expensive luxury vehicles and real estate. In Cardi B's first Number 1 hit, "Bodak Yellow," she raps: "I don't dance now, I make money moves." Throughout this song, Cardi points out her rise from poor to wealthy class status by reminding us that she no longer needs to work as a stripper to support herself. Cardi B also raps about her "red bottoms" in "Bodak Yellow." In the chorus, she points out that she can afford multiple pairs of Christian Louboutin shoes.[9] In verse two of "Bodak Yellow," Cardi B raps, "Got a bag and fixed my teeth, hope you hoes know it ain't cheap." This line signals that her financial success does not only allow her to obtain designer shoes, but she can now afford to invest in dental care, which is cost-prohibitive for most people in the trap.

In "Get Up 10," Cardi B gives more details about her rags-to-riches story. Her lyrics contain her history of choosing stripping as a profession given the lack of opportunity and poverty she experienced while growing up in the trap. She traces a life that advanced from humble beginnings to a life of fame when she raps that she "went from making tuna sandwiches to making the news." To accomplish the feat of moving up from hustling in the trap to being the number one female rapper in the country, Cardi B points to her unstoppable work ethic and her use of strategies outside of the conventionally prescribed mechanisms of going to college and getting a white-collar job.

While we find these examples of a trap feminist standpoint in her music, Cardi B's lyrics also show how some of the behaviors she describes are in tension with conventional gender expectations. As a hustler who tapped into stripping and rapping to provide for herself and elevate herself out of poverty, her strategy detours from the conventional routes of upward social mobility for women. Promoted by mainstream society and discussed in sociological literature, these conventional routes include marriage, education, and employment (Haveman and Smeeding 2006; Oppenheimer 1997).

Cardi's path to success also violates Latinx and US gender expectations that define good women as virginal caretakers who rely on men for financial stability and support. Traditional gender expectations of Latinas include the idea that putting yourself out front as a woman and flaunting your success in front of men is a no-no; if women self-define and flaunt their path to success, they are emasculating their men (Gil and Vazquez 1996). Cardi B's drive to be financially successful on her own breaks from both conventional ideals and cultural traditions.

While we can surmise that Cardi B is an independent woman who is self-defining her role in society, the lyrics on *Invasion of Privacy* also reflect Cardi B's desire to fulfill her role as the dutiful daughter, a tenet of marianismo. In "Get up 10," Cardi raps, "The pressure on your shoulders/ feel like boulders/when you gotta make sure that everybody straight." This lyric points to the assumption that in many Latine households, women are responsible for the entire family's well-being (Gil and Vazquez 1996). As the designated family caretaker, Latinas are expected to cook, clean, and cater to the needs (and wants) of their husbands, brothers, and offspring. As women move away from these rigid guidelines of girlhood and woman-hood, they are often conflicted about shirking these responsibilities (Gil and Vazquez 1996). Financially subsidizing her extended family may be viewed as a creative way that Cardi remains true to her assumed duties as a Latina without compromising her independence. In this way, Cardi B models one of the creative and original ways that trap women navigate the tension between being a trap feminist and a dutiful daughter. As we have learned in this book, trap feminism is truly complex and inclusive; in our next theme, you'll see there is room for both traditional and nontraditional conceptions of gender roles and womanhood.

Open Discussions About Sexual Behavior: "I Call My Own Name During Sex"

The second theme that emerged from our analysis was openness about sexuality. In ten out of the 13 tracks on *Invasion of Privacy*, there are lyrics about sexual performance, sexual prowess, and sexual desire. The references are often overt and graphic. For example, in "Bartier Cardi," Cardi raps about having sexual intercourse and oral sex with her husband, Offset: "Cardi put the pussy on Offset/Cartier/Cardi B brain on Offset." Sex positivity is a trap feminist attribute. In Chapter 1, we learned through other Hip Hop lyrics that trap feminism's sex-positive stance centers Black women's agency, which enables them to embrace their sexuality even though white society dictates shamefulness in this area.

On the other hand, sex positivity and the idea of a woman enjoying sex is the antithesis of marianismo. The mother of Jesus is considered perfect because she was a virgin. Therefore, a gender role that aligns with the idea of the virgin Mary—marianismo—is asexual or embraces sexual activity as only useful for procreation. According to this ideology, Black women who embrace their sexuality are viewed as hoes; if a woman has financial expectations of her sexual partners, she is called a gold-digger.

One of the subthemes of openness about sexual behavior is found in Cardi's lyrics about exchanging sex for financial gain. In many songs, Cardi B's lyrics promote sexuality as another way to boost a woman's income, a resource that can be swapped for money or gifts. In "Bodak Yellow," Cardi raps one of her most famous lines, "I'll let him do what he want/he buy me

Yves Saint Laurent."[10] In the stanzas right before and after this one, Cardi B tells the story of receiving expensive gifts of designer clothes and a sports car in exchange for allowing a man to perform oral sex on her. She elevates the stakes in the song "Bickenhead," when she talks about her quid pro quo: "vag for a bag," "ass for a Raf," and an orgasm for money. In her lyrics, Cardi expresses her willingness to perform certain sex acts for specific gifts and money. This scenario could be read as immoral sex work or oppressive bartering. But in our analysis, we label sex for money and gifts as a trap feminist hustle. The lyrics of James Brown's song "Hot Pants" are apt here: "She used what she got to get what she want."

Another subtheme of openness about sexuality emerged in the lyrical data–sex and attractiveness as a competitive sport. The woman who is more attractive and better at sex wins the prize of affection and resources from men. Cardi B boasts in multiple songs about the superiority of her sexual performance and her looks. In "Money Bag," Cardi B tells a woman that because of looks and reputation she (Cardi) can "take your man/won't give him back." In these lyrics, Cardi threatens to out-woman her competition which reflects a belief in a zero-sum game within the arena of sex: there can be only one sexual goddess that accepts offerings from men. Although feminism more broadly advocates for sisterhood among women, it appears that the competitive nature of hustling—a tenet of trap feminism—may outweigh feminists' desire for universal solidarity. This is easier to understand when we connect Cardi's competitive streak to trap feminism. Our sociological imaginations remind us that trap feminism is undergirded by the very real need to survive in a place where people typically die young. Therefore, a life-or-death survival instinct may lead to a willingness to push another woman (who is not or who is no longer in the sister circle) out of the way in order to get a man with money. We must also keep in mind that one-upmanship cannot be decoupled from Hip Hop as a musical genre or a lifestyle (Price 2006).

Owning one's sexuality and using sexuality to one's advantage in a male-dominated world are trap feminist characteristics that challenge gender norms and also defy the respectability politics we learned about in Chapter 2. However, a trap feminist perspective also provides space for Black women in and from the trap to self-define womanhood and sexuality without being stigmatized. Refusing to bow to the conservative ideology of restraint, trap feminists demonstrate knowledge about both the pleasure and the power of their sexuality (Morgan 2015). Cardi B flaunts her sexuality to make money, and she does not hide the fact that she worked as a stripper. On the other hand, Cardi's lyrics also describe her deeply painful feelings about and powerful reactions to infidelity and other negative aspects of her relationships with men and women.

Negative Experiences in Romantic Relationships: "You Might Have a Fortune, But You Lose Me, You Still Gon' Be Misfortunate"

In three songs on *Invasion of Privacy*, Cardi's lyrics describe negative experiences in relationships, the third theme in this analysis. Like the lyrics quoted here, the lyrics in these songs include multiple references to men's infidelity and abandonment. Taking the angry view of a long-suffering, scorned woman, Cardi's lyrics provide examples of the emotional trauma that results from bad relationships.

As in all of our themes in this chapter, there is complexity here. In "Be Careful," Cardi B raps about the impact of infidelity on a woman's sense of self, "You even got me trippin'/you got me lookin' in the mirror different/ Thinkin' I'm flawed because you inconsistent." In this same song, Cardi B reminds her lover of her feelings for him, tells him how his actions are affecting her, and cautions him to stop before she leaves him. This decline in self-esteem stands in stark contrast to the air of superiority reflected by most of the tracks on *Invasion of Privacy*. Cardi B's understanding of the complexities of relationships is demonstrated by lyrics that go from having any man she wants in "Bodak Yellow" to having hurt feelings after she discovers infidelity in "Be Careful." Even in the life of a financially independent and sexually assertive woman like her, Cardi notes the importance of love and loyalty.

In addition, Cardi B's lyrics tell us about retaliation for partner betrayal. In "Through Your Phone," Cardi B provides examples of the "woman scorned" responses often seen in television shows like *Snapped* (Jupiter Entertainment 2004–2023) and *Fatal Attraction* (Jupiter Entertainment 2013). Modeling the dark thoughts that often arise when women find evidence of their partner's unfaithfulness, Cardi details her desire for vengeance by threatening her cheating partner; her lyrics describe her thoughts of stabbing and poisoning him, destroying his property, and calling his mother. Violent threats are common to Hip Hop lyrics in general. And when matters of the heart are discussed, these threats may seem warranted to many, as symbolized in the adage "all is fair in love and war."

Stories about self-esteem and competition with other women also surface as a thematic element in Cardi's lyrics about infidelity when she raps about the degradation of the side chick (the woman with whom her man cheated). She refers to side chicks as hoes, bitches, and lower-quality women; in "Through Your Phone," she tells her partner: "You don't even cheat with no badder bitches." Cardi B goes on, threatening to expose the nude photographs a side chick sent to her partner's phone. This attack on other women is contradictory to a traditional feminist practice and an example that demonstrates the complexity of trap feminism. Cardi's threat is far from the ideals of even a Black feminist practice. However, this is a practice that occurs frequently in the hood where women must compete for scarce heterosexual Black men who have not fallen victim to the scourges of high unemployment and mass incarceration. Therefore, many poor Black women may go after their women peers instead of their cheating partner.

Showing a more sensitive yet still violent side, Cardi B's lyrics in "Through Your Phone" exemplify a yearning for a long-term relationship. Here we see another example of the tension between gender expectations and trap feminism. Her desire to be in a monogamous, heterosexual relationship aligns with the gendered expectations of women within most cultures. Black women and Latinas are traditionally expected to be the long-suffering wives who silently accept their husbands' bad deeds to keep the family together (Gil and Vazquez 1996; Jones 2009).

On the one hand, the lyrics infer that to some degree, Cardi B ascribes to this gender norm because she is giving warnings and reevaluating herself to understand her partner's behavior. On the other hand, Cardi B is *not* suffering in silence. Cardi violates marianismo gender norms by admonishing her cheating partner and considering revenge against him and the side chick. Under the lens of trap feminism, Cardi's lyrics reflect the multifaceted nature of Black women in the trap. Even though they hustle to be independent, trap feminists still desire love and relationships.

Many people paint the poor with a broad brush, questioning the possibility and the validity of relationships and families within the construct of poverty. However, when all you have to give is love, love becomes a valuable commodity (Edin and Kefalas 2005). Seeing life through the lens of trap feminism removes the class boundaries from love. A trap feminist standpoint reveals the creativity and determination of Black women in the trap, who build and dismantle relationships within the confines of a society that does not even believe that poor Black women deserve love and families.

The Word "Bitch" As Empowering and Degrading: "Bad Bitches Do What They Want"

Now, let's move onto our fourth and final theme, Cardi's frequent use of the word "Bitch" in her lyrics. The word "bitch" is sprinkled throughout *Invasion of Privacy* like the Swarovski crystals on Cardi B's nails. To be specific, Bitch appears 123 times across the 13 songs on the album. While featured artists on the album are responsible for 17 "bitches," Cardi B raps the word 106 times. In "Bartier Cardi," a song performed and co-written with the rapper 21 Savage, the word is used 31 times.

Throughout *Invasion of Privacy*, the word "bitch" is most often used as a derogatory term for other women. It is used alone, as in lines like "Bitch, I'm the mayor!" or accompanied with adjectives to infer another woman's inferiority. For example, the phrase "lil bitch" is used two times in the famous lyrics of "Bodak Yellow." "Said, lil bitch/you can't fuck with me/ if you wanted to" and "My pussy glitter is gold/tell that lil bitch play her role." In both of these examples, the use of the word "little" before the word "bitch" signifies the subordinate place of another woman. Part of the culture of rap is one-upmanship. Therefore, in this context, the word "bitch" is used to insult and diminish peers in the rap industry and haters, who are predominantly other Black women.

Cardi B also uses bitch as a compliment and an indication of superiority. When we look at the context within which "bitch" is used positively, we observe that it is accompanied by words like "bad," "boss," and "that." As adjectives, these words change the connotation of bitch into something more uplifting, especially when Cardi B refers to herself. For example, in "Drip," Cardi raps "I've been that bitch since pajamas with footies." Being *that* bitch is positive while being *a* bitch is negative. Similarly, the use of "real" before "bitch" speaks to Cardi's claims of authenticity.

Within 15 bars of "I Do," featuring singer SZA, Cardi uses the word bitch in three different ways: to compliment herself and other women, as a neutral synonym for a woman, and to degrade other women. In fact, the phrase "boss bitch" was used as a statement of superiority and applied to symbolize the oppositions' inferiority. For example, in the first verse, Cardi refers to herself as a boss bitch, then says, "you aint a boss bitch, move." These lyrics also align with the braggadocious way rappers present themselves and their material positions as enviable symbols and examples of success that others should emulate even though they might never get there.

We don't see a universal love for other women in *Invasion of Privacy* lyrics. Many Black feminist scholars speak to the elevation of women without intragroup conflict. But Cardi B's lyrics will call a woman a bitch just as quickly as the male rap group NWA.[11] Cardi raps about openly competing against other women and uses the same degrading language as male Hip Hop stars.[12] Most self-proclaimed feminists would find Cardi B's use of the word bitch antithetical to feminism. However, if Cardi B frames her feminism as the ability to be equal to men, then by using the word bitch she is engaging in high-level feminism by claiming her right to do what male rappers do. From the original rap battles in New York to contemporary rap beefs (like Remy Ma and Nicki Minaj), rappers' songs degrade their opponents in an attempt to come out on top. Although the language Cardi uses toward other women would not be appreciated by some feminists, Cardi B's use of bitch and other negative lyrics simply confirms her statement at the beginning of this chapter, "a woman can do things the same as a man."

Anti-women rhetoric is not addressed in the gender norms dictated by marianismo. However, in a US context, competition sustains society's relationship with individuality. Individuals are prompted to be the best at whatever they do as a part of US exceptionalism.[13] By promoting herself as a woman who has reached the zenith as the hardest working, richest, most beautiful, smartest woman of all, Cardi is demonstrating her buy-in to the US idea of our society as a meritocracy. The standpoint theory of trap feminism extends this merit-based narrative to things that have value among women outside of the conventional marketplaces,[14] like the ability to attract men and have "better" pussy. As poor Black women self-define womanhood and compete for resources, trap feminism allows us to expand the definition of merit in a society where the intelligence, beauty, and strong work ethic of poor Black women are devalued at best.

Conclusion

In this chapter, we set out to better understand what a Cardi B-style feminism might look like based on her song lyrics. We examined Cardi B's debut album, *Invasion of Privacy* to uncover themes or signposts that infer Cardi's proximity to current feminist ideology as well as the ways she resists cultural gender expectations. Four themes emerged from Cardi's song lyrics that help us understand her unique feminist stance: financial success; open discussions about sexual behavior; negative experiences in romantic relationships; and the word bitch as empowering and degrading. Ultimately, Cardi's art reflects a complicated relationship with what most scholars define as feminism. This tension between subscribing to gendered expectations and self-determination can be understood by using a trap feminist framework.

Evident in all of the themes that emerged from the lyrics of *Invasion of Privacy* is the pushback against traditional expectations of women. Cardi B violates the gender expectations of marianismo and the white patriarchy by representing herself as someone who makes her own money, enjoys a stellar career in Hip Hop, loves sex, vocalizes her relationship issues, and demands respect. Read as a continuous text, the lyrics on *Invasion of Privacy* also convey Cardi's primary alignment with US cultural ideals of self-reliance, independence, and a Protestant work ethic, which are usually reserved for men. Although we noted Cardi B's adherence to the "dutiful daughter" expectation of Latinas, Cardi makes it clear that she does not subscribe to other traditional expectations of women. She can earn money, use her sexual prowess to get what she wants, and even degrade other women by using the word "bitch" at the same levels as male rappers. Therefore, her lyrics reflect a belief in gender equality, one of the primary principles of Cardi's feminism.

But, while her lyrics exemplify gender equality, Cardi's lyrics also reflect the diversity of emotions commonly associated with women. Her lyrics show how she copes with feelings of low self-esteem while at the same time she asserts herself as a highly motivated, self-confident woman who embraces, utilizes, and maximizes her leadership skills and talents. Women and girls from the trap are forced to be independent due to their circumstances while still embracing the role of the "trap queen" to the trap king. This both/and perspective of the trap feminist shows the complications of a feminist practice rooted in survival instead of liberation. Trap feminism for poor women is more about choices that can lead to survival than freedom because trap feminists do not have the luxury of simply standing against the principles of patriarchal oppression. Trap feminists are born into a culture that demands resistance no matter what—simply put, there isn't room or time to don a pussy hat[15] and march against some far-off notion of the patriarchy. Women in the trap are busy using all the tools at their disposal to fight for their lives and their rights to exist and be recognized by society.

That brings us back to our central question: What kind of feminist is Cardi B based on her song lyrics in *Invasion of Privacy*?

Well, she is certainly not the bra-burning, coochie-hat-wearing kind of feminist. Her feminism is complicated and multifaceted. We see glimpses of gender equality across most of her songs; whether it's about how she makes money or how she competes with other women. We also see remnants of the traditionally feminine attributes of caretaking, issues with self-confidence, and desires for a long-term heterosexual relationship. Yet, when the full picture emerges, we see that Cardi's feminism is aligned with survival; you cannot expose your sensitive side for too long if you want to survive in the trap.

A trap feminist standpoint honors the lived experience of economically and socially constrained Black women of and adjacent to the trap who go out there and get it because no one is coming to save them. Trap feminism embraces the courageous women who hustle as hard as men to keep a roof over their head. Trap feminism addresses the full spectrum of womanhood in poor communities, including the human desires for love and pleasure.

Cardi B's feminism is a feminism that emerged from her life in the streets of New York where conditions conspired to mow her down, her heritage as the daughter of immigrants with rich histories of female resistance and conformity, and her embrace of the self-reliant narrative embedded in US culture. In the next chapter, we will show how Cardi B has also faced backlash for presenting her race and ethnicity in a way that does not align with US norms. We can conclude that Cardi B doesn't just talk the talk of feminism, she walks the walk by espousing a trap brand of feminism on her biggest platform. Like we said at the end of our preface, and like Cardi said in front of millions, "Bad bitches do what they want."

Notes

1 In Hip Hop, Lauryn Hill, Mumu Fresh, Noname, Queen Latifah, and Rapsody are examples of Black women artists whose social and political messages are clear in their lyrics.
2 The data was analyzed using qualitative content analysis and grounded theory methodologies. For more information on these analytical methods, see Sharlene Hesse-Biber's 2017 book, *The Practice of Qualitative Research: Engaging Students in the Research Process,* and Kathy Charmaz's 2014 book, *Constructing Grounded Theory.*
3 She endorses the song that she releases. She embodies them in her performances and in her engagement with social media. Her tweets and Instagram lives are also endorsements.
4 With this long-lasting success, Cardi B inherited the crown from the former record-holder, Lauryn Hill (Devin 2020).
5 Complexity is a hallmark of trap feminism – in the trap, feminism is about survival while inadvertently defeating the patriarchy. It takes bravery to seek long-term partnerships and hustle.
6 This information in the 1695 report to the Crown from the oral history of the Santo Domingo people. The facsimile of this document can be found on the City College of New York Libraries website in the Dominican Studies Institute section.
7 Maroon societies are remote hidden communities, usually in undeveloped areas, created by Black people who escaped from slavery.
8 Black feminism, third-world feminism, Hip Hop feminism, hood feminism, and Chicana feminism to name a few.
9 The phrase "red bottoms" refers to the distinctive red soles that mark Christian Louboutin shoes, which often retail for $3000 a pair.
10 In a television interview with Jamie Foxx, Denzel Washington recited this particular lyric in a televised interview. In fact, he says he loves Cardi B.
11 NWA is a rap group that began in the late 1980s who recorded "A Bitch Iz A Bitch."
12 For example, in "She Bad", Cardi raps "Bitch say that she gon' try me, how come I ain't seen it yet?" and in "Bartier Cardi", "Bitch, you a wannabe Cardi. Red bottom MJ, moonwalk on a bitch."
13 The idea that the United States is the best country in the world. For more on this concept, see Donald Pease's 2009 entry, "The New American Exceptionalism," in Oxford Bibliographies.
14 The conventional marketplaces include educational and job-related spaces.
15 The women's march, held on January 21, 2017, was a protest to the election of Donald Trump. During this predominately white feminist demonstration, women wore pink knit hats called "pussy hats" as an emblem of solidarity.

4

POLICING CARDI B'S BLACKNESS

In August 2023, Belcalis Marlenis Almánzar (Cardi B)[1] became the first Afro-Latina to be featured on the cover of *Vogue México*. When the magazine interviewed Cardi about the contents of the designer purse she wore when photographed for the cover, she mixed Spanish and English in her responses (Vogue México y Latinoamérica 2023). A Twitter user then responded to the video of the interview, saying:

> Ok so I wanna point out something . . . everyone knows I'm not a CARDI fan but seeing her speaking Spanish and embracing her roots and just not trying be something she's not (black) like I really like to see her in this element.
>
> *(Twitter user; 08/23/2023)*

This tweet reflects how folks often associate Blackness in the United States with English-language fluency while framing Spanish-language use as a non-Black practice associated with Latinxs. Cardi B's bilingualism marks her as a supposed outsider to US Blackness which, paired with her appearance, has led many to question her legitimacy in Hip Hop, an unmistakably Black musical genre. In Chapter 3, we applied the standpoint of trap feminism to understand how the lyrics of Cardi B's songs reflect her unique relationship to feminism. Here, we examine another facet of Cardi's identity: her race and ethnicity. We use an instrumental case study method along with a trap feminist theoretical framework to study the public policing of Cardi B's Blackness and to analyze how Cardi B has challenged this policing.

DOI: 10.4324/9781003184980-5

To properly analyze the public debates about Cardi's Blackness and Cardi's public reactions to these debates, we first need to include the entirety of the African Diaspora. After all, Cardi B is the daughter of Caribbean immigrants from the Dominican Republic and Trinidad and Tobago who raised her in New York City. Put simply, diaspora refers to the dispersal of peoples from their homeland to two or more outside locations (Butler 2001), while the African Diaspora refers to the specific dispersal of peoples from the African continent, which was significantly shaped by the Trans-atlantic Slave Trade spanning the 16th–19th centuries. Over 12 million enslaved women, men, and children were trafficked from Africa on ships that carried them not only to the present-day United States but also to the present-day Caribbean and Latin America. The ancestors of African Americans, Afro-Caribbeans, and Afro-Latinos have defined themselves and been defined by others differently depending on the cultural contexts in which they experienced the horrors of enslavement and fought for their freedom, human dignity, and civil rights. Therefore, it's important to begin our discussion of Cardi B's Blackness by noting that the African Diaspora includes Africans and their descendants *across* the globe, including the Latin American/Caribbean birthplaces of Cardi's parents.

In this chapter, we argue that debates about Cardi B's Blackness reflect conflicting ideas about race and Blackness across the Americas as well as concerns about Black authenticity in a US context. To reach this conclusion, we first address the overlap and differences between race and ethnicity as social constructs. We then apply three theories to analyze the policing of Cardi B's Blackness in online spaces and to determine the sociological foundations and importance of Cardi's reactions to this policing: (1) Blackness as performance; (2) Diasporic Blackness; and (3) Trap feminism.

To discuss the theory of Blackness as performance we build on E. Patrick Johnson's claim in *Appropriating Blackness: Performance and the Politics of Authenticity*, that Blackness "does not belong to any one individual or group. Rather, individuals or groups appropriate this complex and nuanced racial signifier in order to circumscribe its boundaries or to exclude other individuals or groups" (2003:2–3). This theoretical approach allows us to understand that Blackness does not simply exist as a "fact" but rather that people adopt a performance of Blackness to signal their racial identity and their alignment or nonalignment with different groups of racialized peoples.

The Meanings of Race and Ethnicity

Before analyzing Cardi B's performance of Blackness, we need to define race and ethnicity and understand how these terms are conflated in discussions about Cardi B. The public discussion around Cardi's Blackness (or lack thereof) is commonplace—a quick Google search for "Cardi B Black" produced 102 million results—and reflects the confusion people have around the social construction of race and ethnicity. For example, in a YouTube video titled "20 Things You Didn't Know About Cardi B," the first topic discussed is Cardi's "looks." The text in the video states, "Cardi B's looks leave many people wondering what her ethnic background is. Her father is of Dominican descent and her mother is Trinidadian. That means our girl has Caribbean roots" (TheThings Celebrity 2018). We found this "clarification" interesting and lacking. What do Cardi's Caribbean roots tell us about her looks? Not everyone in the Caribbean looks the same, and being from the Caribbean doesn't automatically assign a person to a specific race.

When people "wonder" about Cardi's background based on her physical appearance, they are attempting to assign her to a racial group. Therefore, TheThings Celebrity's video makes the common mistake of conflating ethnicity with race (or of displacing race with ethnicity). Ethnicity is a capacious concept that includes one's culture, language, and customs while race is a system created with the intent of distributing resources, privileges, and rights based on pseudo-biological understandings of ancestry and physical appearance. Therefore, stating that Cardi B has Caribbean "roots" does little to settle the online debates about Cardi's race or the authenticity of her Blackness.

Race and ethnicity also get conflated through the racialization of language use. Some have used Cardi B's knowledge of Spanish as evidence that she is not Black. Take for example the tweet at the beginning of this chapter, where the commenter says they enjoy seeing Cardi "speaking Spanish and embracing her roots and just not trying be something she's not (black)." This comment presents Spanish language-use and Blackness as mutually exclusive: Cardi embracing her roots and speaking Spanish means she is not Black and is instead being her authentic self. But why can't she be Black and also speak Spanish (as most of the 150 million Afro-descendants in Latin America do)? Scholars have discussed this treatment of Spanish-language use and Blackness as markers of identities that do not overlap. For example, Afro-Dominican scholar Torres-Saillant draws on his own lived experiences and points out how "the perception of a Hispanic person's different linguistic ancestry in the United States seems to disqualify [them] from easy entrance into [white and Black] communal . . . spaces" (2000:15). The fact that language-use can be, and often is, racialized in the United States (Flores and Rosa 2015) is another example of how people treat race and ethnicity as interchangeable.

The conflation of ethnicity and race is due in large part to the social and political nature of these concepts. Race is a social construction that can change, shift, and morph over time to meet the needs of those seeking power. An example of race as a changing social construction is how the US Census categories for race and ethnicity have changed drastically over time. The term "white" was strategically expanded to include Eastern and Southern European immigrants over the course of the 20th century. In contrast, the categories "Mulatto" and "Quadroon" accounted for those of mixed African and European ancestry before government officials narrowed these categories into the singular designation of "Negro" in 1930. That year, at the height of Jim Crow, US Census enumerators were instructed to strictly follow the one-drop rule, or hypodescent, when racially categorizing those living in the country. The specific instructions were "A person of mixed white and Negro blood should be returned as a Negro, no matter how small the percentage of Negro blood" (Parker et al. 2015).

Like race, ethnicity can morph and change over time, with existing groups creating and adopting new ethnic and pan-ethnic categories such as "Italian American" (Waters 1990) and "Hispanic" (Mora 2014). To make matters even more confusing, we can also pair ethnicities with racial designators to create racialized ethnicities like "African American" and "Afro-Latino" (Hordge-Freeman and Veras 2020).[2]

Therefore, to understand how Cardi B is racialized and how she pushes back against that racialization, we first need to understand how she is slotted into socially constructed racial and ethnic labels that are messy to begin with. To address how people view her Blackness, we need a deeper understanding of what we mean by Blackness and an awareness of the context in which her Blackness is being judged; in other words, we need to know the standpoint of those doing the evaluating.

Blackness as a "Fact" and as a Performance

Our desire to know whether someone is "actually" Black is often rooted in specific cultural, personal, and societal ideas about Black authenticity. What does it mean to be Black? And what metrics do we use to determine someone's Blackness? Our answers to these questions (and most questions about race) are dependent on context; divergences in history and politics, as well as our specific life experiences, lead us to different conclusions and definitions of Blackness.

One way of assessing whether a person is Black is to look at how they perform Blackness. This usually involves two steps: (1) establishing a set of markers (e.g., cultural, political, socioeconomic, physical, and ancestral) that we associate with Blackness *in a particular context*; and (2) measuring the extent to which a person exhibits those established markers of Blackness. The process of determining the "markers" or "standards" for assessing someone's Blackness is political and depends upon the context in which we are making these assessments. If we are not careful, it is easy and common to fall into the trap of oversimplifying the complexities of Blackness into a fixed "essence" of Blackness. Cultural theorist Stuart Hall (1993) points to the dangers of racial essentialism, stating that "The moment the signifier 'black' is torn from its historical, cultural, and political embedding and lodged in a biologically constituted racial category, we valorize, by inversion, the very ground of the racism we are trying to deconstruct" (111). Hall argues that racial essentialism—in this case, the act of describing Blackness as a static, fixed, genetic, and/or biological category—reinforces racism rather than challenging it. Research confirms Hall's theory: social psychologists have found that, because essentialism promotes a view of racial hierarchies and inequalities as natural, white and Black Americans who had essentialist views of race were more likely to hold prejudiced views of Black people (Mandalaywala, Amodio, and Rhodes 2018). In contrast, thinking of Blackness through the lens of performance allows us to avoid racial essentialism by centering on the historical, cultural, and political contexts in which Blackness is (re)produced.

The idea of Blackness as a performance might lead some to think that being Black is simply an act that can be turned on and off at will. But most people don't have this much personal power over how they are racialized—that is, how they are assigned by outsiders as belonging to one "race" or another (Roth 2016; Torres-Saillant 2009). Further, the idea that Blackness is so flexible that people can hop in and out of the racial category downplays how people racialized as Black experience higher mortality rates, more police brutality, less investment in their communities, and other negative life outcomes. In short, anti-Black racism is a tool used for the unequal distribution of resources. Therefore, Blackness is not an identity you can simply adopt or reject at will.

Still, viewing Blackness as a performance provides us with an alternative to racialization, which assigns Blackness and all its significations to people regardless of how those people view themselves. We can see how these two approaches to Blackness differ through Fanon's (1952) work. In *Black Skin, White Masks* (1952), Martinican revolutionary and psychologist Frantz Fanon devotes an entire chapter to "The Fact of Blackness." In this chapter, he shares personal narratives of times where he tried to assert his humanity in the face of constant racialization and marginalization by white people (e.g., he learns about the pre-colonial histories of his African ancestors—their civilizations, kingdoms, and customs—and then is questioned by white critics about whether those histories are true).

But Fanon's lived experiences do not reflect the policing *of* his Blackness. No one is accusing Fanon of not being Black. Instead, his traumas are the result of white people policing him *due to* his Blackness. This is not always the case when discussing the lived experiences and racial identity of Cardi B, a light-skinned Afro-Latina of Caribbean descent who many see as not *actually* being Black. However, the disparities in the experiences of Fanon and Cardi B don't support the authenticity of Fanon's Blackness while reflecting the inauthenticity of Cardi B's Blackness. These disparities simply reflect differences in how people have constructed Blackness across time and space.

While the fact of Blackness might seem self-evident, the realities of Blackness are not as clear-cut as they seem. Blackness is not a monolith. Our attention to the diversity within Blackness should prompt us to view Blackness not only as something that is assigned to those racialized as Black but also as a category that is creatively adopted, embodied, performed, and recreated over time and across spaces. Along this vein, Black Performance Studies scholar E. Patrick Johnson (2003) presents a contrast to Fanon's comments about the fact of Blackness, saying,

> The fact of blackness is not always self-constituting. Indeed, blackness, like performance, often defies categorization. . . . Its elusiveness does not preclude one from trying to fix it, to pin it down, however, for the pursuit of authenticity is inevitably an emotional and moral one (2).

Johnson's words provide one explanation for the policing of Cardi's Blackness. Oftentimes, folks will police the boundaries of Blackness to preserve the cohesion of a group that has historically been oppressed and marginalized; unity and solidarity among Black people are at stake when we assess who is part of the in-group and who is an outsider.

The primary contribution of viewing Blackness through the lens of performance is the unsettling of the supposed fixedness of Blackness. Given that Blackness is "contingent on the historical, social, and political terms of its production" (Johnson 2003:3), we can understand the performance of Blackness by looking at when and how it is produced and by acknowledging who has the power and legitimacy to establish its boundaries. In the case of Cardi B, we do this by addressing the unique history of Blackness in the United States, comparing this to the history of Blackness in the birthplaces of Cardi's parents, the Dominican Republic and Trinidad and Tobago, and linking these histories to Hip Hop and trap feminism.

Diasporic Blackness and Hip Hop

Expanding our view of Blackness beyond the United States and including the entirety of the African Diaspora allow us to better understand Cardi

B's trap feminist performance of Blackness. Developing a diasporic sense of Blackness involves broadening our lens to include the experiences of those racialized as Black across the African Diaspora. Stuart Hall's work shows how differences in Black popular culture reflect divergences in the performance of Blackness across the world. Hall argues that Black popular performances "were partly determined from their [African] inheritances; but they were also critically determined by the diasporic conditions in which the connections were forged" (1993:109). One of the "diasporic conditions" Hall refers to is the extent to which European cultures were either incorporated or mixed with African cultures in the Americas. This allows us to consider how, in the Dominican Republic, anti-Blackness and the privileging of whiteness exist alongside African-derived musical styles, religious practices, and other Black everyday practices (Thornton and Ubiera 2019). Hall (1993) also describes the importation of indentured South and East Asians to parts of the Caribbean during European colonialism as a diasporic condition. This history of indentured labor helps us understand why Trinidad and Tobago (the birthplace and former home of Cardi B's mother) still espouses a nationalist narrative of being an Afro-Creole nation, even though almost half of the population is of South Asian descent (Brereton 2007).

To understand Cardi B's performance of a Diasporic Blackness, we also need to consider how Hip Hop itself has African Diasporic origins, while being uniquely shaped by its creation in a New York City context. Hip Hop emerged in the 1970s from the contributions and collaborations of African Americans, Puerto Ricans (many of whom were Black Puerto Ricans), and West Indian immigrants (many of whom were Black) living in poor neighborhoods of the Bronx, New York (Phillips, Reddick-Morgan, and Stephens 2005). Since its inception, Hip Hop has been rooted in a Black diasporic space and has centered on the experiences of people who were both racially and economically marginalized.

Trap feminism, which stems from this longer history of Hip Hop, gives us space to address the many complexities of Diasporic Blackness. Cardi B's lived experiences with race represent these complexities: First, her mother is a lighter-skinned Afro-Trinidadian woman, and her father is a lighter-skinned, mixed-race Dominican man; this has led many to question the legitimacy of Cardi's Blackness and her place within Hip Hop culture (as we discussed in Chapter 2 regarding Nicki Minaj's framing of Cardi as being outside of Hip Hop/Black culture). Those in the industry, as well as consumers, might question Cardi's status in Hip Hop simply because she is a woman in the male-dominated world of rapping. But Cardi's status as a "hood chick from the Bronx" (Price 2022) means she is closely connected to the birthplace of Hip Hop, which provides some legitimacy to her claims of belonging in the culture (Forman 2002).

Like many of the creators of Hip Hop, Cardi is a second-generation immigrant and a native New Yorker. She is also simultaneously Black, mixed race, Caribbean, Afro-Latina, and American (i.e., from the Americas and the United States). Cardi also practices a trap feminism that challenges the idea of "respectable womanhood" adopted by middle-class Black/Caribbean/Latinx people. In the following, our findings and analysis show how Cardi performs what Afro-Latinx Studies scholar Omaris Z. Zamora refers to as an "urban working-class transnational Black diasporic feminism that continues to push the boundaries of blackness" (2022:55).

Cardi B and Racial Ideologies in the Caribbean, Latin America, and the United States

To acknowledge who has the power and legitimacy to assess the Blackness of others, particularly high-profile celebrities like Cardi B, we examine conversations on Black Twitter—the decentralized social media space in which Black people across the country and the world engage in debates concerning the boundaries and politics of Blackness (Brock Jr 2020; Maragh 2018).

In social media spaces, and particularly on Black Twitter, people perform their Blackness by exhibiting cultural knowledge specific to Black Americanness—what scholars refer to as the linguistic practice of "signifyin"[3] (Florini 2014). Therefore, when Cardi B engages with the public on social media, others usually measure her performance of Blackness against Black American cultural norms.

We argue that the policing of Cardi B's Blackness in online spaces is mainly driven by the public's broader lack of knowledge on how racial ideologies and identities developed differently across the Americas—and particularly in the Caribbean versus the United States. Put simply, racial ideologies are powerful uses of language and ideas that work to reinforce the racial status quo in a specific context (Bonilla-Silva 2003). Given that the racial status quo across the Americas is informed by white supremacy and anti-Blackness, it's tempting to use the same measures to analyze race and racism across these spaces. But the legacies of Spanish and British colonialism in the Caribbean, and British and American colonialism in the United States, led to crucial differences in how folks in these spaces understand race and Blackness.

In the United States, race is commonly understood as a product of one's ancestry, with Blackness seen as tied not only to one's appearance but also, importantly, to one's culture and lineage. What is not always clear in social media discussions concerning Blackness (especially on Black Twitter) is that the racial ideologies underlying those discussions were shaped by the unique history of racism in the United States. As we briefly discussed earlier with the census, the one-drop rule was enshrined into law in the early 20th century and was used to categorize who was Black and who was white—with a firm boundary separating these groups (Hollinger 2003). Even today, the one-drop rule informs how Blackness is understood in the United States.

Arguments about Cardi B's supposed non-Blackness rest heavily on how outsiders view her parents and their race—reflecting a US view of Blackness as tied to ancestry and lineage. Once Cardi B released pictures of her parents, online commenters were quick to point out their racial "ambiguity."[4] For some, Cardi having a parent from the English-speaking Caribbean was a marker of her Blackness. Given that her mom is Trinidadian, and Trinidad and Tobago is a (presumably) Black nation, Cardi was, at the very least, half-Black or "mixed." On the other hand, her father's Dominican roots marked Cardi as non-Black in the eyes of many. Comments online claimed that having a Trinidadian mom and a Dominican father made Cardi half-Latina and half-Black. Here, though, we see the continued conflation of ethnicity with race. Latino is a pan-ethnic label, so saying Cardi is half-Latina doesn't clarify her place in the United States racial hierarchy or even her racial self-identification.

In June 2019, Cardi directly addressed her racial identity on Instagram live, stating that her lighter skin color did not mean that she was not a Black woman. In the video, she says,

> People just don't be understanding shit. It's like, "Cardi's Latin, she's not Black." And it's like, "bro, my features don't come from . . . two white people fucking, okay?" And they always wanna race-bait when it comes to me . . . I have Afro features. "Oh, but your parents are light-skinned" . . . all right, but my grandparents aren't.
>
> *(DiversityInc 2019)*

By directly challenging people's views of race and ancestry as tied to her parents alone, Cardi is pushing back against racial essentialists and challenging their ways of "testing" her Blackness. More specifically, Cardi is adopting the US racial ideology of the one-drop rule to challenge her critics—if ancestry matters for determining one's Blackness, and the one-drop rule persists in the US, then Cardi's grandparents' Blackness should provide enough proof of her own race.

FIGURE 4.1   Cardi B and her father, Carlos, attending the CARDI B "Gold Album" Release Party at Moxy Hotel on April 10, 2018 in New York City.

Source: Johnny Nunez/Getty Images.

We argue, though, that Cardi B's assertion that her "features" do not come from "two white people fucking" reflects a combination of the one-drop rule and the dominant racial ideology in Latin America, *mestizaje*. Mestizaje centers the importance of appearance, features, and mixedness for assessing someone's race (Telles and Paschel 2014). During the 19th-century-nation-building period in Latin America, political elites argued that mestizaje was a positive way to mix races and cultures and present as unified nations on the global stage. Scholars have since shown that political elites in the region strategically used mestizaje to whiten Latin American populations, a process known as *blanqueamiento* (Godreau et al. 2008). Since the nation-building period, mestizaje has been the dominant racial ideology in Latin America and is still hegemonic today (Telles and Garcia 2013).

In contrast to the United States, Spanish colonialism in Latin America and the Caribbean was not followed by a period of legalized segregation like the Jim Crow era. Instead, white supremacy and anti-Blackness were often enforced socially and culturally rather than legally. During the post-abolition period, white establishments socially excluded Black Latin Americans from entering and gaining membership. In addition, there were concerted government-driven efforts across Latin America to ban African religious practices and African musical performances (Butler 2000). It was not until the 1970s that Black social movements across the region began to make inroads in challenging the tenets of mestizaje, which made room for Black Latin Americans to fight for racial equality and civil rights (Paschel 2010). Mestizaje, in contrast to the one-drop rule, privileges an assessment of individuals' features and appearance over their lineage in assessing race. In addition, Latin American mestizaje often frames race in terms of a skin-color continuum (e.g., Indigenous to white; Black to white) rather than as a set of discrete, mutually exclusive categories (Black versus white) (Telles and Flores 2013). Therefore, Cardi's comments about her "Afro" features reflect a Latin American sensibility around appearance and race while her argument about her parents not being white draws on the US one-drop rule.

Online commenters have also pointed out Cardi B's hair as a marker of either her authentic Blackness or, conversely, her "mixedness." The connection between hair and race is evident across the Americas (Sims et al. 2020), and Dominican Studies scholar Ginetta Candelario argues that hair is the main indicator of race for those in the island nation and its US diaspora (Candelario 2007). In March 2020, Cardi posted a photo of herself rocking her natural hair from four years prior, in 2016 (Carter Jr 2020). This photo[5] features Cardi wearing a teal halter top and large, silver hoop earrings, and highlights her natural afro, resembling a halo surrounding her face. The photo has since gone viral on several occasions.

This photo appeased some of her online critics while also reflecting the fact that visual "signals" and "features" are as important in US assessments of Blackness as they are in Latin America. We might ask, though: Is Cardi B Black because her natural hair is Type 4 (coily and/or kinky)? Or is this the bar established for Cardi because her parents are lighter-skinned and from the Caribbean? Do Afro-Caribbean women and Afro-Latinas need to meet a higher burden of proof due to existing views of the Caribbean as a "mixed-race" space or given that Latinxs are often viewed as automatically not Black?

Since her rise to fame, Cardi B has kept followers and fans updated on her attempts to make her natural hair healthy and long. But these posts are often met with critiques—specifically, people argue that Cardi's natural hair journey is easy given her racial "mixedness." For example, Cardi posted a natural hair selfie to Instagram in late 2021 and offered her fans a recipe for the hair mask she used to help her hair grow. The photo[6] is a bathroom mirror selfie, and features Cardi with a black sports bra and no makeup. Her natural hair is blown out and reaches her waist.

Some online commenters stated that Cardi being racially mixed was the explanation behind her long natural hair rather than the hair mask itself. Cardi replied at length in an Instagram comment, saying,

> Why every time I post my natural hair I hear "you're MIXED you're supposed to have long hair"? That's not true and very misleading. I been posting pics of my hair journey for years and being mixed don't mean your hair is always long and curly, that wasn't my case. Since I was a child I have problems with managing my hair and couple years ago I find different methods that work for me and look at my length now. They'll try to make us believe our hair won't grow this long it's not true. A lot of hair products we used back then wasn't good for our hair but that's all we had to choose from also we couldn't afford to get to the salon regularly, if at all. now everybody is getting better options, making affordable GOOD products, learning from natural hair YouTube and TikTok about how to care for our hair better. I want women of color with tighter curl patterns to know that you don't have "BAD HAIR" there's no such thing as bad hair. and "good" hair don't mean a certain texture. ALL HAIR IS GOOD.
>
> *(Instagram, @iamcardib, 12/13/2021; Turner 2021)*

Here, Cardi does not challenge others' views of her as being mixed-race, which is the dominant racial ascription (i.e., assigned race) in Latin American spaces. In a US context, though, those who adopt a mixed-race identity are often seen as existing outside of, or at best adjacent to, Blackness.

Scholarship on mixed-race Black people has shown that their membership in Blackness is often questioned, which leads to divergences in how mixed-race Black people identify racially—those with darker skin color being more likely to identify solely as Black and those with lighter skin color being more likely to identify as mixed-race (Campion 2019).

In addition to reflecting her racial self-identification, Cardi's comments reflect her trap feminism. By detailing her struggles with her natural hair texture, and stating that "ALL HAIR IS GOOD," Cardi B is reflecting a trap feminist orientation that seeks to uplift women of color,[7] as they grapple with white beauty standards. She does this while keeping class issues central, pointing out how women of color often struggle to care for their hair due to the costs associated with salon visits and hair products. These comments show how Cardi uplifts other women, and particularly Black women, from a trap feminist standpoint that acknowledges how poverty can affect their ability to meet society's (white) beauty standards.

In addition to using the physical appearance of Cardi and her parents to assess the rapper's race, online commenters have also referred to Cardi's Caribbean ethnic background as proof of her (non)Blackness. But the metrics used by locals to decide who counts as Black differ when we are in Trinidad and Tobago, the Dominican Republic, or the United States. In the following, we argue that Cardi B's performance of Blackness represents the merging of racial ideological frameworks from all three of these contexts.

"They Don't Understand Caribbean People or Our Culture": Performing Diasporic Blackness in the United States

While Cardi B embodies her identity as an Afro-Latina unapologetically, and "without explanations or translations" (Zamora 2022:57), the rapper has also received significant backlash for how she has explained her race and ethnicity to the public. But even when she feels the need to explain herself to outsiders, Cardi's responses reflect a "knowingness" that is rooted in her lived experiences, showing how trap feminists are inherently knowledge producers.

In response to people questioning her Blackness due to her Caribbean ancestry, Cardi B points out the absurdity of the comments about her "non-Black" ethnic origins in an interview with actor Zendaya. As a mixed-race Black woman herself, Zendaya has also experienced identity policing on social media. During the interview, published in the March 2018 issue of *CR Fashion Book*, Zendaya asks Cardi, "Is there anything that people don't ever ask you that you want somebody to ask you?" Cardi responded passionately, saying,

> One thing that always bothers me is that people know so little about my culture. We are Caribbean people. And a lot of people be attacking me because they feel like I don't be saying that I'm black. Some people want to decide if you're black or not, depending on your skin complexion, because they don't understand Caribbean people or our culture. I feel like people need to understand or get a passport and travel. I don't got to tell you that I'm black. I expect you to know it. . . . I expect people to understand that just because we're not African American, we are still black. It's still in our culture. Just like everybody else, we came over here the same fucking way. I hate when people try to take my roots from me. Because we know that there's African roots inside of us.
>
> *(Zendaya 2018)*

Cardi B's response reflects an understanding of Blackness that combines Latin American, Caribbean, and US racial ideologies. First, Cardi argues that her Blackness should be a given due to the widespread enslavement of Africans in the Caribbean and the impact of this history on Caribbean cultures. She highlights this history of African enslavement in the Caribbean by stating, "Just like everybody else, we came over here the same fucking way." These comments emphasize Cardi's knowledge of her African ancestry and, at the same time, challenge the views of those who equate Blackness with Black Americanness. By pointing out that people exclude her from Blackness due to her lighter skin color, Cardi also assumes the US one-drop rule to argue that her Blackness should be common sense due to her Afro-Caribbean ancestry—"I don't got to tell you that I'm black. I expect you to know it." Through this comment, Cardi argues that her Blackness is evident if we use US metrics to assess her race. By referencing her knowledge of the history of Blackness in the Caribbean and Latin America, Cardi B helps us understand transnational racial ideologies and how they lead to her social exclusion from US Blackness.

As we discussed at the beginning of this chapter, another way folks in the United States assess someone's Blackness is by looking at their ethnic background. Given that people often conflate race and ethnicity, those in the United States whose ethnic background is not African American are often categorized as non-Black. Still, exceptions to this rule are often made for people from places that are viewed, in the public imaginary at least, as majority-Black nations. Despite the centrality of racial mixedness (or creolité, mestizaje, mulataje etc.) in Caribbean racial ideologies, many in the

United States see the English-speaking Caribbean as predominantly Black while viewing the Spanish-speaking Caribbean as non-Black. Remember, Cardi B is of Dominican and Trinidadian ancestry. Many conceive of Trinidad and Tobago, and the rest of the former British West Indies, as Black nations. In contrast, many see the Dominican Republic as a "Hispanic" nation, with explicit ties to Spanish culture and Catholicism. This begs the question: What makes the Dominican Republic a Latino/Hispanic nation and Trinidad and Tobago a Black nation in the US public's imagination?

The Dominican Republic is a majority Afro-descendant nation—Torres-Saillant (2000) argues that up to 90% of the country's population are descendants of Africans. That said, Dominicans are often typecast as self-hating Afro-descendants due to their supposedly collective disavowal of Blackness in favor of a mixed-race identity. This idea of Dominicans being non-Black, however, is a narrative established by the nation's elite to distance the Dominican Republic from its neighboring nation, Haiti, the world's first Black republic (Thornton and Ubiera 2019). Knowledge about the history of contention and violence between the Dominican Republic and Haiti is crucial to understanding evolving racial ideologies among Dominicans. Today, many in the Dominican Republic identify as mixed-race (of African, Spanish, and Indigenous ancestry) and not solely as Black, though this might be changing due to heavy migration between the Dominican Republic and the United States, where Dominican migrants are often racialized as Black (Telles and Paschel 2014).

In contrast to the Dominican Republic, Trinidad and Tobago is broadly conceived of as a Black nation, even though a sizable proportion of the population is of South Asian and East Asian descent. Current racial demographics of Trinidad and Tobago describe the population as 40% Afro-descendant and 40% South Asian-descendant, with the remainder of the population being European and East Asian descendants (Brereton 2010). Despite this diversity, nationalist narratives have framed Trinidad and Tobago as an Afro-Creole nation since its independence in 1956. According to Brereton (2007), this Afro-Creole narrative

> came from a view of Trinidad's history which saw the descendants of the slaves, and of the free Blacks and "Coloureds," as the people who had been in the island for the longest time . . . and who enjoyed the moral and historical "right" to succeed the British in the governance of the new nation (175).

Like the Dominican Republic, Trinidad and Tobago is a country where nationalist narratives conflict with racial realities on the ground. Widespread views of Trinidad and Tobago as a Black country and the

Dominican Republic as a (non-Black) Hispanic country are informed by nation-building narratives scripted by elites on these islands (Brereton 2007; Thornton and Ubiera 2019).

The fact that nationalist narratives shape our understanding of race in different countries highlights the need to analyze Cardi B's performance of Blackness by adopting a broader, diasporic view of Blackness. Trying to understand Cardi B's race by using only a US view of Blackness would frame her racial self-identification as deviant, deficient, or just messy. Instead, we gain a foundational understanding of Cardi B's Blackness by acknowledging the complexities of her various backgrounds as well as her lived experiences. By pushing against the boundaries of US Blackness, Cardi B is urging us to broaden our view of Blackness if we want to understand her identity. Cardi does not do this from a place of insecurity but from a place of self-knowledge and accountability—she performs a trap feminism informed by the overlaps, contradictions, and historical divergences of Diasporic Blackness.

Cardi B's Trap Feminist Performance of US and Diasporic Blackness

When we look at how Cardi navigates the complexity of her identity as a Black woman, we have to keep in mind that she is expected to perform her Blackness in a way that is legible to Black Americans, Latinxs, and Afro-Latinxs, all while being a trap feminist stigmatized for her sex positivity and artistry. In our analysis of Cardi's music, videos, and online posts, we find ample evidence of her proudly performing her Blackness. However, these performances prompt critiques from online commenters and other celebrities that show these tensions.

For instance, we can talk about the messy public beef between Cardi B and Black American rapper Azealia Banks. Banks is no stranger to controversy—to date, she has had public feuds with figures ranging from Pharrell and Erykah Badu to Beyoncé. In an interview with Hip Hop radio show "The Breakfast Club" (2018), host Charlamagne tha God asks Azealia Banks whether she had called Cardi B an "illiterate rat" in another interview. After hesitating and calling Charlamagne an instigator, Banks said,

> I feel like two years ago, the conversation surrounding Black women's culture was really reaching an all-time high . . . Beyoncé came out with Lemonade.[8] There was just this really really intelligent conversation going on nationally, and then, everything just kind of changed and then it was like, Cardi B, you know what I mean?
>
> *(Breakfast Club 2018)*

Later in the interview, Azealia said that Cardi B was a "caricature of a black woman that black women themselves would never be able to get away with," explicitly framing Cardi as a non-Black person who was pretending to be Black by adopting a stereotypical persona. Going back to the original question of Cardi being "illiterate," Banks also claimed that "If my spelling and grammar were that bad, I would be canceled."

In the 24 hours following the Breakfast Club interview, Cardi B and Azealia Banks called each other out in a flurry of social media exchanges. Responding to Banks, Cardi began by addressing the claim that she was "illiterate," tweeting, "I speak how i speak .My mom speak broken English my dad speak Spanish and i use a lot of hood slang .thats that!" (Twitter; @iamcardib; 05/11/2018). After some back and forth, Cardi responded at length to Banks with an Instagram post that included the following:

> The difference between me and you, I've never pretended to be or represent someone I'm not! I've made it where I am for being myself and staying true to that. . . . I know who I am! A daughter to a Hispanic father and a carribean mother and I'm proud of that! . . . I've been this way, always! . . . How smart are you if you don't know that the meaning of illiterate means to not know how to read or write. I can do both, and speak 2 languages fluently. Just because I mix a few words up forget to use commas or misspell a few words doesn't make me stupid. And because I laugh a little harder or talk a little louder doesn't make me a caricature!
>
> *(Instagram; @iamcardib; 05/11/2018)*

Here, Cardi B is keepin' it real, which is a central mark of authenticity in Hip Hop culture (Forman 2020). Cardi argues that her authenticity lies in her realness ("I speak how I speak" and "I've been this way, always!"). Cardi also denies the claim that she is a caricature by saying that this is her genuine personality—she just "laughs a little louder" and "talks a little louder." Using a trap feminist standpoint, we can read this as Cardi pushing back against the confines of respectability that constrict Black women's behavior to meet "acceptable" and usually white [American], middle-class norms (see Chapter 2 for more on the impact of the white gaze on Black people's behavior).

In her response to Azealia, Cardi also notes that she is "not stupid" due to her grammatical mistakes, but rather that she mixes up words given her fluency in Spanish and English. Research shows that bilingual Latinxs are often stereotyped by monolingual English-speakers as being deficient in both their English and Spanish use (Cummins 2013; Flores and Rosa 2015). In her interview with Zendaya, discussed earlier, Cardi B pointed out how being a bilingual rapper has affected her career, stating, "You know I have Caribbean parents, so my vocabulary is a little bit different. So, I always ask people, 'Hey do this make sense? Can you say this word? Is this even a word?' [Laughs]" (Zendaya 2018). Cardi's bilingualism, therefore, presents a slight barrier to producing Hip Hop in the United States, where she has to fit the linguistic parameters of US English to succeed. In Chapter 3, we noted the inclusion of Spanish lyrics throughout *Invasion of Privacy*. These bilingual moments, while genuinely representing Cardi's ethnic background, reduce the perceived authenticity of Cardi's Blackness in a US Hip Hop culture that is commonly associated with Standard and Black Vernacular English. Cardi B's experiences reflect how Afro-Latinxs work to legitimize their Blackness in Spanish-speaking and English-speaking contexts, even as those spaces both erase and overdetermine their status as Black.

Another common critique of Cardi's performance of Blackness surrounds a specific use of language in the United States—her use of nigga in her lyrics and interactions. Online commentators have pointed to this as an issue, especially given their view of Cardi as not Black. For example, one Twitter exchange included the following comment and quote-tweeted response:

I'm really trying to figure out why the culture lets Cardi B fly with saying "N*gga" lol.

Looks like you gotta go far back to see any black in the bloodline. Look like Spanish settlers blood in that DNA.
(Twitter user; 12/02/2017)

She Dominican and Trini which both have African roots. So [questioning face emoji].
(Twitter user; 12/02/2017)

The question of whether Cardi should be allowed to say nigga asks us to consider how the word has been used in Black spaces and in Hip Hop. In one of her earlier interviews, a white male interviewer from VladTV asked Cardi about her frequent use of nigga and brought up the backlash against (non-Black) Latina artist Jennifer Lopez after she used the word in her song "I'm Real." When asked to talk about her use of the word, Cardi struggled to articulate her thoughts, saying,

It seems like it's something that is like so normal, which is bad, but like, it is what it is. And if it comes to the fact that [Jennifer Lopez is] Latina, you know, I'm, my, my, parents, my father's side, we're Spanish, we're Hispanic and everything. But it's like, where do them Hispanic people came from? Where them Latina people came from? They mixed people! You know, we, we mixed with African, European, uh, what is it? Uh, Mulatic [sic] and everything. And it's just like, what am I considered? At the end of the day, like, Latinos and Hispanics, they are considered a minority. Like, you think white folks see Hispanic and Black people like, "oh yeah, they're Hispanic, they're Black?" No, we are all considered the same to them so it's like—you know what I'm saying?

(VladTV 2017)

This portion of the interview is cringe-worthy—and, in fact, Cardi visibly cringes while the interviewer is posing the question. When she says, "It seems like it's something that is like so normal," we might interpret this as a reference to the common use of nigga in the neighborhoods where Cardi was raised. On the other hand, her discussion of Latinxs as "mixed people" rests on the Latin American racial ideology of mestizaje. So Cardi might see her own use of the word as legitimized by her experiences growing up poor in the Bronx, as well her mixed-race ancestry.

We should note that this was one of Cardi's earlier interviews, though. In 2021, she referred to her lack of knowledge on this topic by responding to one of her online critics with a clip from the VladTV interview mentioned earlier. Along with the video clip, Cardi said,

I'm also leaving this here because in the same interview I also said how Latinos are mix with African and like [I] previously stated I had to educate myself between the difference of race, nationality & ethnicity because our school system failed us.

(Twitter, @iamcardib; 03/29/2021)

We include this because it shows Cardi taking accountability and acknowledging her own growth in learning about race and ethnicity. As knowledge producers, trap feminists must be capable of getting it wrong and later self-correcting.

So, should Cardi B be allowed to say nigga? Some might argue that Cardi shouldn't use the word because it's not part of her cultural history in the same way that it's part of Black Americans' cultural history. Here, we might return to Diasporic Blackness, and its focus on the cultural, social, and political histories of Blackness, to inform our views on who can say the word. Given that nigga is a rewriting and reclaiming of a term used during a period of racial terror in the United States, some might argue Cardi B doesn't have the right to use the word. On the other hand, we have to consider how and where a person grew up to understand their use of the word. Despite being the child of immigrants, Cardi is the descendant of enslaved Africans, and she has been racialized as Black in a US culture where saying nigga is normalized among people racialized as Black. Therefore, her use of the term might be understood as a product of the historical processes of Diasporic Blackness, which includes the impact of changing demographics and cultural influences on the development of Black identity. We do argue, though, that Cardi's use of nigga should be paired with a commitment to a politics of Black liberation (and we show how she does this in Chapter 6). Blackness is not just a racial or cultural category; it is also inherently political.

Finally, we should remember that in the United States, Hip Hop is viewed as a site of Black authenticity; if saying nigga is common in Hip Hop, then using the word adds to an artist's perceived authenticity as Black *and* as a Hip Hop artist. Therefore, the use of nigga is both common and incentivized in mainstream Hip Hop, where being authentically Black contributes to artists' success. We're not arguing that Cardi B is using the word strategically, since she's already noted that she grew up using the term. We're simply pointing out that Cardi's success in mainstream Hip Hop hinges in part on her authenticity—to be genuine and real, Cardi uses terms that she grew up with, based on how she was racialized while refusing to cave in to others' exclusion of her from US Blackness.

Conclusion

In this chapter, we theorized that people online and elsewhere police Cardi B's Blackness due to the prevalence and privileging of US-centered notions of race, as well as the persistence of essentialist views of race that shape what we consider to be "authentic Blackness." In a US context, Black Americans (in spaces like Black Twitter) often have the social influence to define Blackness and its attributes. In contrast, post-emancipation Black immigrants and their descendants have to navigate the murky cultural waters of wanting to signal their Blackness to others while being policed for their performance of Blackness when it doesn't conform to US Black norms.

Is gatekeeping Blackness in the United States about protecting Black people and Black culture? Or is it part of a struggle to claim whatever power we have to define ourselves given the violent and extractive nature of racism? Johnson argues that concerns over Black authenticity are, in fact, central to Black culture, stating that "the mutual constructing/deconstructing, avowing/disavowing, and expanding/delimiting dynamic that occurs in the production of blackness is the very thing that constitutes 'black' culture" (2003:2). Therefore, far from driving a wedge in Black culture, the debates surrounding Cardi B's race are "the very thing that constitutes 'black' culture." We agree with this statement and urge you, the reader, to question your parameters for Blackness; how do you define and assess Blackness? And how do history, politics, and context inform those parameters? The unstable nature of Blackness doesn't mean that any artist or person should be allowed to adopt and profit from Black culture, but it does show us how Blackness is inherently a political category that many are invested in preserving and protecting—and often for good reasons.

Whether the policing of Cardi B's Blackness is about protecting Black people or not, we should consider how context plays a role in people's assessments of racial identity. Diasporic Blackness asks us to expand our understanding of race by acknowledging the social, cultural, and political histories that have shaped the development of Blackness across the Americas. Cardi B challenges her fans and critics to consider their own frameworks of race when they police her Blackness—insisting that her Blackness should be assumed given the one-drop rule commonly used in the United States. On the other hand, she pushes critics to understand the transnational nature of Blackness that has shaped her views and ideas of race as a Black, mixed-race, Caribbean, Afro-Latina, trap feminist rapper.

Cardi B's lived experiences with race show us that outsiders question the authenticity of her Blackness because she performs her Blackness in a diasporic and transnational way that does not completely conform to US racial ideologies. This is just one of the ways Cardi has been policed, though—she has been policed for many of her behaviors on- and off-stage as well. In the next chapter, we'll learn about Cardi's experiences with motherhood and how her behaviors have been policed in that realm of life—we contextualize this with a history of how Black women have been affected by controlled reproduction during and after slavery and show how the policing of Cardi's motherhood, like the policing of her Blackness, can be traced to broader histories of racism.

Notes

1 As Cardi B rose in popularity, fans and critics took to social media to discuss her background, including her legal name. One Twitter user joked, "I just learned today that Cardi B's real name is belcalis almanzar. I said that shit out loud and my furniture started floating" (Twitter user; 01/09/2023). That tweet garnered over 300,000 likes, 100,000 retweets, and thousands of comments, including, "lmfao Cardi B's real name really do sound like a spell from Harry Potter tho." These tweets were not surprising—to many people outside of the Spanish-speaking Caribbean, Belcalis Almánzar is an ill-fitting or "weird" name for a rap icon. We argue that Cardi B's real name also marks her as a supposed outsider to US Blackness.

2 Afro-Latinos are individuals with African ancestry who are from Latin America. The term was created by activists to specifically highlight the importance

of African culture and heritage in Latin America, where it has been (and still is) often erased from current understandings of the region.

3 Sarah Florini explains signifyin' on social media as,

> an interactional framework that allows Black Twitter users to align themselves with Black oral traditions, to index Black cultural practices, to enact Black subjectivities, and to communicate shared knowledge and experiences. Signifyin' generally involves elements of humor and displays of wit, and at times may seem frivolous to the uninitiated. But, even at its most lighthearted, signifyin' is a powerful resource for signaling racial identity, allowing Black Twitter users to perform their racial identities 140 characters at a time.

(2014:224)

4 For a photo of Cardi B and her mother, Clara, visit (https://cardib.fandom.com/wiki/Clara_Alm%C3%A1nzar).

5 Photo source: Instagram; @iamcardib; 03/14/2020. While this post has since been deleted, the same photo can be accessed here (www.instagram.com/p/CWO_gYMs-Lx/?utm_source=ig_web_copy_link&igsh=MzRlODBiNWFlZA==).

6 Photo source: Instagram; @iamcardib; 12/13/2021. While this post has since been deleted, a video from the same day can be accessed here (www.instagram.com/p/CWO_gYMs-Lx/?utm_source=ig_web_copy_link&igsh=MzRlODBiNWFlZA==).

7 It's not clear here whether Cardi views "women of color" as synonymous with "Black women" or if she uses it to be inclusive of mixed-race women. We contend that the term "women of color" is not synonymous with "Black women" and that the conflation of these terms obscures the anti-Blackness directed at Black women from non-Black women of color (e.g., non-Black Latinas and Asian women).

8 Despite her positive comments about Beyoncé here, Banks said the following after the release of Beyoncé's album *Lemonade*, "She's not an artist, she's a poacher," and, "She takes food out of darker skinned women's mouths & pretends to be inspired" (Peters 2016).

5

CARDI PUT THE WAP ON OFFSET

Trap Feminist Motherhood

Cardi B set the internet ablaze when she officially unveiled her first pregnancy on the April 7, 2018, episode of Saturday Night Live after dealing with months of public speculation about the cause of her weight gain and the status of her relationship with Offset.[1] For her second performance as the skit comedy show's musical guest, she appeared on stage in silhouette with a bright light shining behind her. As she began to perform "Be Careful," a single spotlight focused on her upper body, revealing her only from head to chest until she finished the first verse and chorus of her song. Then the spotlight expanded to reveal Cardi's baby bump underneath the ruched fabric of her white dress which had been designed especially for this occasion by Project Runway Champion Christian Siriano. Spontaneous cheers erupted from the live SNL audience when they realized Cardi was pregnant. Even though Cardi B and Offset had been public about their relationship for months, fans and haters posted jokes, opinions, and memes after Cardi revealed her pregnancy—not only about Cardi's pregnancy but also about her marital status and even the identity of her baby's father.[2]

A flurry of 280-character think pieces about Cardi's choices were posted on Twitter. Some social media commenters even incorporated Cardi's lyrics into their tweets. For example,

> cardi b is only pregnant to prove that she does in fact *put the pussy on offset.*
>
> *(Twitter; @eivvil; 4/9/2018)*

DOI: 10.4324/9781003184980-6

Other commenters defended Cardi's choices. For example,

> Why are people bashing Cardi B for getting pregnant? Half of yall got pregnant 3 weeks after meeting your baby daddy. Cardi is financially stable and it's her body who tf cares.
>
> *(Twitter; @ssoto; 4/9/2018)*

Just as the social media world cooled into ambivalence about her pregnancy reveal on SNL, Cardi reignited the flames with her April 15, 2018, Coachella performance.[3] Emerging on the stage again in white, she brought her baby bump to the desert outfitted in an aesthetic that paid homage to the late Lisa "Left Eye" Lopes of the 1990s supergroup TLC.

For roughly 35 minutes on one of the most famous stages in the world,[4] Cardi B performed songs from *Invasion of Privacy* and mixtapes. She included platinum artists Chance the Rapper, 21 Savage, and other well-known artists as her guest performers. Her pregnancy did not seem to be a constraint during her Coachella performance even though Cardi was close to her third trimester, a time many women experience back pain, swelling, shortness of breath, and fatigue. Instead, Cardi incorporated her pregnancy to supercharge her lyrics. For example, she changed her original lyrics on "No Limit" with G-Eazy from "fuck him then I get some money" to "fuck him then I got a baby." Once again, internet users flooded the comments section on blogs, YouTube, and social media sites with their opinions about Cardi's performance; online conversations mainly zeroed in on the fact that Cardi decided to twerk on stage while visibly pregnant with her daughter Kulture.

Many social media commenters expressed seemingly strong opinions about the inappropriateness of twerking while pregnant. For example,

> I get that Cardi B is trying to prove that you can be pregnant and still have a career. But I DONT wanna see a pregnant woman twerking, it's unattractive and doing too much.
>
> *(Twitter; @LaTera; 4/16/2018)*

The sentiment expressed in this tweet reflects a patriarchal perspective that shapes public opinion about pregnant women in our culture. In the patriarchal culture of the United States, pregnancy is considered to be the antithesis of sexuality; pregnant women are expected to be the epitome of reserved femininity. Under the influence of these patriarchal views, the public sees a sex-positive act like twerking during pregnancy as uncouth and unsavory (Welter 1966). The sentiment expressed in the previous tweet by @

Latera reflects the patriarchal perspective that shapes public opinion about pregnant women. In this case, twerking was seen as "doing too much" as in this behavior is too sexual for the public. In this chapter, we argue that responses to Cardi B's pregnancy ranged from opinions grounded in traditional white heterosexual family norms to a trap feminist stance of self-definition and self-actualization for women.

The analysis in this chapter is focused on Cardi B's behavior and the public reaction to her behavior during and after two focal events during 2018: Cardi's SNL pregnancy reveal and her subsequent performance at Coachella. We argue that during this time, many of the opinions expressed on Twitter seemed to be based on the standards supported by traditional white heteronormative ideals, while other opinions skewed in the direction of trap feminism by supporting Cardi's (and all women's) agency in the areas of family formation, reproductive choices, and motherhood. We lay the foundation for our theorizing by illuminating the socio-historical understandings of the Black family, Black motherhood, and Black women's sexuality. Trap feminism then helps us to expand our lens beyond the patriarchal norms that influenced and continue to influence so many opinions about Cardi B's performances and the behaviors of all Black women. We analyze the feminism and complexities of Cardi's sex-positive performances and her initial presentation of nonnormative (unmarried) reproductive choices.[5] Next, we bring to light three major themes of debate that emerged from our analysis of social media commentary[6] in the days directly after Cardi's performances:

(1) choosing to have a child with Offset
(2) choosing to have a baby at all
(3) choosing to remain sexual

We conclude this chapter by noting the alignment between Cardi's nonconformist choices and the trap feminist perspective of motherhood and erotica and we use the standpoint of trap feminism to further clarify the embedded sexism and racism so prevalent in the dominant public opinions about Black women's (and Black men's in the case of Offset) familial and reproductive choices.

By focusing our scholarship through the lens of trap feminism, we emphasize the resourceful use of agency as evidenced by both Cardi B's sex-positive and more conservative choices. We also demonstrate the influence of socialization on public opinions that express resistance or adherence to patriarchal social norms. Most importantly, a trap feminist lens shows us how to support and respect the motherhood and lifestyle choices made by marginalized Black women.

When It's White, It's Right—Mothering in the United States

From children's stories to social policies and laws, expectations about sexuality, marriage, and reproduction are woven into our society. From a young age, girls are told how their life course "should" be lived and that there is a right way to mother—usually, a heteronormative script of love, then marriage, and, finally, children. Essentially, the "correct" way to build a family is outlined in children's songs and stories, and then this patriarchal script is used as a norm or a judgmental standard; if a family does not adhere to the societally approved "standards" for family formation, they are stigmatized. However, most families across races do not follow this structure in their family formations, especially considering the increase in cohabitation, births outside of marriage, divorces, and combined families since the 1970s (Risman and Rutter 2015).

US society is built around specific ideas of white, patriarchal, heterosexual, middle-class nuclear family formation as the standard (Cherlin 2004). The nuclear family includes a working husband as the breadwinner, a nonworking wife as the caregiver, and their biological offspring. The primary caregiver of the biological offspring is the mother. In this framework for the family, standards of motherhood are institutionalized. When a person becomes a mother, the role of mother becomes the primary status behind which all of her other roles in society (like wife, worker, friend, and daughter) must align and take second place. Mothers of color are then judged based on their alignment with the rules set for white middle-class women, who are expected to fulfill the role of homemaker by sacrificing their careers, acting as the primary caregiver, and by devoting their creativity and labor to projects in the home. Furthermore, depictions of middle-class and elite white women's motherhood are usually positive, while depictions of poor Black women's motherhood tend to be negative. Poor Black mothers are stigmatized as lazy if they choose public assistance as a means to stay home with their children and simultaneously demonized for not providing 24-hour supervision if they choose to work outside the home (Collins 2022). Because of their race and socioeconomic status, many Black mothers are constrained from meeting the demands of white middle-class motherhood norms. Yet these dominant white-centric standards still shape how people view and judge Black mothers across all classes.

Our historically grounded analysis of Black motherhood is rooted in the lived experiences of Black women in the United States. We specifically highlight the ways that Black women have always been expected to use their emotional and physical labor to serve the white supremacist, patriarchal, and capitalist structure of this country. This social structure was created to limit Black women to the roles of laborers and sexual reproductive objects, with other traditional ideals of womanhood and motherhood being reserved for white women.[7] Black women were and are still fetishized, commodified, objectified, and used as tools of social control—all of which are factors of dehumanization. In the following, we trace the historical constraints that shaped Black motherhood in the United States throughout enslavement, the Jim Crow era, and the age of welfare reform in the 1980s. This socio-historical overview demonstrates how the white capitalist patriarchal structure of the United States sought to socially control Black womanhood and Black motherhood.

"Ain't I a Woman?"—Mothering During Enslavement

For generations, enslaved mothers were not seen as women or human for that matter. Enslaved Black people were regarded as property and required by law to work their entire lives as guaranteed "free" labor. The laws and practices created and instituted during enslavement were centered on social control and included the subordination, abuse, rape, and murder of African people and their offspring. In Chapter 4, we reviewed the facts about forced reproduction; the US economy relied on the ability of Black women to bear children, but under the laws of the state, Black women were considered property, not human (Davis 1972). To institutionalize the domestic enslavement industry and the role of enslaved Black women, US lawmakers enacted national laws that only applied to enslaved people. For example, womb laws proclaimed that the legal status of Black mothers—whether they were freed or enslaved—determined the legal status of their newborns even in cases of rape by white men (Davis 2011). To the contrary, the legal status of children born to white mothers was determined by the legal status of the white father.

Profit-seeking during the domestic slave trade created a hierarchy of economic value which was assigned to enslaved Black women. If an enslaved woman was deemed capable of giving birth to many children, she could be sold and insured[8] for higher prices than an enslaved women who could give birth to fewer or no children. In addition, Black women who did not birth enough children or who could not have children endured the very real fear of being sold and separated from their existing families (Roberts 1997). Because the value of an enslaved Black woman depended on her capacity to reproduce "free labor," enslavers inflicted severe punishments on enslaved women who would not or could not reproduce at the rate deemed acceptable by the enslaver. This differential valuation and treatment speak to the damage done by the commodification of reproduction as well as the pressure placed on Black enslaved women to have children during this period.

In the profit-oriented calculations of enslavers, Black women's main role during enslavement was to reproduce more "slaves," not to mother them (Roberts 1997). Because enslavers forced Black mothers to work both during their pregnancies and immediately after giving birth, they had little time to raise and nurture their babies. Ironically, enslaved Black mothers were considered human enough to mother, breastfeed, and be the primary caretakers for their white captors' white babies and white children (McKittrick 2014). To ensure that enslaved mothers would not run away or rebel, enslavers threatened to sell enslaved children to different plantations (McKittrick 2014). This cruel tactic is just one of many tools of social control that disrupted the ability of Black women to mother and protect their children.

Black women's legal status as property not only rejected their womanhood but also denied the legitimacy of their motherhood in the eyes of the state (Roberts 1997). Because they had no parental rights or any human rights under the laws of the land, enslaved mothers could not protect their children from the discriminatory laws of the state. These laws and practices placed Black mothers in a precarious situation where their children were perpetually in danger. Still, there are some examples of Black mothers who attempted to petition the courts to win freedom for their enslaved children. In fact, Sojourner Truth succeeded in her attempts to seek freedom for her son in the courts (Accomando 2003) prior to performing her well-noted speech "Ain't I a Woman." Overall, Black women were relegated by law to permanent subordinate status, which rendered them powerless as people and as mothers. Enslaved Black mothers were not only denied power over their reproduction and motherhood, but they were also denied personhood since they were not considered human under the law.

Still Not Free—Mothering After Emancipation and Reconstruction

After the Civil War and the Emancipation of enslaved people in 1865, Black people hoped to be viewed as humans who had access to the basic rights of life, liberty, and the pursuit of happiness. Recently freed Black people expected to be free—to have civil rights and the freedom to make their own choices about having and maintaining a family without the interference of the white power structure. During the Reconstruction era after the Civil War, northern and southern states attempted to institute policies that benefited recently freed Black people. Although some of these efforts were successful, the impact of most of these policies was short-lived. In response to Black people's progress during Reconstruction,[9] white leaders in the south developed and instituted new methods of social control to put the recently emancipated population "back in their place." To maintain white supremacy, many states instituted Black Codes followed by Jim Crow,[10] both of which contained new rules, laws, policies, and social norms for Black people to obey. At the same time, the rise in policing and the use of prison systems mimicked the conditions experienced during enslavement and became new methods of controlling and policing Black people and their labor.

For Black women, these new laws, systems, and practices meant that their mothering would also be under the watch of the white gaze—the concept discussed at length in Chapter 2. The increased criminalization of Black life prevented Black mothers from self-determining the practice of mothering outside of the confines of slavery (Haley 2016). From the mid-1800s to the early 1900s, Black women were arrested, charged, and incarcerated for minor offenses such as public drunkenness, profanity, public quarreling, dumping dirty water in the streets, keeping an unkempt home, and vagrancy. These "crimes" helped create a free labor system that mimicked slavery through the use of prison labor and convict leasing.

Black women were arrested and jailed for these crimes at a much higher rate than white women, and these disparate rates of incarceration continue to persist today (Haley 2016; Mitchell and Davis 2019). Research conducted by *The Sentencing Project*[11] shows us that even today, Black women are overrepresented in the number of incarcerated women, compared to white and Latino women. This disproportionate incarceration has shaped and continues to shape Black mothering in different ways including the development of *othermothers*—family members, most often Black women, who care for the children while the mother is incarcerated. The community value of other mothering is further discussed in Chapter 6. In addition, the incarceration of Black mothers severely strained their mother–child relationships. Black women's perceived criminality was also used as a justification for the state to remove children from the homes of Black mothers who were convicted of the minor crimes listed earlier. Black mothers who were arrested were seen as a detriment to their children. The state justified removing Black children from their homes and placing them in workhouses and forced apprenticeships by asserting that Black women were bad mothers whose life and sexuality were deviant and, therefore, out of control (Haley 2016).

In the post-Reconstruction and Jim Crow eras, Black mothers with large families were seen as unruly and irresponsible and were often punished both socially and legally. In fact, Black mothers who birthed more than two children were viewed as bad mothers (Haley 2016). In the criminal court cases against Black women, judges ruled that poor Black mothers were unfit to raise their children and decided that these children would be better off with the state or in workhouses or orphanages, where they would receive "proper" mothering—meaning mothering from white-centric standards. These beliefs about Black motherhood derived from racial and gender stereotypes that frame Black womanhood as uncouth and criminal. Also, white people profited from the incarceration of Black mothers by forcing Black children and mothers to perform unpaid labor via chain gangs, forced apprenticeships, and in workhouses. At the same time, the stereotypes of Black mothers perpetuated white fear that Black children would grow up to be criminals and a threat to whites. Once again, society and the law denied the womanhood and personhood of Black mothers in the United States.

The practice of rehoming Black children or children of color and placing them with the state continues today. The US Congress determined that the removal of Black children from their homes was a noble effort to prevent the intergenerational spread of deviant and criminal behavior (Haley 2016). However, in practice, Black mothers and their children were being used as a free labor force to compensate for capitalists' loss of profits following the abolition of slavery. This exclusion of Black women from legitimized motherhood often manifested through increased criminalization of Black mothers and children. The afterlives of slavery constrained Black mothers from self-determining the practice of mothering outside the confines of social control (Haley 2016).

Baby Need a New Pair of Shoes—Mothering While Poor and Unmarried

Negative narratives about Black motherhood persisted past the Jim Crow era and through the Reagan era. During this time, stereotypes such as the matriarch and the welfare queen became nationally known images for Black mothers (Collins 2022). The public image of poor Black single mothers toward the end of the 20th century centered on negative narratives about Black mothers, ignoring the fact that Poor Black single mothers must juggle many challenges as breadwinner, loving caregiver, and sole parent invested in their children's futures. Manufactured by politicians to gain the support of white voters while also further criminalizing and stigmatizing Black families, these stereotypes pointed to poor Black mothers who received economic benefits from the state as the root of the problems within the Black community.

Leaning on the "analysis" presented by the infamous Moynihan Report (Moynihan 1965), politicians blamed poor Black single mothers for the state of the Black community in inner cities. By incorporating discriminatory terms and biased ideas into their public discourse, politicians created a false narrative about Black women. By labeling Black mothers as overbearing, hyper-independent "matriarchs," politicians and others were able to place blame for Black family dysfunctions solely on inner-city Black mothers and their parenting methods. If a Black father abandoned his family, it was because of the matriarch at home. Then, if a Black mother worked to provide financial support, she was labeled as domineering and emasculating. Black women as the breadwinners for their families do not fit the ideal type of nuclear families where the men are supposed to be the breadwinners.

The patriarchal perspective that men should be the head of the household places women in a subordinate position under men. The mismatch caused by a woman assuming the head of the household is then labeled as the cause of chaos erupting across all Black families. Moynihan's report inferred that Black women were replacing Black men's role in the family and that this replacement had led to social disorganization in Black communities. Further, Moynihan concluded that the Black community would have less violence and poverty if Black families followed the order of the nuclear family. However, one very important factor to note is that Moynihan did mention the influence of policies as a factor in the social position of Black families, but the politicians who utilized the findings of the Moynihan Report almost completely ignored the institutional actors of oppression. In other words, the role of oppression, social control, enslavement, segregation laws, and the incarceration of Black women and mothers was disregarded by law and policymakers when assessing and conveying the status of Black families.

Different stereotypes about Black mothers continued to be perpetuated throughout the media and policies in the United States during this time. For example, the welfare queen stereotype of the Black mother emerged from the stereotype of the matriarch. The welfare queen is described as a single Black mother who is lazy, promiscuous, and immoral (Collins 2022). This narrative paints low-income Black mothers who live in neighborhoods of concentrated disadvantage (the trap) as women who would rather live on small government stipends than go to work (Collins 2022), the welfare queen stereotype also promotes the belief that poor Black women have more children to increase their income from government assistance programs. Again, single Black mothers are blamed—not only for causing their own poverty and the poverty of future generations but also for higher crime rates, juvenile delinquency rates, and other problems faced by the entire Black community (Moynihan 1965).

Welfare was created so that mothers could stay at home with their small children. However, when Black women started to receive welfare in the 1960s due to northern migration and looser welfare rules, the characterization of poor Black unmarried mothers was used by many politicians to justify welfare "reform" policies, like benefit limits, work requirements, and even placing a cap on the number of children per family that are eligible to receive state benefits (Bobo and Charles 2009; Gilens 1999). Republican presidents Richard Nixon and Ronald Reagan successfully used "welfare queen" campaign messaging to garner votes (Cammett 2014; TWS 1976) by using dog-whistle tactics to blame Black people for their poverty rather than institutions. In addition, President Bill Clinton, a Democrat, created the largest welfare reform policy under the auspices of increasing poor people's self-sufficiency. With support from both sides of the aisle, the Personal Responsibility and Work Opportunities Act of 1996 reified racist welfare policy stances that had been discussed for decades. Underlying this harmful policy was a goal to target people who "used the system" by having babies in order to receive a check from the government. Despite being untrue, Black women, specifically mothers, were once again blamed rather than supported. During and prior to this period, it was apparent that the negative perception of Black mothers was one topic on which Republicans and Democrats agreed. Policies created by both political parties demonstrated that their shared belief that the social status of Black families was to be blamed on the mother.

In sum, historically and contemporarily, these policy initiatives are rooted in racism by way of negative racial stereotypes. The idea that Black families are responsible for their own poverty ignores institutional and structural factors such as enslavement, sharecropping, Jim Crow laws, Black Codes, chain gangs, and mass incarceration. In addition, discriminatory factors such as hiring practices, racist housing policies (redlining), racist bank policies (blackballing), and racist educational policies are also left out of the conversation about Black poverty. All of these laws and policies have disproportionately harmed generations of Black families, who remain stuck at the bottom of the social hierarchy where they lack wealth, social mobility, and opportunities. Meanwhile, the entire system results in the unjust enrichment of whites which perpetuates the unjust impoverishment of Black families (Feagin 2006). Therefore, the overwhelmingly negative discourse about Black motherhood is nothing more than a reflection of the white patriarchal supremacy that frames the narratives surrounding Black families, especially those headed by single mothers and/or living in poor neighborhoods.

Trap Feminist Mothering

Throughout this book, we use a trap feminist framework that aims to disrupt expectations of how Black women should behave, speak, and act in public spaces. We challenge the expectation, rooted in respectability politics (Higginbotham 1993:185–230), that Black women should not be seen, heard, nor have any form of agency regarding their actions and how they are politicized. In this chapter, we use a trap feminist perspective to center the hood chicks, ghetto girls, and the ratchet women who live and embody the trap to more deeply understand the family formation choices and motherhood of poor Black women. This trap feminist approach not only challenges normative notions of motherhood but also disrupts negative stereotypes placed on Black mothers (e.g., the matriarch, the welfare queen). Furthermore, a trap feminist standpoint carves out a space in which we can discuss—without the white gaze, male gaze, or respectability politics—the sexuality and partnering choices of Black women and mothers. Trap feminist mothers express and discuss their desires regardless of judgment from people who ascribe to heteronormative patriarchal ideals. Additionally, analysis grounded in a trap feminist perspective helps us to understand the choices made by Cardi B and those of mothers who are living in or adjacent to the trap, whose behavior is deemed deviant and frowned upon by people who subscribe to white patriarchal beliefs about motherhood.

By studying mothering through the lens of trap feminism, we acknowledge that Black mothers are held to a standard that they cannot easily achieve; as a result, they structure their mothering to fit the environment of the trap for the benefit and survival of their children. However, the family formation and mothering choices of poor Black women are most often scrutinized through a narrow white microscope. Therefore, we need the wider lens of trap feminism to see that individual trap mothers are not the problem—the problem is the structural responses to low-income Black single mothers. Instead of addressing the structural roots of poverty, the public stigmatizes the adaptive solutions of Black mothers.

Even though the public already knew Cardi B was a hood chick, many still expected to follow the script of the nursery rhyme—to fall in love, get married, have a baby, and make her primary identity "mother." People stay mad at Cardi B because she refused to shape her life according to their preferred mold. This was exemplified when the public continued to criticize Cardi's family formation choices even after it was revealed that she had, in fact, used the traditionally accepted route to build her family: love, marriage, then baby carriage. (A vivid example of the adage "you can't win for losing.") In the following sections, we further unpack examples of the way that Cardi is stuck in between a rock and a hard place with the public's opinions about her husband, her child, and her career.

The responses to Cardi's pregnancy outlined in this chapter came from Twitter users with both white and Black presenting profile pictures. Most people would expect this scrutiny from groups we consider more conservative like white people and older Black people (aka Boomers).

However, Black Millennials[12]—the same age cohort as Cardi B—also made negative comments that reflected their adherence to white patriarchal views on family. These comments also reflect the ways that Black people police each other; as we learned in Chapters 2 and 4, Black people police each other due to the fear that one person's actions will badly reflect on the entire race (Higginbotham 1993). On the other hand, many Twitter users supported Cardi B during this period by calling out the hypocrisy of her critics and by supporting Cardi's use of agency to form a family in the way she chooses. The tweets analyzed in this chapter draw attention to both the stigmatization and the support of the adaptive practices inherent to trap feminist mothering.

Reactions to Cardi B's Trap Feminist Mothering

Here, we analyze two central moments that help us understand how Cardi B's mothering has been discussed online: The 2018 pregnancy reveal on Saturday Night Live and the Coachella performance. When examining the online discussion after these events, three main themes emerged in the debates about Cardi's choices in (1) the fathering of her child, (2) the timing of her motherhood, and (3) the act of twerking in public while pregnant. Our analysis of these tweets is grounded in historical and contemporary expectations of mothering as well as trap feminism, which we use as a lens to better understand the online discussions about the adaptive practices used by mothers in the trap. We argue that many of the negative comments about Cardi B's pregnancy are rooted in anti-Blackness, while supportive comments are rooted in support and understanding of the utility of trap feminist mothering as it operates within the Black community. For each theme, we present evidence that negative rhetoric about unmarried Black mothers thrives in online spaces while trap feminism also enters the chat to disrupt this anti-Black Discourse.

Choosing to Start a Family with Offset

Cardi B's love life had been on full display during her two seasons on reality show *Love and Hip-Hop New York*, where Cardi was shown dating a man in jail,[13] while flirting with DJ Self,[14] and participating in an explosive love triangle with music producer Swift.[15] Although Cardi met Offset at a music industry event in 2016 and publicly announced their relationship at the 2017 Superbowl in Houston, Texas, bloggers and social media users posted assumptions about another fling that would never last. Since 2017, Cardi B's relationship with Offset has remained in the public eye through all its ups and downs. In this section, we focus our analysis on the SNL pregnancy reveal.

Her choice to have a child with Offset was the most prevalent theme that emerged in the online debates about Cardi B's pregnancy. Many of these tweets focused on the fact that Cardi made a bad decision when she chose Offset as a partner and as a father to her child because Offset had already fathered three children with three other women.

> love cardi B . . . but girl looks stupid with a dude that already has 3 kids with different baby mommas.
>
> *(Twitter, @aangelaaXO; 4/8/2018)*

Users asserted that Offset was a bad choice to father Cardi's children because he had so many children in different households. One Twitter user pointed to what seemed to be the frequency with which Offset changed partners and had children, posting that Cardi B's child was "about to have 37 stepmoms" (Twitter; @memyrin2; 4/9/2018). On the other side of the debate, social media users pushed back in support of Cardi B's choice by asserting that Offset had a good relationship with his other children and that he had more than enough financial resources to support all of his kids, unlike "y'all letting broke ass n****s bust in y'all every week" (Twitter; @ ItsVinnyBro; 4/8/2018). Based on information found in social media posts, Offset seems to be very involved with his children. In addition, the financial success of his rap career means that Offset probably has the means to support all of his children.

The online debates about Cardi's choice to have a child with Offset also centered on Cardi B having a baby with a man after allegations of infidelity. Many online commentators did not agree with Cardi's decision to start a family with Offset because of his alleged affairs. One Twitter user posted:

> So cardi b got cheated on by offset, stayed with him and got pregnant LMAOOOOOOOOOOOOOOOOOOOOO.
>
> *(Twitter; @Salvi1k; 4/9/2018)*

Another comment about Cardi B's choice of a supposedly unfaithful partner read "cardi b pregnant by the man who cheated on her. her biggest hit song is about cutting a man off" (Twitter; @nickdelfenty; 4/9/2018). This is a reference to the hit song we analyzed in Chapter 3, "Bodak Yellow." Cardi B's lyrics in the chorus read: "I'm quick, cut a nigga off, so don't get comfortable." The difference between the sentiment expressed in her lyrics and having a child with a man who was unfaithful to her was heavily scrutinized by the public. Another user tweeted, "Whos idea was it for cardi b to announce she's pregnant performing a song about getting cheated on by the dad lol" (Twitter; @rip_rlb; 4/10/2018) while another Twitter user wrote, "Imagine being Cardi B, got cheated on and got pregnant all in the same year smh tragic" (Twitter; @CoralGivenchy; 4/9/2018).

Internet commentators propagated a narrative of disappointment in Cardi B's choice of a father for her child, and these narratives were rooted in their belief that Offset lacked moral character. However, others defended Cardi B's choice of Offset as a partner and a father. These commentators discussed the double standards when it comes to the expectations of celebrities compared to their own lives. One online user tweeted: "I can't judge Cardi B for getting pregnant by Offset after he cheated on her. If my mom didn't stay with my dad after he cheated, I wouldn't be here" (Twitter; @Chellyxboo; 4/10/2018). Other users mentioned that some of the women who were ridiculing Cardi's choices were voluntarily having children with married men. These internet users were not stigmatizing Cardi B for choosing Offset. They allowed space for alternative family styles and self-defining what a suitable mate looks like. This trap feminist way of thinking pushes back against society's ideology of the traditional nuclear family.

The primary narrative to emerge in our analysis of the social media responses was that Cardi, as the child bearer, should have known better, chosen more wisely, and discontinued her relationship with Offset because of his behaviors and his existing children. The brunt of the negativity was aimed at Cardi B, a Black woman; there was almost no outrage aimed at Offset for getting Cardi B pregnant in spite of Offset's multi-partner fertility and rumored infidelity. There was also clear lack of online comments admonishing Offset for having more children out of wedlock. None of the SNL-related Twitter posts aimed at Offset in our analysis spoke against him for his infidelity. This double standard is the product of the patriarchy which encourages male domination and socializes women to be pure and resistant to the advances of unsuitable men while explaining away men's behavior with "boys will be boys" (Collins 2004). It is acceptable (if not expected) for a man to have sex before marriage and to have multiple families because it speaks to his prowess as a man as well as his legacy,[16] but a woman who has sex before marriage and/or has multiple children with different fathers is stigmatized as sexually deviant. Men like Offset are not judged in this manner since heterosexual men's masculinity is often based on their number of sexual partners, the more the better, especially in their young adulthood (Collins 2004; hooks 2004).

Offset did receive some criticism from the public—not for his family formation choices or his rumored infidelities—but for starting a family with Cardi B, a former stripper. Although Offset's actions directly align with the allegations that Black men are hypersexual beings who indiscriminately procreate without establishing a solid foundation for support (Collins 2004; hooks 2004), internet users were outraged that Offset was "trying to make a hoe into a housewife," an adage that discourages Black men from partnering with sexually liberated women like Cardi B.

The themes in this section reveal how Twitter users debated Cardi B's choice of a partner. Examining these debates also showed us how the public assesses the partnering choices of Black women as well as their beliefs about who is a suitable partner. When viewed through the lens of the dominant ideology surrounding Black families in general, and Black mothers specifically, we can see that the public's disdain for the pairing of Cardi B and Offset is steeped in anti-Blackness as well as classism (Muhammad 2011). Today, Black mothers from disadvantaged neighborhoods are still stereotyped as unintelligent and lazy people who have children with irresponsible men who do not take care of the families they help create (Moynihan 1965). Through our analysis, we discovered that many people labeled Cardi B as an unintelligent woman because they judged her under a patriarchal lens—therefore, they were sure she was having a child with a man who was likely to abandon her and her child. These expectations show that many people's beliefs align with the idea that women from the trap knowingly choose bad fathers for their children and therefore should be stigmatized.

However, the other side of the debate brings forth the variation in experiences of those who chose a conventional path that failed as well as those who chose a less acceptable path with success. Using a trap feminist lens, we see how Cardi B's choice of Offset shows how Black women are open to less than perfect partners. There is room for love, acceptance, forgiveness, and redemption in the trap as reflected in the reintegration of those who are formerly incarcerated or recovering from drug addiction, which is also stigmatized in the mainstream. The trap feminist approach to partner selection also reflects how Black women in communities devastated by mass incarceration expand their partner pool to include Black men with multiple families as well as known philanderers because Black marriageable men are considered scarce in the trap (Lichter, LeClere, and McLaughlin 1991).

The fact that Black trap love does not mimic the white middle-class picket-fenced fantasy makes Black love political. Black families, even blended ones, are a form of resistance to the historical systematic dismantling of Black humanity (hooks 1981). Even as millionaires, Cardi and Offset were scrutinized by the public based on their Hip Hop aesthetic, which emerged from poor Black communities; their new economic-class background was not enough to save them from the scrutiny of the public. However, those who have a trap feminist way of thinking embrace Black trap love and the families that emerge from it because *love stories have always happened* in spite of the challenges endured by people who live in disadvantaged neighborhoods or the trap—a largely loveless environment.[17]

Choosing Kulture

Cardi B revealed her pregnancy to the world on Saturday Night Live after denying it for months. In a now-deleted Instagram post, Cardi responded to a user's post asking if she was pregnant saying "No bitch I'm just getting fat. Let me fat in peace" (Arnold 2018). Her initial response to questions about her pregnancy can be situated among all the other aspects of her life at that current moment. Cardi B was surfing the wave that "Bodak Yellow" created in the Hip Hop world. She was also recording *Invasion of Privacy* and preparing for its debut in April 2018. Lastly, Cardi B's performance calendar was full to promote her upcoming project. She may have been reluctant to announce another life-changing event that seems counterintuitive to her professional goals. Eventually, Cardi decided to reveal her pregnancy to the public on SNL and after she finished her performance and came off stage, she expressed feelings of freedom. It was probably a relief that the public's speculations were confirmed, and any pressure that may have been associated with hiding her pregnancy was alleviated.[18] In this section, we focus on the initial responses to her pregnancy with her first child, Kulture.[19]

Another major theme that emerged across the internet chatter about Cardi B's 2018 pregnancy was Cardi's decision to get pregnant and remain pregnant. One way this was discussed was in reference to the timing of her pregnancy. One of the major trains of thought about timing was focused around Cardi's decision to get pregnant before marriage.[20] Many of the comments seen on Twitter reflected negative opinions about Cardi's choice of family formation outside of the bonds of marriage. Other users admonished her for voluntarily becoming a "baby mama," alluding to her supposed unmarried pregnant status. Social media users called Cardi B things like stupid and irresponsible. One clear example was posted on a recently deleted post on Twitter:

> Ya'll was really happy when Cardi B announced she was pregnant like she was married lmaoooooo.
>
> *(Twitter, @HezSoKrayzee; 4/9/2018)*

Other commentators who objected to the timing of Cardi B's pregnancy pointed out that Cardi B had the resources to avoid an out-of-wedlock pregnancy. One social media commenter even suggested that she obtain a late-term abortion. This suggestion implied that Cardi's economic status should have excluded her from being an unmarried mother because apparently baby mamas are only low-income Black women, which we know is false.[21] Clearly, these posts epitomized the responses of those who expect others to adhere to traditional family formations. Marriage is a social institution that regulates sexual behavior and reproduction per ideology in the United States, which is supported by religion. This perspective speaks to puritanical views of sex, which tell us first, that sex is sacred, and second, that sex should be reserved for marriage (Cherlin 2005; Welter 1966). Similarly, online comments referenced Cardi's former employment as a stripper as well as her alleged drug and alcohol use as potential reasons for her "poor" decision-making leading to her 2018 pregnancy.

Online commenters with less rigid ideas about procreation spoke out in support of Cardi B's choice to get pregnant. Most posts used sarcasm and anecdotes to point out the hypocrisy of those who believed that Cardi B's life should be packaged in a conservative wrapper, which has never been a part of her public persona. One tweet read:

> This girl in my office is really talking shit about cardi b having a baby before marriage meanwhile she got married and pregnant at 18 and now she's divorced
>
> *(Twitter, @fuckdeanna; 4/9/2018)*

This post points out that getting married before having a family does not always lead to the mythical "happily ever after" that many believe it will. Others highlighted that Cardi's status as an unmarried mother was different from that of your average single mother based on her economic status. Some commenters also emphasized that Offset had a fathering relationship with his other children and that Cardi B was engaged to the father of her unborn child, so she's technically not a single mother.

Social media users' degradation of Cardi B's choice to be an unmarried mother—despite her actually being married—is rooted in negative narratives surrounding the welfare mother, who chooses to have children out of wedlock (Collins 2022). This seemingly voluntary decision is seen as deviant and immoral. Those who assert it is immoral to have a child without being married to the child's father believe in the institution of marriage. However, marriage does not benefit Black women from the trap in the same way that it does white middle-class women (Pate 2010). The unification of two poor people in a marriage does not lead to the same economic and social benefits as marriages combining two middle- or upper-class individuals. From the trap feminist perspective, the supporters of Cardi B's choice to have a child are challenging dominant views of family formation by making space for multi-partner fertility, which is not inherently deviant. As previously mentioned, multi-partner fertility was an economic benefit to slaveholders before Emancipation. Then when it no longer benefited capitalists, multi-partner fertility gained its negative connotations. Trap feminism allows us to expand our definition of family to include multi-partner and other family formation choices that emerged (and still exist) as a means to survive poverty.

Another subtheme that emerged from online discussions of Cardi B's pregnancy was the speculated impact that the timing of her pregnancy would have on her career. Cardi B officially announced her pregnancy one day after the release of her studio album, *Invasion of Privacy*. Her fans and critics expressed extreme disappointment that she chose to start a family when her career was on the rise. One Twitter user expressed anger at the timing of Cardi's pregnancy, posting:

> Perfect example of women being dumb no matter how amazing they are: Cardi B drops such an amazing album but gets pregnant 🤦‍♂️🤦‍♂️🤦‍♂️ I WAS WAITING FOR THE TOUR DATES NOW ALL A MA GET IS A DUE DATE 😩😔😫
> *Twitter, @_DJLindo; 4/9/2018*

This tweet is an exemplary response representing those who believed Cardi's pregnancy to be ill-timed relating to her career. Individuals across the internet called Cardi's family planning both irresponsible and selfish. As mentioned earlier, commenters assumed that her pregnancy would preclude Cardi from all performances and stall what seemed to be a promising career. Those involved in the internet chatter felt as though Cardi would not be able to sustain her career while being a mother. They argued that if she did continue to perform, her performances would be lackluster compared to those of a not-pregnant Cardi. This stance is again rooted in antiquated white, middle-class, gendered expectations of mothers. White pregnant women were seen as delicate and incapable of strenuous daily activities while Black pregnant women were not. Still, Black mothers who work are viewed as bad mothers because they are not at home with their children, who are presumably running amok. At the same time, if Black single mothers do not work outside the home, they are framed as lazy, harkening back to the welfare queen stereotype. These conflicting stances place Black mothers, including Cardi B, into a "damned if you do, damned if you don't" conundrum.

Cardi B's fans and other online commentators also wrote responses that were more accepting of Cardi B determining the timing of her pregnancy. These commenters presented counterarguments about how Cardi's pregnancy was not affecting her career, citing the ongoing promotion of her newly released studio album. Most users pointed out that Black women have always worked while pregnant and continued to work after they became mothers.[22] We argue that trap feminism respects Black mothers' ability to self-determine how their families are structured irrespective of dominant expectations of family formation. One integral part of being a trap feminist is respecting the "hustle." Expecting Cardi B to stop "getting money" while pregnant contradicts this important tenet of trap feminism. Those with a trap feminist consciousness support and expect Cardi B to be a "hustling" mom, which helps expand the way Black mothers are represented and allows Black women to define their own mothering practices.

Choosing to Twerk

The last theme that emerged from the online discussions about Cardi B's 2018 pregnancy was her decision to twerk while pregnant during her Coachella performance. As we discussed, Cardi B gave a high-energy performance that included her signature twerking moves. Her pregnant belly was not concealed under oversized clothes. The content of her performance brought her pregnancy into plain view while also showing that carrying a child will not keep her from giving her audiences her best. She was exhibiting the freedom she proclaimed backstage in New York after her SNL pregnancy reveal.

One would expect online commentators to fill up social media and internet blog comment sections with their opinions about Cardi's choice to continue performing while visibly pregnant based on assumptions about the delicate condition of pregnant women. However, most of the banter revolved around *how* she performed instead of her decision to perform at all. Cardi B is a former stripper known for provocative dancing that aligns with her song lyrics (discussed in Chapter 3). Some of these dance moves may be described as simulating sex acts, particularly twerking, which has been called ghetto and ratchet.

The most common narratives among internet users involved in this conversation that condemned Cardi B for twerking was about the inappropriateness of this behavior for an expectant mother. For example, one Twitter user wrote:

A hot a mess. She's a pregnant mother out here acting a fool 🙍‍♀️
(*Twitter, @SIGNYOBOOBS; 4/16/2018*)

There were many comments like this across the internet in the days immediately following Cardi's performance. Many inferred that she would not be a good mother based on her onstage performance. Others predicted that this video would one day be traumatic for her child, who may then be bullied in school. The main narrative throughout these online comments was that Cardi B's choice to twerk in her performance while visibly pregnant was evidence that she would not be a good mother. Here again, Black women are stigmatized for the shape of their bodies which they cannot control, not to mention owning and expressing their sexuality in public. Patriarchal societies continuously police women's bodies, telling women what they can and cannot do and when and where they can be sexual. In addition, Black women are stereotyped as hypersexual and promiscuous. Many Black women adhere to the rules of the patriarchy (for many reasons including assumptions about safety) then police, chastise, and marginalize other Black women who do not fall in line with these standards.

Many online comments about Cardi B's decision to twerk at Coachella assaulted her personhood. Twitter users in particular made negative comments about her intelligence, upbringing, and morality. These posts used degrading language to describe her performance as well as her as an individual. Words like "ho(e)," "vulgar," "tacky," "disgusting," and even "buffoon" were used in posts referring to Cardi B twerking on stage. This tweet, accompanied by a gif with "Congratulations. You're a disgrace.," the user posted,

> what an idiot she's so vulgar and disgraceful for a bad example for those poor young female.
>
> *(Twitter, @festaga; 4/16/2018)*

As shown here, the comments surrounding Cardi B's choice to twerk while pregnant were mostly negative and related to a lack of class. People online commented based on their personal beliefs, which are informed by dominant ideologies surrounding motherhood and respectability. This ideology speaks to the notion that Black mothers cannot be sexual and, if they do display their sexuality, they are not afforded flexibility in how they express that sexuality. It also speaks to the belief that Cardi's behavior is associated with poor Black single mothers (i.e., the welfare queen).

In contrast, other users embraced Cardi B's choice to perform at Coachella in a manner that is true to her identity and her style. They addressed her condemners, accusing them of having double standards and antiquated beliefs. Comments ranged from being inspired by Cardi's commitment to remain true to herself even while pregnant, to awe that she could pull off the performance during her third trimester. For example, one tweet read: "Cardi B dancing in heels with her baby bump is everything I aspire to be" (Twitter; @d11lxyd; 4/15/2018). Others talked about how free and uninhibited Cardi appeared on stage and expressed a desire for the same type of freedom were they to become pregnant.

Meanwhile, others shot back at Cardi B's character-assassins. They pointed out the hypocrisy of Cardi's haters who often applaud others who do the same things Cardi does. For example, online users pointed out how Beyoncé did not receive the same negative response after she performed during her pregnancy.[23] Others admonished negative commentators by reminding them that Black women have always been active while pregnant. One of our favorite responses is:

> Sooo some dudes gotta problem with cardi b being pregnant and twerk-ing on stage . . . but y'all mamas did the same shit back in 70s and 80s while being pregnant with y'all!better yet! Ask your mama why you and your siblings all got different daddies! #YoMamaWasAStoneColdFluzzy.
> *(Twitter, @MidgeEl; 4/16/2018)*

This Twitter user very clearly pushes back at the morality police who attempt to constrain Cardi B. El Enano points out that many of the people making negative comments about a celebrity they do not know person-ally have similar family formation histories and/or family members who engaged in similar activities. This comment highlights how many are hypo-critical in their critiques of celebrities like Cardi B, expecting her behavior to conform to patriarchal standards that even they do not follow. In other words, people in glass houses shouldn't throw stones.

Conclusion

As a trap feminist mother, Cardi B resists patriarchal expectations of moth-erhood while embracing and staying authentic to who she is as a woman. The relationship between Cardi B's choice of a partner who was deemed unacceptable, the timing of her pregnancy, Cardi's choice to twerk while pregnant, and the public's outrage goes far beyond Cardi just being a preg-nant woman on the public stage. The ways in which people feel comforta-ble talking about what she should and should not do is also associated with the way Black women have always been policed. We are policed at work. Our hairstyle (natural hair is not professional), our clothing (that form-fitting dress is distracting), and our behavior (tone down your voice—it sounds aggressive) have always garnered comments by those who ascribe to the ideals of white patriarchal standards of professionalism and stand-ards of beauty. Black women have historically and contemporarily been told that they should aspire to be more white to be acceptable. The same is true when we think about Black motherhood. We are told to not have children out of wedlock. If we decide to get married, we are told to choose partners who are free from blemishes. We are told that we should not have children while poor. But if we do, we are told that we must work and leave our children in the care of others unlike white mothers who are told to stay home with theirs. If we choose to stay home to care for our children, Black women are seen as lazy and shiftless (welfare queen stereotype).

There has been a long history of condemning and criminalizing Black women and Black mothers. The roots of the stigmatization of Black motherhood began during enslavement, then followed Black women into the Jim Crow era, through the Reagan era, and continues to shape the public's perceptions of Black mothers today. Black women "being too loud" and uncouth translated into Black women being criminalized and incarcerated and thus bad mothers. Now, people discredit Black mothers by using the characteristics to shame who they are as Black women and how they parent. The denial of personhood, womanhood, and motherhood for Black women are intertwined in how people view hood chicks who are mothers and the choices they make for themselves and their family.

As discussed throughout this chapter, Black mothers in the United States have been plagued by stereotypes that paint them as unfit caretakers for their children. The public opposed Cardi's choice of Offset as a partner because his multi-partner fertility and alleged infidelity placed him in the unmarriageable man category. He exists outside the bounds of respectability that white supremacy constructs around manhood. However, Black women's partnering pools are often more shallow because of mass incarceration and other factors (Charles and Luoh 2010). Therefore, women in the trap expand their choices to include men who might be seen as undesirable partners as well as make room for redemption.

We also found that those who admonished Cardi B for choosing to have a baby when her career was just about to blow up were steeped in ideology about mothering. Some believed that Cardi ruined her career because mothers should not work. Others thought that she was careless in her timing even though she had more resources to control her pregnancy, reflecting the belief that upwardly mobile Black women should delay having children to focus on their careers. Both of these beliefs are embedded in white middle-class standards of family formation and gender expectations that never existed for Black women. Historically, Black women have always worked while pregnant; as mentioned earlier when discussing forced reproduction, for some Black women, getting pregnant was their job. Trap feminism teaches us that Black women from the trap must work to take care of their families, not just in conventional jobs but also side jobs or hustles. We do both, mothering and working, while looking like a bad bitch.

Lastly, our data revealed that the people who were deeply disturbed by Cardi B's twerking while pregnant on stage were steeped in respectability politics. Pregnant women are believed to be delicate and frail. They are expected to behave in a manner that white patriarchal ideology prescribes as respectful—quiet, meek, and asexual. When Cardi B gave a performance that was high energy, fun, and sexy, she broke the rules of motherhood, and the public admonished her for it. Yet trap feminism teaches us that trap queens are strong. They face and conquer adversity daily. They also use all of their assets and talents in an effort to survive and ultimately leave the trap. Why would this stop during pregnancy? It wouldn't and to expect that would be dooming Black women to extinction.

Notes

1 Offset, aka Kiari Kendrell Cephus, is an American rapper. He rose to prominence as part of the Hip Hop group Migos, alongside Quavo and Takeoff.
2 Cardi B and Offset were secretly married before the announcement of her pregnancy. A fact that she concealed until after her reveal.
3 Cardi B set the media world on fire again by announcing her second pregnancy at the 2021 BET awards.
4 Coachella is one of the most famous "7 Top Music Festivals Around The World – Tripoetic Blog." Tripoetic Blog. January 31, 2017. Archived from the original on February 23, 2017. Retrieved February 23, 2017.
5 Cardi did not tell the public that she was already married to Offset until after her first pregnancy reveal and her Coachella performance.
6 We used NodeXL software to capture the data from the Twitter search API relevant to the two events highlighted in this chapter: Cardi B's pregnancy reveal on Saturday Night Live and her Coachella performance. Both were in April 2018. This free software package does not retrieve all of the data. However, the assumption is that the resulting dataset is both valid and robust. To delineate the dataset, we used dates and search terms that would extract tweets that were most relevant to the moments under study. In relation to the SNL event, we entered the following criteria into the NodeXL software: Cardi, 4/7/2018, 4/8/2018, 4/9/2018, 4/10/2018, pregnant, and SNL. This search resulted in a dataset of 6,484 tweets referencing to Cardi B's pregnancy. Of these tweets, 52% were retweets including quoted retweets with additional comments. Of these tweets, approximately 30% of these tweets included new content. After removing tweets that only retweeted someone else's comment, our dataset comprised 4,123 tweets. Using the currently acceptable convention (Downing and Dron 2020), we took a 5% random sample (206) of the dataset to conduct the analysis. The same progress was used to capture the data surrounding the Coachella event. We entered the search following search criteria into NodeXL: Cardi, Coachella, 4/15/2018, 4/16/2018, 4/17/2018, 4/18/2018, pregnant, and twerk. This search resulted in 4,327 tweets relevant to Cardi B's pregnancy. Of these tweets, about 53% were retweets including quoted retweets with additional comments. Of these tweets, about 28% represented new content. The final dataset included 2,676 tweets. Again, we randomly sampled 5% (134) of the final dataset to analyze. We conducted qualitative content analysis and grounded theory methodologies to explore the content of online commentary among Twitter users. As a method, the goal of qualitative content analysis is to illuminate the influence of mainstream ideology on how social concepts, like motherhood, are framed (Hesse-Biber 2017). We also used a constructivist

grounded theory methodological approach (Charmaz 2014). The text was read multiple times in order for themes to emerge organically from within. As we read the text, we wrote memos containing notes on the thoughts and revelations that emerged. These memos were later used to develop the links between the theoretical framework and theory. Also, while reading the text included in this analysis, we created codes (labels) to describe the data's relationship with the research question (Hesse-Biber 2017). Examining the SNL dataset, approximately 50 codes emerged from a preliminary analysis. After this round of coding, roughly 30 descriptive codes emerged. I interacted with the data again, this time conducting more focused coding. A sample of the focused codes includes Offset in unfaithful, mad Cardi's pregnant, happy Cardi is pregnant, Cardi looks good pregnant, and Cardi ruining her career. Themes and subthemes became more abstract and allowed for a broader interpretation of what the data was saying. A sample of a few of these more abstract themes (analytical codes) relevant to this analysis includes choosing to have a baby with Offset and choosing to be pregnant at the height of her career. Examining the Coachella dataset, approximately 40 codes emerged from a preliminary analysis. After this round of coding, roughly 27 descriptive codes emerged. I interacted with the data again, this time conducting more focused coding. A sample of the focused codes includes twerking is ghetto, Cardi inspiring women, Cardi will be a bad mom, Cardi has no class, and Cardi is a hustler. Themes and subthemes became more abstract and allowed for a broader interpretation of what the data was saying. The abstract theme (analytical codes) relevant to this analysis includes choosing to twerk while pregnant.

7   However, Black women then and now found ways to show their humanity and live outside of the constraints of their forced inhumanity.

8   Slaveholders insured slaves with property insurance. For more information, see Amy Bride's 2020 article, "Dead or Alive: Racial Finance and the Corpse-Value of the African American Slave Body" in the *Journal of Historical Sociology*.

9   The Reconstruction era lasted from 1865 to 1877. It was a time of Black progress that included federal protection for Black populations in former Confederate states and Black political leadership including a Black governor. For more information, see W.E.B. Du Bois's 1935 book, Black Reconstruction.

10   Jim Crow laws and practices were birthed after the Black Codes were deemed unconstitutional by the Supreme Court.

11   The Sentencing Project is a research and advocacy firm that partners with national and state groups to challenge racial injustice in imprisonment. For more information, visit (www.sentencingproject.org).

12   The profiles of these users, via profile pictures and Twitter (now X) usage, appear to be those of Black Millennials.

13   Love and Hip-Hop New York: Season 6.

14   Love and Hip-Hop New York: Season 6.

15   Love and Hip-Hop New York: Season 7.

16   Nick Cannon may be a relevant example of this.

17   When we say loveless environment, we are talking about the lack of infrastructure, resources, and jobs in the trap that make the environment seem abandoned and cold.

18   As of this writing, Cardi B now has two children, Kulture Kiari and Wave Set. She also masked her second pregnancy until her third trimester.

19   Future research can use our framework to analyze responses to her second pregnancy, when similar conversations occurred.

20 Cardi B was not actually an unwed mother. She and Offset married each other in a private ceremony in September 2017. See France, Lisa Respers. 2018. "Cardi B and Offset were married when he 'proposed'." in CNN: Cable News Network.
21 See Khloe Kardashian and Kylie Jenner as examples.
22 Many Twitter users point to Beyoncé as an example of a celebrity who continued to perform while pregnant.
23 Beyoncé also revealed her pregnancies during performances.

6

CARDI B'S TRAP FEMINIST POLITICS

Trap feminists' experiences with white patriarchal policies and institutions, such as the US government, have been central throughout this book. In Chapter 5, we reviewed the impact of the government-backed Moynihan Report, which incorrectly absolved the government and other state institutions for their role in creating many of the social problems plaguing Black families. This chapter continues to engage with the role of institutions in trap feminists' lives, as we analyze Cardi B's public engagement with politicians and governmental institutions, as well as the social causes she cares about.

In the following messages, two US Senators exchange thoughts about retweeting an Instagram (IG) video posted by Cardi B that argued for an end to President Donald Trump's 2018–2019 federal government shutdown.

> Guys, I'm still holding my breath, are you gonna RT (retweet) Cardi B or not?
>
> *—Senate Minority Leader Charles E. Schumer*
> *(Twitter; @SenSchumer; 01/16/2019)*

> We decided not to—wouldn't be senatorial.
>
> *—Hawaii Senator Brian Schatz*
> *(Twitter; @brianschatz; 01/16/2019)*

Cardi used her IG video to preemptively silence those who argued that Trump was no different than former President Barack Obama, who had also prompted a federal government shutdown during his time in office.

DOI: 10.4324/9781003184980-7

In the video, she explains that Obama's shutdown was in defense of the Affordable Care Act (Obamacare), in contrast to Trump's xenophobic goal of building a wall to keep migrants from crossing the Mexico–US border. In her unique, funny, and relatable tone, Cardi points out that Obama's shutdown was "so your grandma could check her blood pressure and you bitches could go get your pussy checked at the gynecologist with no motherfucking problem." She also criticizes Trump for causing hundreds of thousands of federal employees to work for 38 days without pay.

The senatorial rejection of Cardi's video happened in spite of the fact that the video was immensely popular, garnering six million views and two million likes within hours of being posted (Cheok, Lee, and Chuwiruch 2019). Cardi's words could have helped the senators reach an even larger swath of potential and current Democratic-leaning voters from a wide variety of backgrounds. Instead, the senators' tweets about Cardi's video not being "senatorial" reflected their judgment of Cardi as an unfit political spokeswoman based on her use of "non-respectable" (aka not white, middle-class) language. The senators' tweets illustrate the widespread acceptance of suppressing the civic and political engagement of women like Cardi B. Unfortunately, this incident is just one instance of the continual subjugation of Black women due to the overwhelming dominance of patriarchal white-centric views in our culture.

Senators are not the only people who operate under the influence of a white-centric patriarchal culture: the epistemology of sociological literature, or how sociologists make claims about what counts as knowledge, often ignores, underestimates, and devalues the civic and political engagement of Black women. In fact, scholarship on civic engagement often (and incorrectly) "confirms" that Black people and Black women are less civically engaged than white people (Putnam 2000). However, there is plenty of evidence to the contrary. Black women like Cardi B only *seem* less civically engaged than other racialized groups because the scholarly lens used to interpret Black people's behaviors and activism is tuned to white patriarchal settings (Robinson 2019).

As an expert on her own life, Cardi B recognizes the importance of being civically and politically engaged. In her 2018 interview with *GQ Magazine*, the rapper highlights the importance of civic and political engagement that centers one's community:

> I'm always watching the news. I'm always looking at it on my phone. I hate when you talk about something that's going on in the community, people think, because you're famous, you doing it for clout. But you concerned about it because you are a citizen of America. You are a citizen of the world.

(Weaver 2018)

She further sums up her commitments to civic and political engagement when speaking with David Letterman on his show, *My Next Guest Needs No Introduction*, a few years later:

> I don't really put a lot of political things in my music, but I use the fuck out of my platform . . . I have used my platform even when I was a dancer . . . I feel like I have a responsibility.
>
> *(Steed 2022)*

Cardi clearly understands the political value of her fame.

In this chapter, we explore the contours of trap feminist politics through examples of Cardi B's use of her platform. A trap feminist standpoint reminds us that public and political institutions are disinvested in women like Cardi B due to Black women's marginalized social location at the intersections of racism, classism, and sexism. Therefore, we define trap feminist politics as civic and political engagement that not only emerges from the lived experiences of hood chicks, ghetto girls, and ratchet women but also centers the needs of these women in policy and institutional decisions. To illustrate these points, we emphasize that trap feminist politics encompass three broad categories: (1) activism and advocating for social change, (2) institutional politics such as voting and other actions directed at the government, and (3) community work and volunteering. Trap feminist politics involve not only the political beliefs of trap feminists but also their direct engagement with politics and communities every day.

To explore Cardi B's commitment to trap feminist politics, we first situate her within a long lineage of politically and civically engaged Black women. We then highlight how Cardi B's trap feminist politics are evident in her support for, as well as her arguments against, specific social causes and politicians. Next, we pair these findings with an analysis of how politicians and pundits on *both* sides of the political spectrum have marginalized, ignored, or outright attacked Cardi B for her political engagement. Throughout the chapter, we show how Cardi B's trap feminist politics are best understood and appreciated when we take a trap feminist standpoint that expands beyond the white-centric lens of conventional politics to encompass the lived experiences and knowledge production of poor Black women. This helps us recognize that hood Black women (like Cardi B before her rise to fame) are essential contributors to civic life and politics despite historically being the most impacted by the failings of our democracy. The chapter concludes with a broader discussion about the importance of encouraging and acknowledging marginalized women's agency within the political and civic sphere. Adopting a trap feminist perspective of civic and political engagement ensures that we see and support trap feminists as women with voices and who can make their own choices rather than as passive subjects in political issues.

The Lineage of Trap Feminist Politics

Black women have consistently envisioned and worked to create an equitable world even when our civic and political engagement has been thwarted by racism, sexism, and classism. We have advocated for social change, participated in institutional politics, and volunteered our efforts individually and in groups across a wide spectrum of social and political organizations. One of the challenges we faced as the authors of this book was choosing examples from the seemingly endless stories of Black women from diverse socioeconomic backgrounds who use(d) their voices to affect civic and political change despite the white supremacist, patriarchal culture of the United States. At best, this dominant culture is hostile to Black women, and at worst, it is deadly to us, but we have never stopped pushing for a better world.

Activism and Advocating for Social Change

One aspect of trap feminist politics is activism and advocacy for social change. Broadly understood as actions that challenge existing elements of social and political systems, activism includes a wide range of activities from everyday conversations in homes, neighborhoods, and on social media to the more explicit and contentious activities of marches, protests, and riots (Moss and Snow 2016; Saunders 2022). Cardi B's activism is an extension of the activism of Black women throughout US history. Black women have participated in activism with the aim of achieving the rights and responsibilities that being a citizen of the United States is supposed to provide.

One of the countless examples of Black women's activism can be found in the actions of Harriet Tubman. While she is widely lauded as a trailblazing abolitionist today, it is important to remember that Harriet Tubman did not follow the rules of "respectable" political participation. She did not push for social change through traditional legal means such as political lobbying or organized protests. Tubman broke the law (United States Fugitive Slave Law 1850)[1] when she helped enslaved persons escape to freedom via the Underground Railroad. She then translated her lawbreaking abolition work into leadership during the Civil War. She is not only recognized as the first woman in history to lead a military operation but also acknowledged for her concurrent service as a spy for the Union Army (Brown 2021). In spite of no formal education or traditional military training, Tubman transformed a society built on and by enslavement into one that recognized the horrors of the practice by not playing by the "rules" (Brown 2021; King 2022).

In the introduction to this book, we acknowledged how Ida B. Wells-Barnett made critical contributions to Black sociology by paving the way for Black women to serve as scholar-activists at the turn of the 20th century (Allen 2021). In the words of Cardi B, Wells-Barnett "used the fuck out of her platform" as an investigative journalist to speak out against lynching, massacres, and the intimidation of Black-owned businesses during the violent Reconstruction era following the US Civil War (Duster 2021; Giddings 2009; Pulitzer Prize 2022). Her works, *The Red Record: Tabulated Statistics and Alleged Causes of Lynching in the United States* (1895) and *Southern Horrors: Lynch Law in All Its Phases* (1892) are some of the first texts to systematically bring attention to white terrorism in the South. In the preface to *Southern Horrors*, Wells-Barnett states:

> The Afro-American is not a bestial race. If this work can contribute in any way toward proving this, and at the same time arouse the conscience of the American people to a demand for justice to every citizen, and punishment by law for the lawless, I shall feel I have done my race a service.

Ida used her pen as a tool for social change in the same way that Cardi B uses her videos and tweets.

By the mid-20th century, activism began to more loudly challenge the social and political systems that marginalized Black people and Black women specifically. Classroom discussions about the Civil Rights Movement often center the contributions of men, inadvertently casting a shadow over the traditional and nontraditional leadership of Black women during this time (much like the male-centric culture of Hip Hop we discuss in Chapter 1). For example, Dorothy Height, of the National Council of Negro Women (NCNW), and Diane Nash, a co-founder of the Student Nonviolent Coordinating Committee (SNCC), served as mobilizers for the March on Washington alongside the "Big Six."[2] For the purposes of historical accuracy, the "Big Six" should be expanded to at least the "Big Eight."

As Black Americans shouted "I'm Black and I'm Proud" during the Black Power Movement in the late 1960s and into the 1970s, Kathleen Cleaver, Angela Davis—quoted in the book's introduction—and Assata Shakur were leaders in speaking up for the humanity of Black people and the inclusion of Black women. Not only did they use their voices to speak against social and political inequalities, they also used their clothing and hair as activism; their unique halo afros became visuals of the movement.

In the words of scholar Tanisha Ford in *Liberated Threads*, the use of their images helps us to learn "about the innovative ways that black women responded to state sanctioned violence" (Ford 2015b:21). In short, we figured out how to use our unique style as a symbol and tool in the fight for our rights. These Black women activists served alongside many unnamed Black women as the voices and leaders of organizations and communities, often becoming a bridge between the two (Robnett 2000). Their civic and social activism was not done out of a desire for "clout" but because of a genuine care for our community and all Black people.

Moving into the 21st century, Black women continued to be central mobilizers of social movements. Patricia Cullors, Opal Tometi, and Alicia Garza founded the organization Black Lives Matter and the hashtag #BlackLivesMatter with the aim of using technology to center critical, queer, intersectional praxis in the fight against racist police brutality (Cannady 2022). Soon after, Kimberlé Crenshaw and the African American Policy Forum worked to amplify the hashtag #SayHerName, which represents an organized effort to bring "awareness to the often invisible names and stories of Black women and girls who have been victimized by racist police violence, and provides support to their families" (The African American Policy Forum. n.d.). Like the Black feminists before them, Black women participants, researchers, and activists in #BlackLivesMatter and #SayHer-Name understand an important fact: If we want to create a better society for all people, we must encourage, support, and center the voices of Black women. These examples are just a starting point to consider the reasons why Black women activists and advocates, including Black women living in, adjacent to, and apart from the trap, are not always recognized by non-Black women. We introduced a few of our activist foremothers here as a backdrop for understanding the historical roots of the trap feminist politics practiced by Cardi B and women like her.

Institutional Politics

Trap feminist politics also include institutional politics—voting, engaging in legislation, and running for office. These normative politics are often seen as the only legitimate way to push for social change in the United States (McAdam, Tarrow, and Tilly 2001). In this chapter, we highlight Cardi B's dedication to institutional politics which follows a lineage of unceasing activism of Black women who fought for the right to vote and participate in US governmental institutions. This fight is far from over; despite the many recent publications of academics, activists, and political leaders publicizing Black women's contributions to politics,[3] the voices of Black women continue to be marginalized by white-centric understandings of civic engagement and political participation (Slaughter and Brown 2022). Institutional politics, while seen as the most legitimate way to effect social change, is often the space in which Black women have been most excluded. Yet this exclusion is not due to our lack of attempts to be heard; our voices have been excluded on purpose.

Black women were afterthoughts in 19th-century conversations concerning the suffrage of Black Americans. Abolitionist Frederick Douglass and white feminist Susan B. Anthony ignored Black women in their debates about which racial or gender group should first receive an amendment to support their right to vote, which demonstrates the acceptance of a gendered-raced hierarchy in which Black women are inferior to white women, and all women are inferior to men.[4] Black men received the right to vote via the 15th Amendment in 1870. Even though Black women marched with white suffragettes in the early 20th century to support what would become the ratification of the 19th Amendment in 1920 (Lindsey 2017; Cahill 2020), Black women did not have full access to the vote until the passage of the Voting Rights Act[5] in 1965.

Black women continue to lead the fight for voting rights today. Their participation is credited as being central to the success of Alabama Senator Doug Jones's 2017 election campaign (Naylor 2017) and the triumphant push for political engagement among Democrats in the 2020 elections (Herndon 2020; Perry et al. 2021; Rigueur 2020). Both examples demonstrate the continual and impactful political engagement of Black women.

In addition to voting, legal challenges are central to institutional politics. In the mid-20th century, the political words and works of Black women were essential to the success of the Civil Rights Movement. For example, civil rights activist, legal scholar, and theorist Pauli Murray is credited as the mastermind behind the argument (separate is inherently unequal) that helped the NAACP secure the groundbreaking victory in Brown *v.* Board of Education in 1954 (Crutchfield 2022; Rosenberg 2017; Warren and Supreme Court of The United States 1953). Social psychologist Mamie Clark was also instrumental in the win against the Board of Education. Along with her husband, Kenneth Clark, she created and administered the "doll test," which was used to prove that segregation had a negative psychological effect on Black children. Mamie Clark and Pauli Murray exemplify the power of Black women's unique intellectualism—our ability to think beyond what is assumed as "correct" serves as a cornerstone of roadmaps for legislative change.

Lastly, Black women's engagement with institutional politics includes running for office, even though Black women have been actively prevented from running for office by racism, classism, and sexism. In just one year, 1964, Civil Rights crusader Fannie Lou Hamer described the violence and injustices she had experienced as a Black woman from, and in, the South in her revolutionary speech "Sick and Tired of Being Sick and Tired," ran for a seat in the US House of Representatives to show that "a Negro can run for office," and co-founded the Mississippi Freedom Democratic Party (MFDP) to speak out against the disenfranchisement of Black people in the state's entirely white Democratic Party (Blain 2021; Brooks and Houck 2011; Mills 2007). Ultimately, the Democratic Party, outside of the MFDP, refused to place Hamer's name on the official ballot. But she did not quit in the face of these daunting challenges; in fact, Hamer went on to run for office again and again. She lost both times—in the first attempt, she was unfairly disqualified, and in the second, she was defeated by vote (Blain 2021; Mills 2007).

In 1968, Shirley Chisolm became the first Black woman elected to congress (Curwood 2022). In the past 55 years, we have made scant progress; only 57 Black women have served in congress since 1968. Historically, Black women on average have made up just 0.4% of total congressional membership. In 2022, Black women constituted 7.7% of the US population, but only 5.2% of congressional membership, and none of these seats were in the Senate[6] (Center for American Women and Politics 2022). It is easy to imagine why Cardi B (and Black women in general)—who have the intellectual capacity, passion, dedication, experience, and work ethic for the job—might not see running for political office as a viable career path.

Community Work and Volunteering

The third part of trap feminist politics is Black women's extra-institutional and grassroots community work. We serve our communities not only by giving our time, talents, and energy to volunteering but also by pulling each other up through group organizing and building a sense of unity among Black people. Black actress, writer, and producer Issa Rae used her platform by proclaiming "I'm rooting for everybody Black" at the 2017 Emmy Awards, providing a great example of community work by reminding all of us that Black women loudly support our communities.

The first self-made Black American millionaire Madame CJ Walker was an entrepreneur who specialized in hair care products and cosmetics for Black women, establishing a pathway for Black women to become entrepreneurs. As entrepreneurs, many poor Black women, in the words of Cardi B "make money moves," by selling their own hair care products and cosmetics, too. At the turn of the 20th century, Madame CJ Walker taught us that with more money comes more responsibility through her gospel of giving (Freeman 2020). She pulled Black women into entrepreneurship through her hair colleges, used her lavish estate as a gathering place for the Black community, and donated large sums of money to support Black institutions. Like Cardi B, Walker is an example of a Black woman who was politically engaged through community building and philanthropic endeavors.

In the 21st century, Black women have continued to support our communities by speaking up on behalf of the causes that impact us the most. In December 2014, the University of Notre Dame's women's basketball team showed their support for the developing anti-police-brutality protests around the country by wearing "I can't breathe"[7] shirts, even though it was deeply unpopular to support #BlackLivesMatter at that time. Two years later, in 2016, the WNBA Team Minnesota Lynx wore black warm-up shirts featuring the words "Black Lives Matter," "Change Starts With Us" and "Justice and Accountability," the image of the Dallas police shield, and the names Alton Sterling and Philando Castile,[8] two Black men who were killed by police officers that week.[9] WNBA teams Indiana Fever, New York Liberty, and Phoenix Mercury also expressed their support by wearing black warm-up shirts that year (without any inscriptions). In contrast to the experience of the NBA when their teams participated in similar demonstrations, the WNBA fined these teams and their players. The fines were eventually revoked—although the criticism of their actions remained. Notably, WNBA legend Maya Moore of the Minnesota Lynx continued her dedication to uplifting the Black community when she left basketball to help support the overturning of her friend's prison conviction (Ayala 2020; Gregory 2020), representing an example of the community work off the court as well.

Black women also engage in community work through *othermothering*. Othermothering is any type of mothering in the process of caring for the development of children that extends beyond parental relationships and into a "collective responsibility for nurturance, advocacy, and justice on behalf of others" (Docka-Filipek 2016). In addition to our scholarship, Black women at academic institutions provide immeasurable support for students and colleagues through unpaid labor, including often othermothering (volunteering).

Despite the consistent disregard of our political voices, the histories outlined in this chapter confirm that Black women from all socioeconomic backgrounds have served and continue to serve as cornerstones of civic and political engagement in the United States. Several of the women discussed earlier may appear to fall into the category of "respectable" given their education, income, or occupation, but much like Cardi B, they were and are not often welcomed into white-centric, patriarchal political circles. Audre Lorde is quoted as saying "I am not free while any woman is unfree, even when her shackles are very different from my own." This quote encapsulates the need for Black women to support one another regardless of their background. And this support can only be lent to hood chicks, ratchet girls, and poor Black women everywhere through the understandings provided by an all-inclusive, non-white-centric feminism.

Trap Feminist Politics: A Trap Feminist Framework for Civic and Political Engagement

Trap feminist politics are a political orientation that centers the hood chicks, ghetto girls, and the Black women who live in and embody the trap. Black women, particularly those who grew up in poverty, face significant barriers when attempting to get involved in politics. Ange-Marie Hancock argues that in addition to poor Black women being excluded from political circles, their exclusion also allows politicians to perpetuate incorrect and misguided ideas about Black women (Hancock 2004:5). Often, those in and adjacent to the trap are viewed through controlling images[10] that reinforce the belief that Black women are not to be taken seriously. None of these controlling images, such as the Mammy, Sapphire, Jezebel, and Welfare Queen, depict Black women as intelligent or politically savvy, suggesting that they are incapable of engaging in traditional forms of political and social commentary (Estes, Straub, and León-Corwin 2023; Collins 1991).

In a world that assumes that poor Black and brown women are not invested in broader society, trap feminist politics illuminate the way hood chicks are civically and politically engaged despite assumptions about their style of engagement. Parallel to the stories of Black women discussed earlier, Black women in the hood may not *look* or *act* in the traditional white and male ways in politics, but their engagement is just as valuable as other forms of engagement. For example, the media campaign "Get Your Booty to the Polls," involves Black women strippers and sex workers conducting PSAs and twitter chats to encourage individuals to vote, much to the chagrin of the public (Steadman 2020; Summers 2020). While earnest in its aims, critics still assumed that the PSA was pandering by assuming that Black people are only interested in sex rather than understanding the importance of meeting people where they are (Summers 2020).

Given the United States is a racist, classist, and heteropatriarchal society, it's not surprising to us that trap feminists receive pushback for their engagement. As we noted earlier, when Black women, particularly those who do not fit white, middle-class behavioral norms, engage with politics, their contributions are often devalued and ridiculed. At the same time, those in dominant groups work to put these Black women "in their place" by ignoring them or pointing out the supposed inferiority of their contributions. In short, the public and scholars must address the factors that bias listeners from hearing Black women's voices and acknowledging their civic and political engagement (Clayman Institute for Gender Research 2020; Musto 2020). In the following, we use a trap feminist framework to analyze how and why the voice of Cardi B is consistently marginalized in US politics.

Cardi B's Trap Feminist Political Background

Cardi B has been vocal about her upbringing as a teenager in the Bronx, where she was affiliated with a gang and learned to survive through low-paying jobs and "hustling" (Cardi B Official n.d.). She attended Renaissance High School for Musical Theater and Technology, where she took an Advanced Placement (AP) government class and received a high score on the AP exam (Frazier 2019). At 19, Cardi began stripping to provide herself with the financial means to get out of an abusive relationship and enroll in college. She attended classes at Borough of Manhattan Community College but dropped out before finishing her degree (Cardi B Official n.d.).

Cardi's love of politics has remained central in her life. She stays informed on political and social issues and engages her fans in discussions of these issues—all of which constitute forms of trap feminist political engagement. Since her rise to fame, Cardi has gained access to higher circles of power and has engaged with politics more directly; she has interviewed politicians at the national and state level, engaged in acts of protest surrounding social issues, and encouraged her fans to vote.

Despite Cardi's wealth and fame, she is frequently misunderstood and stigmatized due, in part, to assumptions about her intelligence. This stigmatization is often rooted in the fact that she grew up in a poor neighborhood and then became a stripper. As shown in Chapter 4, Cardi's intellect is often questioned despite (and, we would argue, because of) her bilingualism, while her performance of a diasporic Blackness is misunderstood and used to exclude her from Blackness in the United States. Cardi is also an Afro-Latina millennial[11] which, as we show later, means her political contributions, however deeply informed, are often undervalued, devalued, or ignored.

Another way that Cardi B is stigmatized while expressing her political views is evident in how some focus on her body or sexuality before considering her thoughts. For example, in a 2018 GQ profile interview, Cardi demonstrates her political acumen by teaching the interviewer about Franklin Delano Roosevelt and other presidents; meanwhile, the interviewer starts the article by intently focusing on Cardi's physical appearance:

> With the aid of cutting-edge Millennium science, in the form of orbicular breast implants and illegal buttocks injections, America's sudden

favorite rapper, Cardi B, has built her body for optimal viewing at medium-to-long-distance range. . . . The hills and slopes of her body are so captivating that you might not even notice the delicate beauty of her countenance until it's staring at you head-on from across a dimly lit restaurant booth while you wait to discover what it is that Cardi loves.

(Weaver 2018)

While Cardi is not shy about flaunting her body to her audiences, the beginning of that article shows us that everything that comes out of Cardi B's mouth, no matter how politically savvy or smart, is filtered through gendered, racialized, and classed lenses that position women like her as outside of the norm.

In the following, we unpack Cardi's political engagement by examining four examples of her trap feminist politics: (1) activism and advocacy through uplifting social justice causes; (2) institutional politics by engaging with Democrats to get out the vote and confronting conservative politicians and pundits online; and (3) community work and volunteering by supporting Black women in and beyond the music industry. Using a trap feminist framework to analyze Black women's civic and political engagement helps us shine a light on the everyday political acts of Black women at the margins, as well as the all-too-often dismissal of those political actions by the powers that be.

Cardi B Elevates Social Justice Causes

Cardi B has used her celebrity status and platform to engage in activism and advocacy through uplifting social justice causes—she has interviewed politicians and urged her fans to learn about electoral politics and vote on issues that impact marginalized people, including immigrant rights, Black Lives Matter, the fight against police brutality, economic equality, and gender equality. These social issues are not exhaustive, but they do provide a brief overview of Cardi's politics in relation to her lived experiences as a hood chick, a Black woman, a daughter of immigrants, and a trap feminist.

Immigration Rights

Cardi B has been outspoken about immigrant rights since she took to IG in 2015 to speak about the perils of downplaying the power of Donald Trump as a presidential candidate. Speaking from her bedroom, with a bob-style wig with bangs (and before she got a bag and fixed her teeth), Cardi states, "Y'all love fucking foreign bitches—them hoes gonna get deported if Trump is president, hoe. How about that?" (Wolfson 2019). Cardi uses humor to encourage her fans to vote while also critiquing Black patriarchal notions of desirability that present "foreign" or "exotic" women as status symbols for male rappers (G 2016). Cardi's lived experiences as the daughter of immigrants, paired with her experiences as an Afro-Latina who has likely been exoticized herself, present a trap feminist ethos of centering marginalized women (in this case, immigrant women) while decentering and critiquing the male gaze (Bowen 2021).

Cardi's advocacy for immigrant rights is also evident in her conversations with politicians. In a 2019 conversation with senator and presidential-hopeful Bernie Sanders, Cardi asked the politician about immigration and DREAMers,[12] saying,

> There's a lot going on when it comes to the immigrants. It's a very tough situation. I met a fan in one of my concerts and he was telling me how he's a DREAMer and he was approved by DACA and everything, and now he have to get deported to Mexico, to a country that he don't know nothing about. What are we gonna do when it comes to the DREAMers in this country?
>
> *(Sanders 2019)*

In her question to Sanders, Cardi grounds her truth in lived experiences—she personalizes her question by mentioning a fan she met at a concert who received DACA but was now facing deportation. Her personal storytelling and the fact that she herself has two parents who had to contend with the US immigration system reflect the Black feminist and trap feminist arguments that lived experiences are central to Black women's assessments of truth or epistemology (Bowen 2021; Collins 1989). Cardi also uses an appeal to empathy to present her concerns about immigration during the interview. Her centering of emotional narratives when discussing immigrants' rights highlights one of the four main tenets of Black feminist thought: an ethic of care (Collins 1989). Espousing an ethic of care means that Black women see emotions and empathy as crucial to validating what counts as truth. This Black feminist ethic of care runs counter to dominant (usually rich, white, male) approaches to truth validation, which tend to frame emotions as "irrational" and "illogical," when, in reality, they are centering and uplifting our communities.

Black Lives Matter and #SayHerName

In the tradition of Black women committed to speaking out, Cardi B's trap feminist politics have included her outspoken fight against anti-Black state violence through the #BlackLivesMatter and #SayHerName movements.

Her opposition to police brutality turned into direct action in late 2019, when she refused an invitation to perform at the 2020 NFL Super Bowl Halftime Show.[13] Cardi publicly stood in solidarity with Colin Kaepernick in his kneeling protest against police brutality,[14] stating "I got to sacrifice a lot of money to perform. But there's a man who sacrificed his job for us, so we got to stand behind him" (Associated Press 2019).

Trap feminism helps us understand Cardi's activism against police brutality, given she centers her lived experiences in the hood as a source of knowledge and impetus for activism. Cardi grew up as a poor Black Latina in the Bronx, where she was likely exposed to over-policing and anti-Black police violence (Forman 2002:43). Further, she is married to rapper Offset, a Black man who has been incarcerated (Singh 2020). Hence, her concerns about police brutality stem not only from the popularity of the Black Lives Matter Movement but also from her own lived experiences with policing and the criminal justice system.

In 2020, Cardi B continued advocating for racial justice by taking a stand against police brutality in the wake of the murder of Breonna Taylor, a 26-year-old EMT who was killed by police during a no-knock warrant at her home in Louisville, Kentucky. After learning about Taylor's death, gun control advocate Tamika Mallory arranged a phone call between Breonna Taylor's mother, Tamika Palmer, and notable celebrities including Cardi B (Carter 2020). Shortly after the phone call, Cardi changed her profile picture to the name "Breonna Taylor." She then joined several other women celebrities in posting a video asking, "Do you know what happened to Breonna Taylor?" Each video included a brief introduction from the celebrity, followed by a call for action from Breonna's mother.[15] Cardi added a personalized call to action when she posted the video on her page, stating in the caption, "This is why we gotta keep fighting. Breonna Taylor was one year younger then me. Pose, dress, live her life how we do! Imagine if this happens to YOUR FRIEND, YOUR SISTER" (IG; @iamcardib; 06/10/2020).

By conveying a sense of sisterhood and similarity between herself and Breonna Taylor, Cardi's activism reflects her trap feminist politics. Trap feminism is attuned to the ways that poor Black women are uniquely marginalized due to the intersecting forms of oppression they face. Specifically, Cardi's statements about the similarities between her and Taylor represent the trap feminist ethos of centralizing lived experiences and sisterhood when calling for social change. Rather than distancing herself from these issues as she became richer, Cardi has continued to engender empathy and inspire action against police brutality by standing in unity with other Black activists.

Cardi B's Institutional Politics

Vote for Daddy Bernie

Like the Black women activists before her, Cardi B participates in institutional politics by speaking out for those who share her social position, including Black women from the trap, while also garnering the interest and support of those in positions of power. In the run-up to the 2016 Democratic Presidential Primary, Cardi voiced her preference for Senator Bernie Sanders over other democratic hopefuls by posting a video to[16] IG page complimenting Sanders and urging her followers to "vote for daddy Bernie, bitch!" (Stewart 2019). Two years later, in 2018, Sanders retweeted a post from the nonprofit organization Social Security Works that included a photo of Cardi with the following quote from her GQ interview, "FDR is the real 'Make America Great' president because if it weren't for him, older Americans wouldn't even get Social Security" (Twitter; @SSWorks; 04/09/2018). In addition to his retweet, Sanders said, "Cardi B is right. If we are really going to make America great, we need to strengthen Social Security so that seniors are able to retire with the dignity they deserve" (Twitter; @SenSanders; 04/18/2018).[17]

Cardi's interactions with Bernie Sanders have often involved each of them legitimizing the other to their respective audiences. In the lead up to the 2020 Democratic Presidential Primary, Cardi scheduled an in-person interview with Bernie, who was again a presidential hopeful. Prior to their meeting, Cardi asked her social media followers, "If you had the opportunity to have a question answered by a democratic candidate, what would it be?" From these, she picked the most popular questions to ask Bernie during their interview. By gathering questions, Cardi was sharing her direct access to politicians with her fan base—most of the people posing questions would not have this access without Cardi's political reach. Additionally, the questions from her followers centralized their life experiences and attempted to evoke empathy in both the politician and the listeners of the interview (see the previous example of Cardi asking Bernie about DREAMers).

The rapper and senator finally met in person on July 29, 2019, in Detroit, Michigan at the Black-owned salon TEN Nail Bar. Cardi is known for her long, detailed full sets; speaking in the nail salon meant that Bernie, a white male, was brought into a Black-woman-owned space familiar to Cardi. Cardi and Bernie discussed a myriad of issues, including Sanders's plans to cancel student debt, address climate change, and raise the minimum wage (Grayer 2019). Following the meeting, Cardi emphasized the importance of political education and encouraged young people, who were Sanders's biggest base of support, to vote for the candidate during the primaries. She did this by posting a photo[18] of her speaking with Bernie to her social media pages and including the following caption:

> Not me, US. Thank you, Senator Bernie Sanders for sitting with me and sharing your plans on how you will change this country. . . . Stay tuned to see how he will fight for economic, racial, and social justice for all. Together, let's build a movement of young people to transform this country. LETS LEARN OUR CANDIDATES!
>
> *(IG; @iamcardib; 07/29/2019)*

Cardi's meeting with Sanders and her subsequent comments showed her fans that Black women, and in particular hood chicks, are an integral part of the political process. Prior to meeting Cardi, Sanders emphasized this very point, saying, "Cardi B is deeply concerned about what's happening in the country. She knows what it's like to live in poverty and struggle, and it would be great for her to bring that experience to politics" (TMZ 2020). While some may praise the fact that Sanders worked to legitimize Cardi's voice, we need to remember that Cardi B knows and owns her own political power. As a well-known rapper and a star who was voicing the concerns of young and marginalized people, Cardi legitimized Sanders's perspectives to his biggest voting bloc.

Later, in April 2020, Cardi B met virtually with Bernie Sanders just months into the Coronavirus pandemic. She opened the conversation by expressing her disappointment with Bernie's primary concession to Joe Biden. After that, Cardi demonstrated her political commitment by stating that she would vote for Biden, "because I cannot see . . . the next step of America being ran by number 45" (Corcoran 2020). She went on to clarify her political concerns, saying, "I think we're going to enter a recession. . . . So many people are unemployed right now. And I feel like . . . not everybody is going to get their job back when America opens back up." Here, Cardi is demonstrating a trap feminist political commitment to voice the concerns of the marginalized. By directly voicing these concerns to elected officials, Cardi is serving as a bridge between the powers that be and her community. Further, by discussing economic inequality and poverty, Cardi is signaling her concern with the economic well-being of people who are struggling, a concern tied back to her lived experiences growing up poor in the Bronx.

Engaging with Joe Biden

Cardi continued to get out the vote in 2020 despite Sanders exiting the race. In August 2020, just months before the presidential election, and immediately after the release of her song "WAP" with Megan Thee Stallion, Cardi met virtually with Joe Biden in a conversation mediated by *ELLE Magazine* (ELLE 2020). In her passionate opening remarks, Cardi reiterated her desire to get Trump out of office while being frank with Biden. Her demeanor reflected what many in the United States were feeling at the time, frustration and confusion at the handling of the pandemic. She used the rest of her opening statements to talk about her desire for free universal health care, free college education, and an end to anti-Black police brutality. This interview highlights how women from the trap undoubtedly engage with the political process when provided the space to do so. Cardi's direct engagement with prominent politicians shows how trap feminists contribute a critical standpoint and knowledge base; when marginalized Black women speak on political issues, their ideas and suggestions oftentimes benefit everyone. As Anna Julia Cooper wrote, "Only the BLACK WOMAN can say 'when and where I enter, in the quiet, undisputed dignity of my womanhood, without violence and without suing or special patronage, then and there the whole Negro race enters with me'" (Cooper [1892] 1988:31).

Engaging with Conservatives

In addition to being a supporter of a self-proclaimed democratic socialist— Bernie Sanders—and a centrist Democrat—Joe Biden, Cardi B has also been openly critical of right-wing politicians and their policies. This is most notable when we look at Cardi's commentary about Donald Trump. Even before the 2016 election, Cardi posted a cautionary video to her IG page, where she warns her followers about the perils of manifesting Trump's election by "visioning it" and "gassin' it" (Wolfson 2019).

Following the 2016 election, Cardi made periodic comments about Trump's policies and actions on social media, including criticism of the government shutdown spanning from December 2018 to January 2019 that we discussed in the introduction of this chapter. The video did not only resonate with democrats—conservatives challenged Cardi's comments about the shutdown and critiques of Donald Trump. In a reply to Cardi four days after she posted her video, conservative commentator Tomi Lahren stated, "Looks like @iamcardib is the latest genius political mind to endorse the Democrats. HA! Keep it up, guys. #MAGA2020." Cardi's response to Lahren was both concise and memorable: "Leave me alone. I will dog walk you." The exchange didn't end there, though. Lahren replied, "I'm sure you would. Still doesn't make your political rambling any less moronic. #BuildThatWall." At this point, it became clear that Lahren's argument was not simply about a disagreement with Cardi on policy matters but rather that Tomi viewed Cardi as uneducated and stupid. Cardi, also not one to hold her tongue, replied at length, saying,

> You're so blinded with racism that you don't even realize the decisions the president you for is destroying the country you claim to love so much. You are a perfect example on no matter how educated or smart you think you are you still a SHEEP!
>
> *(Wolfson 2019)*

Tomi's attempt to ridicule Cardi was hypocritical if we look at her support of the 45th president, who himself constantly misspelled words on Twitter and once stated that he "loves the uneducated" (Fares and Cherelus 2016). It is important to recognize that Lahren's comments devalue the views of a Black Latina who grew up marginalized in numerous ways: racially, economically, and based on her gender, to start. Therefore, the repercussions of this exchange go further than Cardi or Tomi. The back-and-forth negatively impacts all hood chicks seeking to engage with politics in this country while sending a clear message that if you do not fit the mold of a white, middle- or upper-class politician, you will be policed and ridiculed for your civic and political engagement.

Like Tomi, other conservative pundits have pushed back against Cardi's trap feminist politics by ridiculing her for her supposed lack of intellect, leaning on the idea that Black women can't be civically and politically engaged if they don't use the "correct" language. For example, Cardi mentioned her desire to engage in institutional politics through a run for congress in a January 2020 tweet, saying, "I do feel like if I go back to school and focus up I can be part of Congress" (Twitter; @iamcardib; 01/13/2020). One of the top comments underneath this post was from Mindy Robinson, a Trump supporter and conservative pundit, who used the opportunity to "correct" Cardi's grammar and syntax. In the comment, Robinson posts a photo of the tweet with corrections in red. The corrected tweet reads

> I felt like if I went back to school and really focused I could get voted into Congress. I have so many ideas that make sense [Robinson adds "(I doubt)" under this]. I just need a couple of years of school and I can shake the table [Robinson adds "(You need more than that.)" next to the sentence].

In addition to the screenshot of the "corrected" tweet, Robinson added the following comment: "You're going to need more school than that [white 'okay sign' emoji]. Your spaces are off too . . . but hey, how can we hold you accountable for kindergarten level sh*t, am I right?" (Twitter, @iheart-mindy, 01/13/2020).

This conservative commenter's post was a clear attempt to mock Cardi. (The corrections were not grammatically correct, though, which led many to joke about the pundit's attempt to put Cardi "in her place.") This form of conservative backlash is rooted in white supremacist thinking that exalts "standard" English as the norm while devaluing Black Vernacular English and the linguistic practices of Spanish–English bilingual speakers (Flores and Rosa 2015). In line with trap feminist politics, we argue that Cardi shouldn't have to conform to white, middle- and upper-class standards of speech or behavior to take part in the US political process.

The deliberate exclusion of poor Black women from the political process is rooted in what Ange-Marie Hancock calls a "politics of disgust." According to Hancock,

> A politics of disgust is first marked by traditional signposts of inequality; for example, members of marginal groups, even when granted the power of speech, find their voices devalued or disrespected, increasing their isolation and alienation from the public sphere.
>
> *(Hancock 2004:4)*

Despite Cardi being a now-wealthy artist, and despite Twitter being a pseudo-democratic platform where marginalized voices can be amplified, there are still ways in which the powerful can and do promote the alienation of Black women seeking to voice our political views.

Cardi B Supports Black Women by Building Community

In addition to publicly and passionately advocating against police brutality and economic injustice, and in favor of immigrant rights, Cardi B's trap feminist politics are also evident in her support of women and queer people in her artistry and within the music industry. Black women in Hip Hop are often pitted against each other in ways that strain attempts at feminist solidarity (Richardson 2021). Cardi is not immune to these conflicts, as shown by our discussion of her public beef with Nicki Minaj in Chapter 2. That said, Cardi is also known for "putting other women on." One example of putting other women on includes Cardi's high-profile collaborations with Black women artists, including Normani on "Wild One" and Megan Thee Stallion on "WAP." The videos for these two singles center the Black women artists along with other women—in fact, they almost entirely exclude men (see Chapter 1 for a deeper discussion of WAP).

Cardi B has also shown her commitment to trap feminist politics by publicly and privately supporting fellow Black women artists as sisters and not just as business partners. Essential to trap feminist politics is ensuring that Black women support each other through our relationships, both professional and personal, which includes volunteering our time to speak up and supporting one another. Yet Cardi does this by still espousing a spirit of hustling and encouraging her peers to play the Hip Hop game smartly. For example, Cardi showed her support of R&B singer Summer Walker in the artist's song "Bitter." At the end of the song, which deals with the pain of having her personal issues exposed on social media and tabloid sites like the ShadeRoom, Summer includes what sounds like a voicemail from Cardi B:

> Well, Summer Walker, you know, I been seeing . . . all the bullshit that's been going on with you today and, I don't know if the rumors are true. I don't know, I don't care, it's not my business. But if it is true, don't let bitches . . . feel like they have a one up by destroying your moment by fucking telling your business to the world. . . . And put that shit in your music and make money off it in your music. Fuck these hoes!

Cardi B encourages Summer to not retaliate against her haters in a spiteful way but rather to respond through her music in a way that will positively build her platform as an artist. Cardi's message to Summer Walker reflects a trap feminist politics that center Black sisterhood—a sisterhood that is emotionally supportive while staying attuned to the realities of the hustle. The message also shows Cardi's trap feminist politics on the issue of gender equality, given that Black women have to care for each other both emotionally and financially due to the many social structures in place that keep them from prospering. This trap feminist orientation to gender equality aligns with the literature in sociology that shows how Black women in the United States are especially economically vulnerable. Sociological studies on gender and race inequalities show that Black women with a high school degree earn a median hourly wage that is 68% as much as that received by white men. These income inequalities persist even with a college degree—Black women with a college degree still earn a median hourly wage that is 68% the hourly wage of white men. Therefore, Cardi's trap feminist politics show her support for Black women given the very real economic barriers we face.

Conclusion

Cardi B's involvement in civic and political engagement started in her pre-Bodak Yellow days, when she would take to IG to voice her opinions on "Daddy Bernie" and Donald Trump. Since her rise to fame, Cardi has been even more politically engaged. She has encouraged her followers to vote and stay informed on political and social issues, met with politicians at the national and state level, and boycotted the NFL to support Colin Kaepernick's protests against police brutality, all while being unapologetically herself. Cardi detailed her own civic and political engagement in 2020, stating, "I've been informing y'all about y'all's senators. I've been informing y'all about districts. Midterm elections. Using my own money to meet up with these candidates" (IG; @iamcardib; 11/18/2020). That said, Cardi's engagement with politics shows the barriers Black women, and especially those from the hood, face when they attempt to enter the US political sphere. By highlighting Cardi's trap feminist politics and the public's positive and negative responses to it, we uncover the need for a more inclusive democracy.

Despite the negative reactions to her civic and political engagement, Cardi B has continued to speak truth to those in power. As she said recently, "Even when y'all's crying like, 'But she don't represent us!' Yes I do . . . I represent America. I wanted a change, and that's exactly what the fuck I did" (IG; @iamcardib; 11/18/2020). In short, Cardi B insists that she represents the country because hood Black chicks are also representative of the United States.

Cardi B's civic and political engagement and the negative responses to it reflect the need to protect and celebrate trap feminists' political voices. To conclude, we share a quote from Black feminist sociologist, Patricia Hill Collins, to drive home that point:

> When Black women choose to value those aspects of Afro-American womanhood that are stereotyped, ridiculed, and maligned in academic scholarship and the popular media, they are actually questioning some of the basic ideas used to control dominated groups in general. It is one thing to counsel Afro-American women to resist the Sapphire stereotype by altering their behavior to become meek, docile, and stereotypically "feminine." It is quite another to advise Black women to embrace their assertiveness, to value their sassiness, and to continue to use these qualities to survive in and transcend the harsh environments that circumscribe so many Black women's lives.
>
> *(Collins 1986:17)*

Notes

1

   Any person who shall knowingly and willingly obstruct, hinder, or prevent such claimant, his agent or attorney, or any person or persons lawfully assisting him, her, or them, from arresting such a fugitive from service or labor, either with or aforesaid; or shall to rescue, such fugitive or labor, or from the custody of, his or her agent or attorney or other persons or persons lawfully assisting as aforesaid, when so arrested, pursuant to the authority herein given and declared; or shall aid, abet, or assist such person, so owing service or labor as aforesaid, directly or indirectly, to escape from such claimant, his agent or attorney, or other person or persons legally authorized as aforesaid; or shall harbor or conceal such fugitive, so as to prevent the discovery and arrest of such person, after notice or knowledge of the fact that such person was a fugitive from service or labor as aforesaid, shall, for either of said offences, be subject to a fine not exceeding one thousand dollars, and imprisonment not exceeding six months, by indictment and conviction before the District Court of the United States for the district in which such offence may have been committed, or before the proper court of criminal jurisdiction, if committed within any one of the organized Territories of the United States; and shall moreover forfeit and pay, by way of civil damages to the party injured by such illegal conduct, the sum of one thousand dollars for each fugitive so lost as aforesaid, to be recovered by action of debt in any of the District or Territorial Courts aforesaid, within whose jurisdiction the said offence may have been committed.

(Fugitive Slave Law 1850)

2 For example, scholars often center the "Big Six" leaders of the March on Washington for Jobs and Freedom in 1963, which included Martin Luther King Jr. (Southern Christian Leadership Conference), James Farmer (Congress of Racial Equality), John Lewis (Student Nonviolent Coordinating Committee), A. Philip Randolph (Brotherhood of Sleeping Car Porters), Roy Wilkins (NAACP), and Whitney M. Young Jr (National Urban League).
3 See Keeanga-Yamahtta Taylor (2016), Tamika Mallory (2021), Stacey Abrams (2020), and Black Lives Matter activists (Cullors and Bandele 2020).
4 For more on these debates, see Leibovich (2008).
5

No voting qualification or prerequisite to voting, or standard, practice, or procedure shall be imposed or applied by any State or political subdivision to deny or abridge the right of any citizen of the United States to vote on account of race or color.

(Voting Rights Act 1965)

6 As of October 2023, under much criticism, Laphonza R. Butler was appointed to replace a vacant senate seat for California.
7 Symbolizing the last words of Eric Garner who was murdered by police in New York City in August 2014.
8 Notably, Castile was from and died in Minnesota.
9 https://time.com/5849780/maya-moore-george-floyd-drew-brees/.
10 Mass media often depicts Black women stereotypically by using "controlling images" such as the Mammy, Sapphire, Jezebel, and Welfare Queen (Collins 1991; Harris-Perry 2011). The mammy is the stereotypical image of a black maid and mother figure—popularized in the 1939 film *Gone with the Wind*—who is submissive and nonsexual (as we unpack in Chapter 5). The Sapphire is a caricature of a sassy, loud, violent, and angry Black woman. The Jezebel stereotypically signifies a hypersexual Black woman. Finally, the Welfare Queen, also referenced in Chapter 5, is seen as a Black woman who exploits social welfare programs for her own gain.

11 For more discussions about the assumptions we make about millennials, please see Allen (2019a, 2019b), Allen et al. (2020), Milkman (2017), Ng and Johnson (2015), Pew Research Center (2010).

12 The Development, Relief, and Education for Alien Minors (DREAM) Act, first introduced in 2001, aims to permanently protect immigrants who came to the United States as children from deportation while offering them a pathway to U.S. citizenship. The Act's temporary counterpart, known as the Deferred Action for Childhood Arrivals (DACA), has provided administrative protection for this group of immigrants.

13 After numerous declined invitations from Black artists including Cardi B, Beyonce, and Jay Z, the 2019 Super Bowl Halftime Show was eventually performed by Maroon 5, with two Black musical guests, Big Boi (from Outkast) and Travis Scott, both of whom were critiqued for their decision to join the show.

14 Colin Kaepernick, a former NFL player for the San Francisco '49ers, started his silent protest in August 2016 by kneeling during the national anthem prior to every game (Boren 2020). His kneeling was a form of protest against police brutality and racial injustice in the country. After a mix of praise and critiques for his actions, Kaepernick has not been signed since that NFL season ended in January 2017.

15 In the video, Tamika Palmer states,

> Three officers on the Louisville Metro Police Department used a battering ram to knock down her door. They fired 22 times. Eight of those bullets landed in the body of the most essential worker I will ever know. Bre was murdered by the Louisville Metro Police Department, and after they killed her, they asked me if she had any enemies.
> (https://thegrio.com/2020/06/10/women-hollywood-breonna-taylor/)

16 Cardi B previously deleted her Instagram account that included this video following criticism (Nunez 2018), therefore this video is no longer there. At the time of writing, she has returned to Instagram, but these posts were not retrieved.

17 Here we can see the power of institutional forces aligned with trap feminism; Social Security works, a well-funded nonprofit and Senator/presidential candidate Bernie Sanders centered an Afro-Latina rapper's voice in politics, providing Cardi B an opportunity to push further.

18 Photo source: Instagram, @iamcardib; 7/29/2019 (www.instagram.com/p/B0h WEaKAa1x/?utm_source=ig_web_copy_link&igsh=MzRlODBiNWFlZA==).

CONCLUSION

Cardi B was told that strippers could not be rappers. She was told that reality TV stars would not have long careers. She was told that instigating a conflict at New York Fashion Week would have her banned from elite events for years to come. She was told she wasn't Black enough. She was told she had ruined her one and only chance of being successful by getting pregnant while (seemingly) unwed. She was told that being too opinionated or political would alienate her audience. In sum, she was told she didn't know enough to have an opinion on her life experiences or to make decisions for herself. As you have read throughout the chapters of this book, none of the things she was told were true. She continues to defy these assumptions and the barriers placed in front of her.

We Trusted Cardi B: A Summary and Look Forward

The Sociology of Cardi B represents the sociology of women like us: Black women and girls who defy narrow definitions of Blackness, womanhood, and Black womanhood. More specifically, it represents an expansion of the concept of trap feminism—defined as a feminism that celebrates and centers the self-defined womanhood of Black women in and adjacent to the trap (Bowen 2021; Miles 2020). The concept represents the ghetto girls, hood chicks, and ratchet women who are often told that who we are is a hindrance to who we want to become or even who we "should" be—yet we defy these beliefs. We persist. We live. We work hard to hold on to our stories and authenticity, because we must truly listen to ourselves to survive and thrive.

DOI: 10.4324/9781003184980-8

This book reminds us that we need to "Trust Black Women." This phrase is not about trusting *solely* Black women but to believe Black women when we tell our stories. Furthermore, the phrase is not about trusting *solely* "acceptable" Black women. With this book, we wanted the reader to recognize the lessons we can all learn from trusting, listening, and *hearing* Black women who are not always heard. We wanted to uplift the art and lesson of paying closer attention to society through the experiences of Black women, and more specifically, centering Black women in and adjacent to the trap. In exploring sociological concepts, we trusted one particular Black woman to guide us, Cardi B.

In each of the book's chapters, we pair the lens of trap feminism with examples from Cardi B's life and work to help readers understand why society does not listen to ghetto girls. By paying attention to narratives about her and being attentive to her words and actions, we found that Cardi's artistry and public-facing stories helped us understand the complicated structures and personal dynamics underlying her choices and other people's responses to her choices. Chapters 1 through 4 provided foundational understandings of the themes of feminism, the white gaze, respectability, and race and ethnicity, while Chapters 5 and 6 applied our understanding of those themes to engage with the topics of motherhood and civic and political engagement. As authors, we often discussed how public conversations around these topics—beyond the life and work of Cardi B—were closely aligned with the issues we covered in this book. We shared with one another countless examples of Black women from the trap, and those within their orbit, defying the odds and embodying trap feminism. In the following, we extend our summaries of the book's chapters and provide a starting place for other applications of the lessons offered by *The Sociology of Cardi B*.

In Chapter 1, we trusted Cardi's belief in herself. With over a century of literature centering Black feminism, the definition of this concept continues to expand as Black women's experiences evolve in relation to structural changes related to race, class, and gender. With this expansion, there continue to be tensions about what a Black feminist looks like and can be. Similar to the expansion of nuanced definitions of Black feminism, there continue to be questions on who a true Hip Hop artist is and what they look like. Black women continue to fight for their voices to rightfully be seen as integral to Hip Hop since the beginning of the genre over 50 years ago. With the emergence of "trap" culture existing in the public imagination within the last decade, we have also encountered the following questions in the public domain: What do Black women from the trap bring to society? What can we learn from the stories they tell? In exploring these questions and bringing Black feminism, Hip Hop, and trap together, Chapter 1 served as a cornerstone for the rest of the book. We outlined how Cardi B practices trap feminism by disrupting gendered norms, expanding the voices of many silenced women, and centering authenticity.

In Chapter 2, we trusted Cardi B's insistence to exist beyond and in spite of the white gaze. Many people were concerned that her clash with another Hip Hop artist at New York Fashion Week would be the end of her due to (white) public perceptions of the event, Cardi B persisted anyway. While Black women in the United States often struggle with how to be authentic in the face of white surveillance and behavioral norms, Cardi B continued to be herself and, as of 2023, has remained successful. This is evident in her collaborations with Patti Labelle, McDonalds, Pepsi, Reebok, and Whip Shots; a Facebook series called Cardi Tries; and a Nickelodeon cartoon character Sharky B in Baby Shark's Big Show.

Extending on Chapter 1 and Chapter 2, we considered other arenas in which Black women excelled despite consistent media conversations about why they were not worthy of success and praise. Even with trailblazers like Cardi B in Hip Hop and the Williams sisters in sports,[1] young Black women at the height of their careers are often challenged by these media portrayals.

As we wrote, we noticed the parallels of the conversations in this book with the responses to Black women athletes Flau'Jae Johnson,[2] Angel Reese, and Sha'Carri Richardson. These are women who would be classified as ghetto girls given their long lashes, nails, hair, and how they communicate. Despite the media's criticisms, they continue to trust themselves and resist outside perceptions (Brown 2023). For example, Sha'Carri Richardson was told that she would never be successful because she chose to run with long nails and bright red hair (Hill 2023). Commentators doubted her ability to be successful despite her appearance reminding many watchers of a 1980s US Olympic athlete with long hair and nails—Florence Griffith Joyner (FloJo)—the 1988 women's world record setter for the 100-meter and 200-meter. In the face of these doubts by others, Sha'Carri qualified for the 2020 Summer Olympics; however, she was disqualified when she was found to have used the common (and legal in many states) recreational drug of marijuana. Commentators felt that they were "proven right," that she was a woman with poor morals and that she would never be successful. Furthermore, they believed that she had ruined her one and only chance to be successful. Sha'Carri spoke up for herself and stayed authentic to who she was, noting that her treatment was different from that given to other athletes with drug use (Chappell 2022). In 2023, she defied the public's assumptions, trusted herself, and chose to resist by existing beyond the white gaze. She qualified for the 2023 World Athletics Championships, winning gold in the 100-meter race (Minsberg 2023). The experiences of ghetto girls in sports are emblematic of how trap feminism manifests beyond Hip Hop and offers one of many avenues through which to apply the findings of *The Sociology of Cardi B*.

In Chapter 3, we trusted Cardi B's lyrics to tell a story. In her debut album (and her only album to date as of December 2023), we found that Cardi's lyrics discussed financial success, sexual behavior, negative experiences with romantic relationships, and how the word "bitch" can be empowering and degrading at the same time. While we use Cardi's lyrics in her first album to illustrate this point, these themes appear time and again in Hip Hop across Cardi's work and that of a multitude of Black women artists. Themes of financial success appear in songs like Cardi's "Money" and Megan Thee Stallion's "Cash Shit"; negative experiences in relationships are discussed in GloRilla's "No More Love"; open sexual behavior is evident in Nicki Minaj's "Freaky Girl," Latto's "Big Energy" and the City Girls' "Twerk"; and both positive and negative uses of the word bitch can be found in Saweetie and Doja Cat's "Best Friend." In further extending Chapter 3, other themes in Black women's lyrics can be found and discussed as well. For example, the themes of confidence, joy, and being free of inhibitions can be found in Cardi's "Up," GloRilla's "FNF (Fuck Nigga Free)," Flo Milli's "Conceited," and Flyanna Boss's "You Wish."

Taken as a whole, the lyrics that Black women trap and Hip Hop artists bring forth rest within a trap feminist framework that encourages nuanced personhood and a rejection of gendered expectations. These decisions are not made without consequence, as the many women who perform (and the many women who enjoy) these lyrics have their morals and values questioned and their autonomy denied. They are accused of centering the male gaze when in many cases men are virtually absent from the underlying messages of their songs and the images accompanying them (See Cardi B's music videos for "Money" or "Bongos" for examples). However, when we trust Black women to tell their own stories in their own voices, we learn more about the multifacetedness of their existence. In choosing the lyrics that they want, Black women artists help to present a new node of feminism, trap feminism, in which they are not shy about discussing all aspects of their lives.

In Chapter 4, we trusted Cardi to understand her own racial and ethnic identities. Conversations around the African Diaspora and about global Blackness continue to be confronted with definitional dilemmas around who "counts" as Black. Throughout Chapter 4, we share details on the long history of enslavement in the Americas and show how and why there continues to be a discussion around who "owns" Blackness in the United States and abroad. As we discussed this chapter among ourselves, we were confronted with our own histories and relationships to diasporic Black-ness, especially as it related to the geographical contexts where we were raised. It is undeniable that the "one drop rule" and visual expressions of Blackness impact how individuals self-identify and their connection to Black people and Black culture (including Hip Hop). Cardi B is not by her-self as we see the expansion of public discussions of Afro-Latinidad in the public and Hip Hop specifically. Hip Hop artist Amara La Negra, with her dark skin, large afro, and undeniable dedication to both her Blackness and Dominican identity, is an example of a Black Latina embracing all aspects of her racial and ethnic identities, despite the public attempting to place her in a box (Meraji and Richmond 2018). There is no-one-size-fits-all when we discuss the boundaries of Blackness. Cardi B consistently identifies as Caribbean, Black, and Latina, despite continued confusion around these identities. Her interviews and openness help to break down the false barri-ers we often place in defining "the" Black experience.

In Chapter 5, we trusted Cardi to recognize when motherhood was appropriate for her. The criticisms regarding when she got pregnant, who she got pregnant by, and how she behaved while pregnant all demonstrate the historical anti-Black and patriarchal forces that try to limit Black women's personal choices. Since the initial backlash to her first pregnancy, Cardi has birthed a son named Wave and gone on to show glimpses of her motherhood on her social media platforms. She has posted videos where she's taking her children to school, feeding them, playing with them, dis-ciplining them, and lavishing them with the birthday parties and holidays that she never received as a child. Cardi has incorporated motherhood in her public image as well, such as when she had her children and stepchil-dren join her and her husband on the cover of *Essence Magazine* (Victorian 2022), or when she, Offset, Kulture, and Wave did voiceover work for an episode of the children's show Baby Shark. More than that, Cardi has dem-onstrated how her identity as a sexually liberated woman does not clash with her ability to mother.

Other Black women in the public eye have also faced similar criticism for their motherhood choices. Lauryn Hill mentions similar criticism in her song "To Zion" on the Miseducation of Lauryn Hill, released in 1998. Recently, Keke Palmer became the topic of scrutiny after her partner took to social media writing, "It's the outfit tho . . . you a mom" in an attempt to publicly shame her for wearing a sheer dress to a concert in Las Vegas after having her son. He went on to talk about "standards and morals," using her motherhood as reasons for why her dress was inappropriate. Pop icon Rihanna was critiqued for giving birth to her sons back-to-back while unwed and was accused of emasculating her partner, rapper A$AP Rocky, when posing for *British Vogue* in March 2023 (Nast 2023) where he held their baby while walking behind her. Up-and-coming rapper Sexxy Red (who embodies the trap in her aesthetic, lyrics, and way of talking) has been criticized for dressing too provocatively and twerking in a bikini while pregnant during her performances (Aniftos 2023). Again and again we see examples of Black women having their motherhood policed in public, a pattern that is not only reserved for celebrities but also applies to all Black mothers in our society. As mentioned in Chapter 2, the white and male gaze is always looming, always attempting to shape Black women's existence. A trap feminist perspective helps us see how women's choices to take on motherhood while expressing their sexuality and maintaining their careers and hustles pushes against the constraints of white normative models of mothering. Trap feminism reminds us that Black women have always had to balance mothering and working and have always had to champion their rights to own their sexuality and reproductive choices.

Lastly, in Chapter 6, we trusted Cardi B to understand the nuances of American political and civic engagement. We defined trap feminist politics as civic and political engagement that both emerges from and centers the lived experiences of hood chicks. In defining this concept, we emphasized that trap feminist politics encompass activism and advocating for social change; institutional politics; and community work and volunteering. In selecting examples for Chapter 6 we found numerous stories of Cardi B getting involved in trap feminist politics on the local and national level that we did not have the space to include. In addition to Cardi's thoughts about health care that we mentioned in the chapter, Cardi has spoken loudly about other ways to create a more equitable country through education. She has previously mentioned the importance of constant learning by reading everything she can get her hands on and has donated to her former middle school (Nast 2022). These few examples further show that her trap feminist politics involve a spectrum of topics and activities that stretch beyond speaking up to direct action.

In addition to Cardi, there are no shortage of examples of Black women and Black artists engaging in civic and political engagement. After all, many women rappers lean heavily on Black Power messages in their videos and lyrics that are linked to politics beyond their music (Carter 2023a, 2023b). For example, Queen Latifah not only cares deeply about Black unity in her music, but she also advocates for Black women by developing programs to challenge racial and gender inequality through the "Queen Collective" and has helped build an affordable housing development in New Jersey (Tribeca Enterprises LLC 2020; Williams 2022). In 2022, rapper Latto received the key to her city, Jonesboro, Georgia, from political advocate Stacey Abrams for her "Win Some Give Some" program that provides resources and self-esteem support for Black youth (Blanchet 2022). A trap feminist lens helps us to see that Black women from the hood are politically and civically engaged despite not always being seen as such or seen doing so.

As readers, we hope that you trusted our expertise as we led you through Cardi B's defiances and around the themes of feminism, the white gaze, race and ethnicity, motherhood, and politics. As the authors, we trusted Cardi, and we trusted ourselves.

We Trust Each Other: Lessons of a Black Feminist Project

In addition to what we learned from trusting Cardi B, we want to discuss how we trusted ourselves and how this book is important as a Black feminist and trap feminist project. Much like Cardi B, throughout this book, we did not stick to everything that we had been told makes for a "good" sociological study. According to dominant narratives in academia, a good sociology project involves working in isolation with a narrow set of literatures and methods, all things we did not do. We recognized early as co-panelists at conferences and then as co-authors that we needed to come together to tell this story in the communal tradition of Black people, Black feminists, and Black feminist collectives. A Black feminist project MUST look different from traditional scholarship, given its commitment to the tenets of Black feminism. With five authors, five approaches, five experiences, five equally valid voices, we were defiant against dominant academic narratives by recognizing that our strength was in our community and that we could trust one another's expertise. Even still, we know that these five voices do not and cannot encompass the totality of Black womanhood(s).

As the authors of this book, we consciously approached our work from a trap feminist standpoint by not allowing the rigid nature of academia to dictate how we produced this knowledge. We actively and intentionally talked about what else was happening in our lives, our feelings about our jobs, current events in society, and our own personal frustrations. We created space for one another to celebrate birthdays, graduations, new jobs, new moves, and personal accomplishments, all while being realistic and critical, yet compassionate, in the ways we held one another accountable. We needed to know about one another's backgrounds and proximity to the trap, as well as how and why we came to know and love Cardi B and what she represents. As we wrote, we actively redefined how professional academic co-authorships operate, in a way that fit our trap feminist ethos.

To approach the book this way was challenging because academia teaches us that "objectivity" is best, that co-authorships should be managed by logic and centered on who gets the most credit, that personhood is secondary to productivity, and that no matter what happens in life, the work must go on. Our Black, trap, and Hip Hop feminist standpoints, however, allowed us to dispel the notion that a book by five Black women could not truly be co-authored. Our feminisms helped us to push past the urge to take ourselves out of the work to legitimize it.

Much like the fact that our experiences as Black women cannot be disentangled from our identities, we also want to mention that as the authors, all trained sociologists, we cannot disentangle our sociological imaginations from our approach to this book. In 2017, we were graduate students working toward PhDs in Sociology at public and private universities across the United States. Some of us were working on comprehensive area exams, a requirement to prove your knowledge of what has been written previously on a sociological topic, while others were completing their dissertation, a project that is the result of intensive research on a subject of your choice. Our exams and dissertation project topics crossed the numerous fields of sociology we discuss in this book, including collective behavior, social movements, criminology, education, families, feminism, media, Black women, race and ethnicity, gender, and stratification. As a result, we have produced not only what we hope is a nuanced analysis with *The Sociology of Cardi B* but also a template for how Black women in academia can and should work together while remaining whole persons. Our five unique experiences as Black women are why this book works.

As mentioned throughout the summaries of the chapters, this book is meant to serve as a springboard into deeper analysis of Black womanhood(s) and the social systems that interact with them. We covered many topics here; however, this text should not be the ending of your understanding of feminism, the white gaze, Blackness, ethnicity, motherhood, or politics. Furthermore, there are other areas of social life that deserve more conversations with and inclusion of hood chicks. The most challenging part of adopting this type of perspective in our work and everyday lives is that it is often not acknowledged or celebrated, and it requires us to unlearn so much of what we've come to know as acceptable knowledge production.

An exciting thing for us as sociologists, whose job is to be writers and producers of knowledge, is to share with you the importance of thinking through knowledge production. As Black feminism tells us that our lived experiences are a source of knowledge, most "traditional" sociology does not go beyond the surface level of what it means to have produced knowledge within the discipline. We acknowledge the limitations of this book to speak deeply to Black women and femme's experiences with queerness, able-bodiedness, health, neurodiversity, and more. Our hope is that this book helps contribute to an existing foundation of work that demonstrates how and why Black feminist, Hip Hop feminist, and trap feminist perspectives are best used to unmask societal processes and inequities.[3]

We Charge Our Community of Readers

As we trusted our expertise on feminism, the white gaze, ethnicity, motherhood, and politics, we trusted Cardi's stories to shepherd us through conversations on those topics. We encourage educators, researchers, and casual readers to trust that you, too, might need to learn more about the topics addressed in this book.

Each reader of this book is likely to have taken something different away from it depending on their identity, when they read it, and their previous understanding of Black feminism and the trap. No matter which chapters or ideas resonated with you most, we hope you use this book to create conversations around how important hood chicks and ghetto girls are to the process of recognizing and dismantling inequality in society. As we talked about how and why ratchet girls have been forced to the margins, we undoubtedly will have to grapple with our own harmful ideologies that are rooted in white supremacy, classism, misogynoir, and more. By not contributing to these institutions of oppression, you make more space for women in the trap and, ultimately, more space for all of us.

When we presented this work in classrooms, from a virtual conversation with Ilka Eikhoff's class at American University in Cairo to Maretta Darnell McDonald's classes at Louisiana State University and Virginia Tech, we encountered students who were a bit skeptical about what they could learn from, and how to make sense of, Cardi B. A football player from Dr. McDonald's class said it clearly:

> I will say at first, with just the course title, I was a little skeptical about everything and the potential course content. But looking back I am very happy I have taken it. The course was overall a dope experience and I feel like I learned a ton of new stuff within fields I have already spent quite a bit of time in.

This student's message is the perfect lesson for us as educators and researchers, too–there's always more to learn and to know.

In addition to recognizing that you can learn more, those of you who are educators should make space (or continue to make space) within your classrooms for those who have to hustle harder, for the girl with the tattoos and fight marks, the one "that don't talk right," the ones with the brightly colored hair. If those groups of women are not taking your classes or are not speaking up in your classes, you might ask yourself what is lost in your classroom if they do not speak and whether you have made this a safe space for them to speak up.

There are countless stories about Black students being steered away from not feeling comfortable in the classroom and being steered away from researching topics that are "non-traditional" because they were not previously in the literature. Dr. Regina Bradley, thankfully had a different experience:

> All that to say, it wasn't until I was in graduate school that I really started thinking about how much the 'Kast and southern hip hop meant to me. We were studying hip hop in my classes and not nan person besides my fellow southern folks—shoutout to Drs. Langston Colin Wilkins and Fredara Mareva Hadley—were asking about how the south fit into these conversations about hip hop. Don't snub us, shawty. I felt snubbed. My mentor and professor, Dr. Portia Maultsby, asked me "well what are you going to do about it?"
>
> *(Jackson 2017)*

Dr. Bradley had peers and a mentor who believed in her and encouraged her interest in the topics of Outkast and the South. Her research, built from her firsthand experiences and knowledge, has assisted in expanding conversations on southern Hip Hop. The point we want our academic colleagues to recognize is that Dr. Bradley's interests were not marginalized or shunned by her mentor and professor but were able to be pushed to help create a more nuanced research topic. While you may not be an expert on a topic that a student introduces to you or completely understand their worldview, you are still able to guide them through how to conduct research. So, when a student comes into your office and says they want to study strippers, the media, Cardi B, or Sexxy Red, do not discourage them.

If you are a researcher, you should have gleaned new ways to think about knowledge, research, academia, and Black women from these pages. Our book pushes researchers into the streets to see, hear, and feel the perspectives, theories, and life experiences of women in, from, and adjacent to the trap. In establishing and expanding your knowledge, this does not mean to go extract from Black women. Nor do we call for academia to sensationalize the lives of women from the trap, as we have seen too many times in ethnographies. We instead want to have hard conversations, understand these communities, and bring more people from these communities into academia—to center them in spaces that are supposedly committed to thinking.

For all readers. For our multiethnic, multi-gendered, multi-classed communities. As you read this book you may have felt some tension or discomfort with some of the ideas presented. While you believe in women's rights to dress and behave as they want, maybe you still hold fast to the idea that certain behaviors are inappropriate, unprofessional, or that they even advance stereotypes. This book encourages all of us to lean into that discomfort; to investigate what makes us uncomfortable and to, at minimum, attempt to understand that the value judgments placed on hood women and girls often ignore their standpoint and experiences. When we begin to view the women in and adjacent to the trap as embodying valuable, worthy, and needed existences, we begin to see them as whole people and stop reducing or writing off their humanity as invalid because it looks different than the white norm. In essence, taking on a trap feminist approach teaches us to be more inclusive, less judgy people who are critical of oppressive systems, not just the actors living within them.

In many ways, this book is a love letter to those who need to see themselves. Yes, the educators. Yes, the researchers. But more importantly, the hood chicks. Hood chicks are often at the forefront of creating and/or popularizing the cultural expressions that others later appropriate: boxer braids, long lashes, acrylics, Chinese store slippers, and more. We have to acknowledge hood chicks for their cultural production, but we should not limit them to only these contributions. We should not caricature them but rather think about their role as knowledge producers that shape how we think about society.

We Have Faith in the Future

Understanding the perspective of hood chicks allows us to extend grace and make room for the evolution of women and girls. Trap feminism is a more inclusive feminism that not only refuses to leave out hood chicks but centers them and asks how their knowledge production offers a unique and critical lens for all of us. Hood chicks do leave the hood—they go to work, school, community events, and more (some of them even got PhDs and helped to write this book). The knowledge and experiences they bring with them when they enter spaces are invaluable. As hood chicks grow and move, they serve as reminders that there are many ways to create knowledge and many ways to exist that don't rest on whiteness or aim to uphold white supremacy.

Through this book, we are speaking to hood chicks to say we trust them to tell their own stories and make sense of the world in the ways that work for them. The goal is not to put them in a box but to acknowledge what they contribute and create space for them to contribute and evolve—to stop looking at them as a problem and to follow their lens and perspective of the world to reevaluate what we can do better. Today, hood chicks have access to recording their narratives in a way that hood chicks of the past did not. Hood chicks have always existed, though. What about the hood chicks of the 1930s? We rarely investigate this long history of Black women in and from the hood, women who often lived "wayward lives," as Saidiya Hartman puts it (2019). The Cardi Bs have always existed in our communities and within Black music.

When you close this book, what exactly will stick with you? Hopefully you go back to your daily life questioning: Who is in my social circle? What voices are not in my circle? How did this come to be? What role do I play in this? Similar to teaching an introduction to sociology course, we want you to have challenged your thoughts and opinions on the social construction of society but more specifically on Black women's relationship to feminism, whiteness, their racial identity, motherhood, and politics. Once you recognize which voices are not included in your life, how can you expand your knowledge for a more nuanced understanding of the world?

In closing, we encourage you to expand your mind. Let's get radical! Let's get ratchet! Let's twerk! Let's use our voices and live our best lives, as Cardi B says. But more importantly, let's engage with a sociology that centers women from the trap.

Notes

1 Those who experienced the 1990s may remember early stories about whether Venus and Serena Williams, two Black girls from Compton, California, were worthy to compete in tennis—a sport often coded for elite white people. Early on, a white male reporter doubted a young Venus Williams, stating "You say (you are confident about beating your opponent) so easily. Why?" As the reporter appears confused about her confidence—as though a young Black girl should not speak up for herself, Venus's father Richard Williams refuses to allow the interview to continue. He tells the reporter that "When she say something, she done told you what's happening," emphasizing that there is no reason to challenge her confidence (Rhue 2018). This clash is much like the clashes that Cardi has with expectations of her and expectations based on the white gaze. Over 20 years from their debut, Venus and Serena Williams are two of the greatest tennis players, with deals and collaboration similar to Cardi B. In Serena Williams's last year of the sport, a white woman reporter asked her if Serena was "surprised" at herself with her level of playing, still doubting one of the greatest players in the world, a Black woman from Compton.

2 Angel Reese and Flau'Jae Johnson, as part of the 2023 Women's College Basketball Champions from Louisiana State University, were told that despite being top athletes, they were hurting their chances with their hair, long lashes, and competitive spirits. Reese, specifically, was told that she hurt her chances of being taken seriously by "intimidating" a (white woman) player, despite that player saying that she felt that the competitiveness was part of the game (Brown 2023; Morse 2023). Within six months of winning and the criticism that followed, these young women were able to negotiate NIL deals with Reebok, Amazon, and PlayStation to name a few. Cardi referenced the LSU team in her feature on the song, "Put in on Da Floor" with the lyric: "I been ballin' so damn hard, could've went to LSU, huh." Angel Reese, dressed in her basketball uniform, with her hair, lashes, and nails done, was featured in the video (HidjiWorld/Latto 2023).

Representing how Black women often see one another in spite of a white gaze. As we mention, this book is not about Cardi B or Hip Hop but about the structures impacting Black women and people's responses.

3 At the time of writing, we conducted a search of all texts that include Cardi B. Since 2018, there have been over 200 academic articles, theses, and books that mention Cardi B. These topics range from Hip Hop history to law, medicine, and sociology. Journal of Hip Hop Studies to Law Reviews. We hope that you seriously engage with those works.

REFERENCES

Abrams, Stacey. 2020. *Our Time Is Now: Power, Purpose, and the Fight for a Fair America*. New York: Henry Holt and Co.

Accomando, Christina. 2003. "Demanding a Voice among the Pettifoggers: Sojourner Truth as Legal Actor." *MELUS* 28(1):61–86.

The African American Policy Forum. n.d. "Say Her Name." *AAPF Website*. Retrieved November 7, 2023 (www.aapf.org/sayhername).

Allen, Reniqua. 2019a. *It Was All a Dream: A New Generation Confronts the Broken Promise to Black America*. 1st ed. New York: Bold Type Books.

———. 2019b. "The Missing Black Millennial." *The New Republic*, February 20. Retrieved March 17, 2020 (https://newrepublic.com/article/153122/missing-black-millennial).

Allen, Richard S., Douglas E. Allen, Katherine Karl, and Charles S. White. 2015. "Are Millennials Really an Entitled Generation? An Investigation into Generational Equity Sensitivity Differences." *Journal of Business Diversity* 15(2):14–26.

Allen, Shaonta' E. 2021. "The Black Feminist Roots of Scholar-Activism." Pp. 32–44 in *Black Feminist Sociology: Perspectives and Praxis*, edited by Z. Luna and W. N. L. Pirtle. New York: Routledge.

Allen, Shaonta' E., Ifeyinwa F. Davis, Maretta McDonald, and Candice C. Robinson. 2020. "The Case of Black Millennials." *Sociological Perspectives* 63(3):478–85. doi:10.1177/0731121420915202.

Allen, Shaonta' E. and Brittney Miles. 2020. "Unapologetic Blackness in Action: Embodied Resistance and Social Movement Scenes in Black Celebrity Activism." *Humanity & Society*. doi:10.1177/0160597620932886.

Alvarado, Steven Elías and Alexandra Cooperstock. 2021. "Context in Continuity: The Enduring Legacy of Neighborhood Disadvantage Across Generations." *Research in Social Stratification and Mobility* 74:100620.

American Sociological Association. 2024. "ASA Presidents | American Sociological Association." Retrieved April 18, 2024 (https://www.asanet.org/about/governance-and-leadership/council/asa-presidents/).

Anderson, Elijah. 2000. *Code of the Street: Decency, Violence, and the Moral Life of the Inner City*. New York: Norton.

Aniftos, Rania. 2023. "Sexyy Red Announces She's Pregnant, Says She Was 'Tired' of Pretending She Wasn't." *Billboard*. Retrieved January 9, 2024 (www.billboard.com/music/rb-hip-hop/sexyy-red-pregnant-1235443786/).

Arnold, Amanda. 2018. "Cardi Just Wants to 'Fat in Peace'." in *The Cut*. New York: Vox Media, LLC.

Associated Press. 2019. "Cardi B Declined Super Bowl Halftime Show With 'Mixed Feelings'." *Billboard*. Retrieved June 18, 2022 (www.billboard.com/music/music-news/cardi-b-declined-super-bowl-halftime-show-kaepernick-8496179/).

Ayala, Erica L. 2020. "Perspective | The NBA's Walkout Is Historic. But the WNBA Paved the Way." *Washington Post*, August 29.

Bernard, Jessie. 1973. "My Four Revolutions: An Autobiographical History of the ASA." *American Journal of Sociology* 78(4):773–91.

Blain, Keisha N. 2018. *Set the World on Fire: Black Nationalist Women and the Global Struggle for Freedom (Politics and Culture in Modern America)*. Philadelphia, PA: University of Pennsylvania Press.

——. 2021. *Until I Am Free: Fannie Lou Hamer's Enduring Message to America*. Boston, MA: Beacon Press.

Blanchet, Brenton. 2022. "Latto Honored with Her Own Day in Clayton County, GA—and Key to the City from Stacey Abrams." *Peoplemag*, December 19.

Bobo, Lawrence D. and Camille Z. Charles. 2009. "Race in the American Mind: From the Moynihan Report to the Obama Candidacy." *The Annals of the American Academy of Political and Social Science* 621(1):243–59. doi: 10.1177/0002716208324759.

Bonilla-Silva, Eduardo. 2003. "Racial Attitudes or Racial Ideology? An Alternative Paradigm for Examining Actors' Racial Views." *Journal of Political Ideologies* 8(1):63. doi: 10.1080/13569310306082.

Boren, Cindy. 2020. "A Timeline of Colin Kaepernick's Protests against Police Brutality, Four Years after They Began." *Washington Post*, August 26.

Bowen, Sesali. 2021. *Bad Fat Black Girl: Notes from a Trap Feminist*. New York: HarperCollins.

Bracey, John, August Meier, and Elliott Rudwick. 1998 (1973). "The Black Sociologists: The First Half Century." in *The Death of White Sociology: Essays on Race and Culture*, edited by Joyce A. Ladner. Baltimore, MD: Black Classic Press.

Breakfast Club. 2018. "Azealia Banks Talks New Single, The State of Female Rap, RZA, Donald Trump + More." Retrieved June 6, 2022 (www.youtube.com/watch?v=r17fqELkv7g).

Brereton, Bridget. 2007. "Contesting the Narratives of Trinidad & Tobago History." *NWIG: New West Indian Guide/Nieuwe West-Indische Gids* 81(3/4):169–96.

——. 2010. "'All Ah We Is Not One': Historical and Ethnic Narratives in Pluralist Trinidad." *The Global South* 4(2):218–38. doi:10.2979/globalsouth.4.2.218.

Brock, André, Jr. 2020. *Distributed Blackness: African American Cybercultures*. New York: NYU Press.

Brooks, Maegan Parker and Davis W. Houck. 2011. *The Speeches of Fannie Lou Hamer: To Tell It Like It Is*. Jackson, MS: University Press of Mississippi.

Brown, Adrienne M. 2019. *Pleasure Activism: The Politics of Feeling Good*. Chico, CA: AK Press.

Brown, DeNeen L. 2021. "Renowned as a Black Liberator, Harriet Tubman Was Also a Brilliant Spy." *Washington Post*, February 13.

Brown, Dr Letisha Engracia Cardoso. 2023. "By Being Herself, Angel Reese Slays Anti-Blackness and Misogynoir in Sports." *First and Pen*. Retrieved January 9, 2024 (https://firstandpen.com/angel-reese-lsu-basketball-black-women-narrative/).

Browne, Simone. 2015. *Dark Matters: On the Surveillance of Blackness.* Durham, NC: Duke University Press.

Brunsma, David L., David G. Embrick, and Megan Nanney. 2015. "Toward a Sociology of Race and Ethnicity." *Sociology of Race and Ethnicity* 1(1):1–9. doi:10.1177/2332649214562028.

Burawoy, Michael. 2021. "Decolonizing Sociology: The Significance of W.E.B. Du Bois." *Critical Sociology* 47(4–5):545–54. doi:10.1177/08969205211005180.

Butler, Kim D. 2000. "From Black History to Diasporan History: Brazilian Abolition in Afro-Atlantic Context." *African Studies Review* 43(1):125–39. doi:10.2307/524724.

——. 2001. "Defining Diaspora, Refining a Discourse." *Diaspora: A Journal of Transnational Studies* 10(2):189–219. doi:10.3138/diaspora.10.2.189.

Cahill, Cathleen D. 2020. *Recasting the Vote: How Women of Color Transformed the Suffrage Movement.* Chapel Hill, NC: The University of North Carolina Press.

Cammett, Ann. 2014. "Deadbeat Dads & Welfare Queens: How Metaphor Shapes Poverty Law." *Boston College Journal of Law and Social Justice* 34: 233–66.

Campion, Karis. 2019. " 'You Think You're Black?' Exploring Black Mixed-Race Experiences of Black Rejection." *Ethnic and Racial Studies* 42(16):196–213. doi:10.1080/01419870.2019.1642503.

Candelario, Ginetta E. B. 2007. *Black behind the Ears: Dominican Racial Identity from Museums to Beauty Shops.* Durham, NC: Duke University Press.

Cannady, Emmanuel. 2022. "Black Lives Matter." Pp. 1–9 in *The Wiley-Blackwell Encyclopedia of Social and Political Movements.* Hoboken, NJ: Wiley-Blackwell.

Cardi B Official. n.d. "Cardi B Bio." *Cardi B Official Website.* Retrieved June 20, 2022 (www.cardibofficial.com/bio).

Carter, Kollin. 2020. "The Politics of Being Cardi B." *ELLE.* Retrieved June 17, 2022 (www.elle.com/culture/music/a33537374/cardi-b-interview-september-2020/).

Carter, Mickell. 2023a. "Queen Latifah and the Legacies of Black Power." *Black Perspectives.* Retrieved January 18, 2024 (www.aaihs.org/queen-latifah-and-the-legacies-of-black-power/).

——. 2023b. "The Transnational Activism of Women in Hip Hop." *Black Perspectives.* Retrieved January 18, 2024 (www.aaihs.org/the-transnational-activism-of-women-in-hip-hop/).

Carter, Terry, Jr. 2020. "Cardi B Revealed Her Natural Hair on Twitter and I Am Mesmerized." Retrieved June 6, 2022 (www.buzzfeed.com/terrycarter/cardi-b-revealed-her-natural-hair).

Center for American Women and Politics. 2022. *Women of Color in Elective Office 2021.* New Brunswick, NJ: Center for American Women and Politics, Eagleton Institute of Politics, Rutgers University-New Brunswick. Retrieved September 30, 2022 (https://cawp.rutgers.edu/women-color-elective-office-2021).

Chappell, Bill. 2022. "Sha'Carri Richardson Sees a Double Standard in Allowing Kamila Valieva to Compete." *NPR*, February 15.

Charles, Kerwin Kofi and Ming Ching Luoh. 2010. "Male Incarceration, the Marriage Market, and Female Outcomes." *The Review of Economics and Statistics* 92(3):614–27.

Charmaz, Kathy. 2014. *Constructing Grounded Theory.* Thousand Oaks, CA: Sage.

Cheok, Melissa, Jihye Lee, and Natnicha Chuwiruch. 2019. "Rapper Cardi B Disses President Trump Over the Shutdown | Time." Retrieved June 20, 2022 (https://time.com/5505409/cardi-b-trump-shutdown-video/).

Cherlin, Andrew J. 2004. "The Deinstitutionalization of American Marriage." *Journal of Marriage and Family* 66(4):848–61.

——. 2005. "American Marriage in the Early Twenty-First Century." *The Future of Children* 15(2):33–55.

Chesney-Lind, Meda and Nikki Jones. 2010. *Fighting for Girls: New Perspectives on Gender and Violence*. Albany: State University of New York Press.

Clayman Institute for Gender Research. 2020, April 30. "Working Girls: Feminist Views on Sex Work [Video]." *YouTube* (https://www.Youtube.Com/Watch?V=1Gz1fQ3LyN8).

Cohen, Cathy J. 2004. "Deviance as Resistance: A New Research Agenda for the Study of Black Politics." *Du Bois Review: Social Science Research on Race* 1(1):27–45. doi: 10.1017/S1742058X04040044.

Collins, Hattie. 2018. "Why the Whole World is Talking about Cardi B." in *i-D Magazine*. London, England: Vice Media Group.

Collins, Patricia Hill. 1986. "Learning from the Outsider Within: The Sociological Significance of Black Feminist Thought." *Social Problems* 33(6):14–32. doi:10.2307/800672.

——. 1989. "The Social Construction of Black Feminist Thought." *Signs* 14(4):745–73.

——. 1991. *Black Feminist Thought*. New York: Routledge.

——. 2000. *Black Feminist Thought: Knowledge, Consciousness, and the Politics of Empowerment*. 2nd ed. New York: Routledge.

——. 2002. *Black Feminist Thought: Knowledge, Consciousness, and the Politics of Empowerment*. New York: Routledge.

——. 2004. *Black Sexual Politics: African Americans, Gender, and the New Racism*. New York: Routledge.

——. 2022. *Black Feminist thought: Knowledge, Consciousness, and the Politics of Empowerment*. New York: Taylor & Francis.

The Combahee River Collective. 1982. "A Black Feminist Statement." Pp. 13–22 in *All the Women Are White, All the Blacks Are Men, but Some of Us Are Brave: Black Women's Studies*, edited by G. T. Hull, P. Bell-Scott, and B. Smith. Old Westbury, NY: Feminist Press.

Cooper, Anna Julia. [1892] 1988. *A Voice from the South*. New York: Oxford University Press.

Cooper, Brittney C. 2012. "(Un)Clutching My Mother's Pearls, or Ratchetness and the Residue of Respectability." *Crunk Feminist Collective*. Retrieved April 19, 2024 (https://www.crunkfeministcollective.com/2012/12/31/unclutching-my-mothers-pearls-or-ratchetness-and-the-residue-of-respectability/).

Cooper, Brittney C., Susana M. Morris, and Robin M. Boylorn. 2017. *The Crunk Feminist Collection*. New York: The Feminist Press at CUNY.

Corcoran, Nina. 2020. "Cardi B Interviews Bernie Sanders about Coronavirus, Healthcare, and Joe Biden: Watch." *Consequence*. Retrieved June 18, 2022 (https://consequence.net/2020/04/cardi-b-interview-bernie-sanders-coronavirus-joe-biden/).

Crutchfield, Joshua L. 2022. "How Pauli Murray Masterminded Brown v. Board—AAIHS." Retrieved November 7, 2023 (www.aaihs.org/how-pauli-murray-masterminded-brown-v-board/).

Cullors, Patrisse and Asha Bandele. 2020. *When They Call You a Terrorist: A Black Lives Matter Memoir*. Reprint ed. New York: St. Martin's Griffin.

Cummins, Jim. 2013. "Four Misconceptions About Language Proficiency in Bilingual Education." *NABE Journal*. doi:10.1080/08855072.1981.10668409.

Curwood, Anastasia C. 2022. *Shirley Chisholm: Champion of Black Feminist Power Politics*. Chapel Hill, NC: The University of North Carolina Press.

Davis, Angela Y. 1972. "Reflections on the Black Woman's Role in the Community of Slaves." *The Massachusetts Review* 13(1/2):81–100.

——. 1998. *Blues Legacies and Black Feminism: Gertrude Ma Rainey, Bessie Smith, and Billie Holiday*. New York: Vintage Books.

——. 2011. *Women, Race, & Class*. New York: Vintage Books.

Demby, Gene. 2013. "Remembering the Woman Who Gave Motown Its Charm." (www.npr.org/sections/codeswitch/2013/10/15/234738593/remembering-the-woman-who-gave-motown-its-charm).

Devin. 2020. "Cardi B's 'Invasion of Privacy' Becomes Longest-Charting Album by a Female Rapper." *Rap-Up*. Retrieved July 16, 2022 (https://www.rap-up.com/2020/08/25/cardi-b-invasion-of-privacy-longest-charting-female-rap-album/).

DiversityInc. 2019. "Cardi B. Sets the Record Straight About Her Race and Ethnicity." *DiversityInc*. Retrieved June 6, 2022 (www.diversityinc.com/cardi-b-sets-the-record-straight-about-her-race-and-ethnicity/).

Docka-Filipek, Danielle. 2016. "Community Other Mothers." Pp. 1–3 in *The Wiley Blackwell Encyclopedia of Gender and Sexuality Studies*. Hoboken, NJ: Wiley-Blackwell.

Downing, Joseph and Richard Dron. 2020. "Tweeting Grenfell: Discourse and Networks in Critical Constructions of British Muslim Social Boundaries on Social Media." *New Media & Society* 22:449–69.

Du Bois, W. E. B. [1903] 2009. *The Souls of Black Folk*. New York: Simon & Schuster.

——. 1961. *W.E.B. Du Bois: A Recorded Autobiography, Interview with Moses Asch*. Washington, DC: Smithsonian Folkways Records.

Durham, Aisha, Brittney C. Cooper, and Susana M. Morris. 2013. "The Stage Hip-Hop Feminism Built: A New Directions Essay." *Signs: Journal of Women in Culture and Society* 38(3):721–37. doi:10.1086/668843.

Duster, Michelle. 2021. *Ida B. the Queen: The Extraordinary Life and Legacy of Ida B. Wells*. 1st ed. New York: Atria/One Signal Publishers.

Edin, Kathryn and Maria Kefalas. 2005. *Promises I Can Keep: Why Poor Women put Motherhood before Marriage*. Berkeley, CA: University of California Press.

ELLE. 2020. "Cardi B Talks Police Brutality, COVID-19, and the 2020 Election with Joe Biden." *ELLE Magazine*.

Entman, Robert M. and Andrew Rojecki. 2000. *The Black Image in the White Mind: Media and Race in America*. Chicago, IL: The University of Chicago Press.

Estes, Michelle L., Adam M. Straub, and Maggie León-Corwin. 2023. "Making the Invisible Visible: Examining Black Women in Black Lives Matter." *Sociological Spectrum* 43(4/5):127–46. doi:10.1080/02732173.2023.2245936.

Evans-Winters, Venus E., ed. 2015. *Black Feminism in Education: Black Women Speak Back, Up, and Out*. New York: Peter Lang.

Fanon, Frantz. 1952. *Black Skin, White Masks*. Revised ed. New York: Grove Press.

Fares, Melissa and Gina Cherelus. 2016. "Trump Loves 'the Poorly Educated' . . . and Social Media Clamors." *Reuters*, February 24.

Feagin, Joe R. 2006. *Systemic Racism: A Theory of Oppression*. New York: Routledge.

Flores, Nelson and Jonathan Rosa. 2015. "Undoing Appropriateness: Raciolinguistic Ideologies and Language Diversity in Education." *Harvard Educational Review* 85(2):149–71. doi:10.17763/0017-8055.85.2.149.

Florini, Sarah. 2014. "Tweets, Tweeps, and Signifyin': Communication and Cultural Performance on 'Black Twitter'." *Television & New Media* 15(3):223–37. doi:10.1177/1527476413480247.

Ford, Tanisha C. 2015a. "The 'Afro Look' and Global Black Consciousness." *Nka Journal of Contemporary African Art* 2015(37):28–37.

———. 2015b. *Liberated Threads: Black Women, Style, and the Global Politics of Soul*: Chapel Hill, NC: The University of North Carolina Press.

Forman, Murray. 2002. *The Hood Comes First: Race, Space, and Place in Rap and Hip-Hop*. 1st ed. Middletown, CT: Wesleyan University Press.

———. 2020. "'Things Done Changed': Recalibrating the Real in Hip-Hop." *Popular Music and Society* 1–27. doi:10.1080/03007766.2020.1814628.

Foucault, Michel. 1977. *Discipline and Punish: The Birth of the Prison*. New York: Random House.

Frazier, Cherise. 2019. "Cardi B's Former AP Government Teacher Says Put Some Respect on Her Name When It Comes to Politics." *MadameNoire*. Retrieved June 20, 2022 (https://madamenoire.com/1058839/cardi-bs-former-ap-history-teacher-gives-us-a-breakdown-you-wont-forget/).

Freeman, Tyrone McKinley. 2020. *Madam C. J. Walker's Gospel of Giving: Black Women's Philanthropy during Jim Crow*. Champaign, IL: University of Illinois Press.

G. 2016. "On Hip-Hop's Intersection of Colorism and Misogyny." *IMPOSE*. Retrieved June 20, 2022 (https://imposemagazine.com/features/on-hip-hops-intersection-of-colorism-and-misogyny).

Giddings, Paula J. 2009. *Ida: A Sword Among Lions: Ida B. Wells and the Campaign Against Lynching*. Reprint ed. New York: Amistad.

Gil, Rosa Maria and Carmen Inoa Vazquez. 1996. *The Maria Paradox: How Latinas Can Merge Old World Traditions with New World Self-Esteem*. New York: Perigee Books.

Gilens, Martin. 1999. "Correlational Framing: Media Portrayals of Race and Poverty." in *Political Psychology Newsletter, Political Psychology Section of the American Political Science Association, Washington, DC.*

Godreau, Isar P., Mariolga Reyes Cruz, Mariluz Franco Ortiz, and Sherry Cuadrado. 2008. "The Lessons of Slavery: Discourses of Slavery, Mestizaje, and Blanqueamiento in an Elementary School in Puerto Rico." *American Ethnologist* 35(1):115–35.

Grayer, Annie. 2019. "Cardi B Joins Bernie Sanders for Campaign Video and Talks Student Debt, Climate Change, and the Minimum Wage." *CNN Politics*. Retrieved June 17, 2022 (https://edition.cnn.com/2019/07/29/politics/bernie-sanders-cardi-b-video/index.html).

Gregory, Sean. 2020. "WNBA's Maya Moore Talks George Floyd, Drew Brees, Police." *Time*. Retrieved November 9, 2023 (https://time.com/5849780/maya-moore-george-floyd-drew-brees/).

Haley, Sarah. 2016. *No Mercy Here: Gender, Punishment, and the Making of Jim Crow Modernity*. Chapel Hill, NC: The University of North Carolina Press.

Hall, Stuart. 1993. "What Is This 'Black' in Black Popular Culture?" *Social Justice* 20(1/2 (51/52)):104–14.

Halliday, Aria S. 2018. "Miley, What's Good? Nicki Minaj's Anaconda, Instagram Reproductions, and Viral Memetic Violence." *Girlhood Studies* 11(3):67–83.

Hancock, Ange-Marie. 2004. *The Politics of Disgust: The Public Identity of the Welfare Queen*. New York: NYU Press.

Hansen, Drew D. 1999. "The American Invention of Child Support: Dependency and Punishment in Early American Child Support Law." *The Yale Law Journal* 108(5):1123–53.

Harrison, Bonnie Claudia. 2002. "Diasporadas: Black Women and the Fine Art of Activism." *Meridians* 2(2):163–84.

Harris-Perry, Melissa V. 2011. *Sister Citizen: Shame, Stereotypes, and Black Women in America*. New Haven, CT: Yale University Press.

Hartman, Saidiya V. 2019. *Wayward Lives, Beautiful Experiments: Intimate Histories of Riotous Black Girls, Troublesome Women, and Queer Radicals*. 1st ed. New York: W.W. Norton & Company.

Haveman, Robert and Timothy Smeeding. 2006. "The Role of Higher Education in Social Mobility." *The Future of Children* 16(2):125–50.

Herndon, Astead W. 2020. "Georgia Was a Big Win for Democrats. Black Women Did the Groundwork." *The New York Times*, December 3.

Hesse-Biber, Sharlene Nagy. 2017. *The Practice of Qualitative Research: Engaging Students in the Research Process*. Thousand Oaks, CA: Sage Publications.

HidjiWorld/Latto, dir. 2023. "Latto—Put It On Da Floor Again (Feat. Cardi B) [Official Video]." Retrieved April 19, 2024 (https://www.youtube.com/results?search_query).

Higginbotham, Evelyn Brooks. 1993. *Righteous Discontent: The Women's Movement in the Black Baptist Church, 1880–1920*. Cambridge, MA: Harvard University Press.

Hill, Jemele. 2023. "The Glorious Exuberance of Sha'Carri Richardson's Hair—The Atlantic." *The Atlantic*, September 23.

Hollinger, David A. 2003. "Amalgamation and Hypodescent: The Question of Ethnoracial Mixture in the History of the United States." *The American Historical Review* 108(5):1363–90. doi:10.1086/ahr/108.5.1363.

hooks, bell. 1981. *Ain't I a Woman: Black Women and Feminism*. Boston, MA: South End Press.

——. 2003. "The Oppositional Gaze: Black Female Spectators." Pp. 94–105 in *The Feminism and Visual Culture Reader*, edited by A. Jones. New York: Routledge.

——. 2004. *We Real Cool: Black Men and Masculinity*. New York: Routledge.

——. 2010. "The Oppositional Gaze: Black Female Spectators." Pp. 93–104 in *The Film Theory Reader: Debates and Arguments*. New York: Routledge.

——. 2015. *Ain't I a Woman: Black Women and Feminism*. 2nd ed. New York: Routledge.

Hordge-Freeman, Elizabeth and Edlin Veras. 2020. "Out of the Shadows, into the Dark: Ethnoracial Dissonance and Identity Formation among Afro-Latinxs." *Sociology of Race and Ethnicity* 6(2):146–60. doi:10.1177/2332649219829784.

Hull, Gloria T., Patricia Bell-Scott, and Barbara Smith, eds. 1982. *All the Women Are White, All the Blacks Are Men, but Some of Us Are Brave: Black Women's Studies*. Old Westbury, NY: Feminist Press.

Hunter, Margaret. 2016. "Colorism in the Classroom: How Skin Tone Stratifies African American and Latina/o Students." *Theory Into Practice* 55(1):54–61. doi: 10.1080/00405841.2016.1119019.

Iglesias, Tasha and Travis Harris. 2022. "It's 'Hip Hop,' Not 'Hip-Hop.'" *Journal of Hip Hop Studies* 9(1).

Itzigsohn, José and Karida L. Brown. 2020. *The Sociology of W. E. B. Du Bois: Racialized Modernity and the Global Color Line*. New York: NYU Press.

Jackson, Panama. 2017. "An Interview with Dr. Regina Bradley, Who Teaches a Class On Outkast." *The Root*, January 9.

Jackson, Sarah J. 2014. *Black Celebrity, Racial Politics, and the Press: Framing Dissent*. New York: Routledge.

Johnson, E. Patrick. 2003. *Appropriating Blackness: Performance and the Politics of Authenticity*. Durham, NC: Duke University Press.

Jones, Jacqueline. 2009. *Labor of Love, Labor of Sorrow: Black Women, Work, and the Family, from Slavery to the Present*. New York: Basic Books.

Jones, Nikki. 2010. *Between Good and Ghetto: African American Girls and Inner-City Violence*. New Brunswick, NJ: Rutgers University Press.

Jupiter Entertainment (producers). 2004–2023. "Snapped." *Oxygen* (https://www.oxygen.com/snapped).

——. 2013. "Fatal Attraction." *TVOne* (https://tvone.tv/show/fatal-attraction/).

Kendall, Mikki. 2020. *Hood Feminism: Notes from the Women That a Movement Forgot*. New York: Penguin Random House.

King, Marissa D. 2022. "Anti-Slavery Movement." Pp. 1–4 in *The Wiley-Blackwell Encyclopedia of Social and Political Movements*. Hoboken, NJ: Wiley-Blackwell.

Kleinman, Sherryl, Matthew B. Ezzell, and A. Corey Frost. 2009. "Reclaiming Critical Analysis: The Social Harms of 'Bitch'." *Sociological Analysis* 3(1):46–68.

Ladner, Joyce A., ed. 1998 (1973). *The Death of White Sociology: Essays on Race and Culture*. Baltimore, MD: Black Classic Press.

Leibovich, Mark. 2008. "Rights vs. Rights: An Improbable Collision Course." *The New York Times*, January 13.

Lichter, Daniel T., Felicia B. LeClere, and Diane K. McLaughlin. 1991. "Local Marriage Markets and the Marital Behavior of Black and White Women." *American Journal of Sociology* 96(4):843–67.

Lindsey, Treva B. 2017. *Colored No More: Reinventing Black Womanhood in Washington, D.C.* Urbana, IL: University of Illinois Press.

Lorde, Audre. 1984. *Sister Outsider: Essays and Speeches*. Trumansburg, NY: Crossing Press.

Love, Bettina L. 2017. "A Ratchet Lens: Black Queer Youth, Agency, Hip Hop, and the Black Ratchet Imagination." *Educational Researcher* 46(9):539–47. doi: 10.3102/0013189X17736520.

Luna, Zakiya and Whitney N. Laster Pirtle, eds. 2021. *Black Feminist Sociology: Perspectives and Praxis*. 1st ed. New York: Routledge.

Mallory, Tamika D. 2021. *State of Emergency: How We Win in the Country We Built*. New York: Simon & Schuster.

Mandalaywala, Tara M., David M. Amodio, and Marjorie Rhodes. 2018. "Essentialism Promotes Racial Prejudice by Increasing Endorsement of Social Hierarchies." *Social Psychological and Personality Science* 9(4):461–69. doi:10.1177/1948550617707020.

Maragh, Raven S. 2018. "Authenticity on 'Black Twitter': Reading Racial Performance and Social Networking." *Television & New Media* 19(7):591–609. doi:10.1177/1527476417738569.

McAdam, Doug, Sidney Tarrow, and Charles Tilly. 2001. *Dynamics of Contention*. Cambridge, UK: Cambridge University Press.

McKittrick, Katherine. 2014. "The Last Place They Thought Of: Black Women's Geographies." Pp. 309–14 in *The People, Place, and Space Reader*, edited by Jen Jack Gieseking. New York: Routledge, Taylor & Francis Group.

Meraji, Shereen Marisol and Justin Richmond, dirs. 2018. "Amara La Negra Confronts Colorism with Her Afro-Latinidad." *Morning Edition*.

Merriam-Webster. 2024. "crossover." Retrieved April 18, 2024 (https://www.merriam-webster.com/dictionary/crossover).

Miles, Corey. 2020. "Black Rural Feminist Trap: Stylized and Gendered Performativity in Trap Music." *Journal of Hip Hop Studies* 7(1). doi: 10.34718/KX7H-0515

Milkman, Ruth. 2017. "A New Political Generation: Millennials and the Post-2008 Wave of Protest." *American Sociological Review* 82(1):1–31.

Mills, Kay. 2007. *This Little Light of Mine: The Life of Fannie Lou Hamer*. Lexington, KY: University Press of Kentucky.

Minaj, Nicki. 2018. "Episode 8." Queen Radio. Apple Music.

Minsberg, Talya. 2023. "Sha'Carri Richardson Is the Fastest Woman in the World." *The New York Times*, August 21.

Mitchell, Michael B. and Jaya B. Davis. 2019. "Formerly Incarcerated Black Mothers Matter Too: Resisting Social Constructions of Motherhood." *The Prison Journal* 99(4):420–36.

Moon, Michelle and Charles D. Hoffman. 2008. "Mothers' and Fathers' Differential Expectancies and Behaviors: Parent X Child Gender Effects." *The Journal of Genetic Psychology* 169(3):261–80.

Mora, G. Cristina. 2014. *Making Hispanics: How Activists, Bureaucrats, and Media Constructed a New American*. Chicago, IL: University of Chicago Press.

Morgan, Joan. 1999. *When Chickenheads Come Home to Roost: A Hip-Hop Feminist Breaks It Down*. New York: Simon & Schuster.

——. 2015. "Why We Get Off: Moving Towards a Black Feminist Politics of Pleasure." *The Black Scholar* 45(4):36–46.

Morris, Aldon D. 2015. *The Scholar Denied: W. E. B. Du Bois and the Birth of Modern Sociology*. Oakland, CA: University of California Press.

——. 2017. "W.E.B. Du Bois at the Center: From Science, Civil Rights Movement, to BlackLivesMatter." *The British Journal of Sociology* 68(1):3–16. doi:10.1111/1468-4446.12241.

Morris, Monique W. 2016. *Pushout: The Criminalization of Black Girls in Schools*. New York: The New Press.

Morrison, Toni. 1975. *A Humanist View*. Portland State University.

——. Interview with Charlie Rose. January 19, 1998. *The Charlie Rose Show*. [YouTube]. https://www.youtube.com/watch?v=-Kgq3F8wbYA&t=4s.

Morse, Ben. 2023. "Caitlin Clark Defends Angel Reese, Says She Shouldn't Be 'Criticized' for Gesture Directed toward Her | CNN." *CNN*, April 5.

Moss, Dana M. and David A. Snow. 2016. "Theorizing Social Movements." Pp. 547–69 in *Handbook of Contemporary Sociological Theory, Handbooks of Sociology and Social Research*. Cham, Switzerland: Springer.

Moynihan, Daniel P. 1965. "The Negro Family: The Case for National Action." Washington, DC: Office of Policy Planning and Research, U.S. Department of Labor.

Muhammad, Khalil Gibran. 2011. *The Condemnation of Blackness: Race, Crime, and the Making of Modern Urban America*. Cambridge, MA: Harvard University Press.

Musto, Michaela. 2020. "Researcher, Activist Examine Feminist Views on Sex Work at Clayman Conversations Event." *The Clayman Institute for Gender Research*. Retrieved June 17, 2022 (https://gender.stanford.edu/news-publications/gender-news/researcher-activist-examine-feminist-views-sex-work-clayman).

Nast, Condé. 2022. "Cardi B Donates $100,000 to Her Former Bronx Middle School." *Vanity Fair*, September 15.

——. 2023. "Rihanna is British Vogue's March 2023 Cover Star." *British Vogue*, February 15.

National Archives. 2021. "Voting Rights Act (1965)." *National Archives*. Retrieved November 7, 2023 (www.archives.gov/milestone-documents/voting-rights-act).

Naylor, Brian. 2017. "'Black Votes Matter': African-Americans Propel Jones to Alabama Win." *NPR*, December 13.

Ng, Eddy S. W. and Jasmine M. Johnson. 2015. "Millennials: Who Are They, How Are They Different, and Why Should We Care?" Pp. 121–37 in *The Multi-Generational and Aging Workforce: Challenges and Opportunities*, edited by Ronald J. Burke, Cary L. Cooper, and Alexander-Stamatios G. Antoniou. Cheltenham, England: Edward Elgar Publishing.

Nunez, Amalia. 2018. "Cardi B Deletes Instagram after Responding to Azealia Banks." *CBS News*, May 12.

Oppenheimer, Valerie Kincade. 1997. "Women's Employment and the Gain to Marriage: The Specialization and Trading Model." *Annual Review of Sociology* 23(1):431–53.

Park, Hoon Ji, Nadine G. Gaddabon, and Ariel R. Chernin. 2006. "Naturalizing Racial Differences Through Comedy: Asian, Black, and White Views on Racial Stereotypes in Rush Hour 2. *Journal of Communication* 56(1):157–77.

Parker, Kim, Juliana Menasce Horowitz, Rich Morin, and Mark Hugo Lopez. 2015. "Chapter 1: Race and Multiracial Americans in the U.S. Census." in *Pew Research Center's Social & Demographic Trends Project*. Retrieved July 30, 2023 (www.pewresearch.org/social-trends/2015/06/11/chapter-1-race-and-multiracial-americans-in-the-u-s-census/).

Paschel, Tianna S. 2010. "The Right to Difference: Explaining Colombia's Shift from Color Blindness to the Law of Black Communities." *American Journal of Sociology* 116(3):729–69. doi: 10.1086/655752.

Pate, David J. 2010. "Fatherhood Responsibility and the Marriage-Promotion Policy: Going to the Chapel and We're Going to Get Married?" Pp. 351–65 in *The Myth of the Missing Black Father*, edited by Roberta Coles and Charles Green. New York: Columbia University Press.

Payne, Ashley. 2020. "The Cardi B–Beyoncé Complex: Ratchet Respectability and Black Adolescent Girlhood." *Journal of Hip Hop Studies* 7(1). doi: 10.34718/PXEW-7785.

Perry, Andre M., Carl Romer, David Harshbarger, and Anthony Fiano. 2021. "Last Night in Georgia, Black Americans Saved Democracy." *Brookings*. Retrieved July 31, 2021 (www.brookings.edu/blog/the-avenue/2021/01/06/last-night-in-georgia-black-americans-saved-democracy/).

Peters, Mitchell. 2016. "Azealia Banks Continues Trashing Beyonce: 'She's Not an Artist, She's a Poacher'." *Billboard*, May 1.

Pew Research Center. 2010. "Millennials: A Portrait of Generation Next: Confident. Connected. Open to Change." Pew Research Center Millennials Report Series. Retrieved June 15, 2019 (https://assets.pewresearch.org/wp-content/uploads/sites/3/2010/10/millennials-confident-connected-open-to-change.pdf).

Phillips, Layli, Kerri Reddick-Morgan, and Dionne Patricia Stephens. 2005. "Oppositional Consciousness within an Oppositional Realm: The Case of Feminism and Womanism in Rap and Hip Hop, 1976–2004." *The Journal of African American History* 90(3):253–77.

Price, Emmett George. 2006. *Hip Hop Culture*. Santa Barbara, CA: ABC-CLIO.

Price, Joe. 2022. "Cardi B Tells David Letterman About Her 'Responsibility' to Speak on Political Subjects." *Complex*, May 20.

Pulitzer Prize. 2022. "Special Citations and Awards." Retrieved June 17, 2022 (www.pulitzer.org/prize-winners-by-category/260).

Putnam, Robert D. 2000. *Bowling Alone: The Collapse and Revival of American Community*. New York: Simon & Schuster.

Queen Radio. 2018. *Episode 8*. Apple Music.

Reddock, Rhoda. 1994. *Women, Labour and Politics in Trinidad and Tobago: A History*. London: Zed Books.

Reed, Wornie and Howard Taylor. 2018. "James E. Blackwell and the Founding of the Association of Black Sociologists." *Issues in Race and Society: Special Issue on James E. Blackwell* 7. doi:10.34314/issuesfall2018.00006.

Rhue, Holly. 2018. "This Reporter Tried to Shatter 14-Year-Old Venus Williams' Confidence. Watch Her Dad Shut Him Down." *ELLE*, August 30.

Richardson, Elaine. 2021. "'She Ugly': Black Girls, Women in Hiphop and Activism—Hip Hop Feminist Literacies Perspectives." *Community Literacy Journal* 16(1). doi:10.25148/CLJ.16.1.010603.

Rigueur, Leah Wright. 2020. "The Major Difference Between Black Male and Female Voters." *The Atlantic*. Retrieved June 5, 2022 (www.theatlantic.com/culture/archive/2020/11/why-black-men-and-women-vote-so-differently/617134/).

Risman, Barbara J. and Virginia E. Rutter. 2015. *Families as They Really Are*. New York: W.W. Norton & Company.

Ritterhouse, Jennifer. 2006. *Growing Up Jim Crow*. Chapel Hill, NC: The University of North Carolina Press.

Roberts, Dorothy E. 1997. *Killing the Black Body: Race, Reproduction, and the Meaning of Liberty*. New York: Pantheon Books.

——. 2017. *Killing the Black Body: Race, Reproduction, and the Meaning of Liberty*. Second Vintage books ed. New York: Vintage Books.

Robinson, Candice C. 2019. "(Re)Theorizing Civic Engagement: Foundations for Black Americans Civic Engagement Theory." *Sociology Compass* 13(9):e12728. doi:10.1111/soc4.12728.

Robnett, Belinda. 2000. *How Long? How Long? African-American Women in the Struggle for Civil Rights*. New York: Oxford University Press.

Rogin, Michael. 1996. *Blackface, White Noise*. Los Angeles, CA: University of California Press.

Romero, Mary. 2020. "Sociology Engaged in Social Justice." *American Sociological Review* 85(1):1–30. doi:10.1177/0003122419893677.

Rosenberg, Rosalind. 2017. *Jane Crow: The Life of Pauli Murray*. Illustrated ed. New York: Oxford University Press.

Roth, Wendy D. 2016. "The Multiple Dimensions of Race." *Ethnic and Racial Studies* 39(8):1310–38. doi:10.1080/01419870.2016.1140793.

Roy, William G. and Timothy J. Dowd. 2010. "What is Sociological about Music?" *Annual Review of Sociology* 36(1):183–203.

Sanders, Bernie. 2019. "Bernie x Cardi B." Retrieved April 19, 2024 (https://www.youtube.com/watch?v=p1ubTsrZFBU).

Saunders, Clare. 2022. "Activism." Pp. 1–3 in *The Wiley-Blackwell Encyclopedia of Social and Political Movements*. Hoboken, NJ: Wiley-Blackwell.

Schultz, Mark. 2005. *The Rural Face of White Supremacy: Beyond Jim Crow*. Champaign, IL: University of Illinois Press.

Sims, Jennifer Patrice, Whitney Laster Pirtle, and Iris Johnson-Arnold. 2020. "Doing Hair, Doing Race: The Influence of Hairstyle on Racial Perception across the US." *Ethnic and Racial Studies* 43(12):2099–119. doi:10.1080/01419870.2019.1700296.

Singh, Abhinav. 2020. "Will Offset Go to Jail Again? A Look at Migos Rapper's Past Legal Issues from Possession of Marijuana to Guns." *MEAWW*. Retrieved June 20, 2022 (https://meaww.com/offset-go-jail-again-look-migos-rapper-past-legal-issues-criminal-history-arrest).

Slaughter, Christine M. and Nadia E. Brown. 2022. "Intersectionality and Political Participation." Pp. 725–43 in *The Oxford Handbook of Political Participation*, edited by M. Giugni and M. Grasso. New York: Oxford University Press.

Steadman, Otillia. 2020. "These Atlanta Dancers Helped Get Out the Vote—Now They're Focused on the Georgia Runoff." *BuzzFeed News*. Retrieved June 17, 2022 (www.buzzfeednews.com/article/otilliasteadman/get-your-booty-to-the-poll-again).

Steed, Michael, dir. 2022. "Cardi B." *My Next Guest Needs No Introduction with David Letterman*.

Stewart, Emily. 2019. "Cardi B's Support for Bernie Sanders, Explained." *Vox*. Retrieved June 17, 2022 (www.vox.com/policy-and-politics/2019/7/30/20747537/bernie-sanders-cardi-b-video-instagram).

Summers, Juana. 2020. "Stripper Polls: The Racy Voting PSA That's Actually All About the Issues." *NPR*, October 5.

Taylor, Keeanga-Yamahtta. 2016. *From #BlackLivesMatter to Black Liberation*. 1st ed. Chicago, Illinois: Haymarket Books.

Telles, Edward and René Flores. 2013. "Not Just Color: Whiteness, Nation, and Status in Latin America." *Hispanic American Historical Review* 93(3):411–49. doi:10.1215/00182168-2210858.

Telles, Edward and Denia Garcia. 2013. "Mestizaje and Public Opinion in Latin America." *Latin American Research Review* 48(3):130–52. doi:10.1353/lar.2013.0045.

Telles, Edward and Tianna Paschel. 2014. "Who is Black, White, or Mixed Race? How Skin Color, Status, and Nation Shape Racial Classification in Latin America." *American Journal of Sociology* 120(3):864–907. doi:10.1086/679252.

TheThings Celebrity. 2018. "20 Things You Didn't Know About Cardi B." Retrieved July 30, 2023 (www.youtube.com/watch?v=IJbYcjwPrCs).

Thompson, Desire. 2016. "Cardi B Responds to Critics Who Doubt Her Feminism—VIBE.Com." *Vibe*.

Thornton, Brendan Jamal and Diego I. Ubiera. 2019. "Caribbean Exceptions: The Problem of Race and Nation in Dominican Studies." *Latin American Research Review* 54(2):413–28. doi:10.25222/larr.346.

TMZ. 2020. "Bernie Sanders Encourages Cardi B to Enter Politics, 'It Would Be Great'." Retrieved October 5, 2023 (www.tmz.com/2020/01/14/bernie-sanders-supports-cardi-b-entering-politics-great-experience/).

Torres-Saillant, Silvio. 2000. "The Tribulations of Blackness: Stages in Dominican Racial Identity." *Callaloo* 23(3):1086–111.

——. 2009. "One and Divisible: Meditations on Global Blackness." *Small Axe* 13(2):4–25. doi:10.1215/02705346-2009-003.

Tribeca Enterprises LLC. 2020. "Queen Collective." *Tribeca*. Retrieved January 18, 2024 (https://tribecafilm.com/queencollective).

Turner, Tasha. 2021. "Cardi B Claps Back at Natural Hair Haters 'There is No Such Thing as Bad Hair. All Hair is Good!'" *The Source*, November 15.

TWS, The Washington Star. 1976. "'Welfare Queen' Becomes Issue in Reagan Campaign." in *New York Times*. New York: New York Times Company.

United States Fugitive Slave Law. 1850. "The Fugitive Slave Law. Hartford, Ct.? s.n., 185-? Hartford." [Pdf] Retrieved from the Library of Congress (www.loc.gov/item/98101767/).

Vernier, C. G. and W. G. Hale. 1920. "Judicial Decisions on Criminal Law and Procedure." *Journal of Criminal Law & Criminology* 11:115–17.

Victorian, Brande. 2022. "Cardi B and Offset." *Essence*, June.

VladTV. 2017. "Cardi B (Full Interview)." Retrieved June 6, 2022 (www.youtube.com/watch?v=l4YT61qLe-Y).

Vogue México y Latinoamérica. 2023. "Cardi B Revela En ESPAÑOL Lo Que Guarda En Su Bolso (y Es Una Locura)." Retrieved October 3, 2023 (www.youtube.com/watch?v=TYfyZX7_YSo).

Walker, Alice. 1983. *In Search of Our Mothers' Gardens: Womanist Prose*. San Diego, CA: Harcourt Brace Jovanovich.

Warren, Earl and Supreme Court of The United States. 1953. "U.S. Reports: Brown v. Board of Education, 347 U.S. 483." [Periodical] Retrieved from the Library of Congress (https://www.loc.gov/item/usrep347483/).

Washington, Valora. 1988. "The Power of Black Women: Progress, Predicaments and Possibilities" [Conference Presentation]. *Anniversary Conference of the Association of Black Women in Higher Education*, Inc. New York.

Waters, Mary C. 1990. *Ethnic Options: Choosing Identities in America*. Berkeley, CA: University of California Press.

Watson, Wilbur H. 1976. "The Idea of Black Sociology: Its Cultural and Political Significance." *The American Sociologist* 11(2):115–23.

Weaver, Caity. 2018. "Cardi B's Money Moves." *GQ*. Retrieved June 18, 2022 (www.gq.com/story/cardi-b-invasion-of-privacy-profile).

Welter, Barbara. 1966. "The Cult of True Womanhood: 1820–1860." *American Quarterly* 18(2):151–74.

Williams, Ebony. 2022. "Queen Latifah's Affordable New Jersey Housing Project Moves Forward." *The Atlanta Journal-Constitution*, June 7.

Wolcott, Victoria W. 2001. *Remaking Respectability: African American Women in Interwar Detroit*. Chapel Hill, NC: The University of North Carolina Press.

Wolfson, Sam. 2019. "'Vote for Daddy Bernie, Bitch': The Political History of Cardi B." *The Guardian*, January 22.

Wright, Earl, II. 2020. *Jim Crow Sociology: The Black and Southern Roots of American Sociology*. University of Cincinnati Press.

Wright, Earl, II and Thomas C. Calhoun. 2006. "Jim Crow Sociology: Toward an Understanding of the Origin and Principles of Black Sociology via the Atlanta Sociological Laboratory." *Sociological Focus* 39(1):1–18. doi: https://doi.org/10.1080/00380237.2006.10571274.

Wright, Earl, II and Aldon D. Morris. 2021. "Introduction to the Special Issue: The Sociology of W. E. B. Du Bois." *Social Problems* 68(2):203–6. doi:10.1093/socpro/spab007.

Yancy, George. 2017. *Black Bodies, White Gaze*. 2nd ed. Lanham, MD: Rowman & Littlefield.

Zamora, Omaris Z. 2022. "Before Bodak Yellow and Beyond the Post-Soul." *The Black Scholar* 52(1):53–63. doi:10.1080/00064246.2022.2007343.

Zendaya. 2018. "Cardi B Opens Up to Zendaya in the New Issue of CR Fashion Book." *CR Fashionbook*. Retrieved June 6, 2022 (https://crfashionbook.com/celebrity-a15943155-zendaya-cr-fashion-book-cover-interview-cardi-b/).

INDEX